Stray Dogs & Lone Wolves

The Samurai Film Handbook

Stray Dogs
& Lone Wolves

The Samurai
Film Handbook

Patrick Galloway

Stone Bridge Press • Berkeley, California

Published by
Stone Bridge Press
P.O. Box 8208
Berkeley, CA 94707
TEL 510-524-8732 • sbp@stonebridge.com • www.stonebridge.com

Front-cover image from *Nemuri Kyoshiro 4: Joyoken,* © 1964 Kadokawa Pictures Inc.

Cover and text design by Linda Ronan.

Printed in the United States of America.

2010 2009 2008 2007 2006 2005   10 9 8 7 6 5 4 3 2 1

LIBRARY OF CONGRESS CATALOGING-IN-PUBLICATION DATA
Galloway, Patrick.
  Stray dogs & lone wolves: the samurai film handbook /
Patrick Galloway.
      p. cm.
  Includes bibliographical references and index.
    1. Samurai films—History and criticism. I. Title: Stray dogs and
  lone wolves. II. Title.
  PN1995.9.S24G35 2005
  791.43'658—dc22
  2005009723

Contents

Part III
Appendix

Foreword

During the writing of *Stray Dogs & Lone Wolves,* whenever the project came up in discussions with friends and acquaintances, I'd notice a funny look, as if to say, "Why on earth would you write a book about samurai movies?" So to all of you who shot me that look, as well as to anyone else who might be wondering, I wrote this book for the following reasons.

First off, I got tired of searching for a book like this, and decided I had to write it myself. The samurai film genre is woefully underrepresented in film criticism, with no popular titles currently devoted exclusively to it. There have been occasional scholarly treatises, but nothing like a handbook for film enthusiasts, a practical reference that's fun to read and use.

Second, I wrote it for the sake of my poor wife, who had become shell-shocked by my nonstop lectures on the sword-fighting prowess of Tomisaburo Wakayama or the superior dramatic performances of Tatsuya Nakadai. By funneling all of my monomaniacal obsessiveness into the book, I found more time to discuss the things that really mattered with her. Yes, this book saved my marriage.

Finally, I wrote it for all the film nuts out there, both long-time fans of the samurai genre as well as newbies looking for a different kind of film experience. There's so much on offer here, so many great films, great stars, superb filmmaking, and

Pat Galloway's private collection

Window With Cat
by Unknown.

the idea of turning people on to it became my mission. My sincerest thanks to Shirley Galloway, my muse and project manager; Peter Goodman for his early interest and continuing support; Greg Dicum for showing me the ropes; Alain Silver for getting the ball rolling; Kanako Takahashi for tracking down images; Tatsu Aoki and Seiichi Sasaki for fine points; Patrick Macias for help and inspiration; Beth Cary for keeping me honest; and Kevin Fellezs for being there.

In compiling movie reviews for *Stray Dogs & Lone Wolves*, I've tried to cover as wide a variety of titles as possible, ranging from traditional, nostalgic period drama to bizarre hybrids and exploitation films. But my real critical focus is on samurai films of the 1960s, the pinnacle of the genre. During this period the forms and conventions of the samurai film were turned inside out by innovative writers and directors inspired by an emerging counterculture and a heightened social consciousness. Imagine a genre that suddenly begins to deconstruct itself, with all the intensity of a samurai, a figurative act of harakiri!

If you're new to these films, you'll find the book will help open up the genre (as well as many aspects of Japanese culture), allowing you unfettered access to the fascinating world of the samurai. If you're already a fan, you will probably find things here to augment your knowledge, as well as trivia, anecdotes, and lots of character/actor attributions that have never before appeared in print (at least in English).

So tighten your topknot, grab your sword, and let the mayhem begin!

Yosh!

Patrick Galloway

Part I
Background

1

The World of the Samurai

This book is all about samurai and samurai films. Therefore it's best to define our terms at the outset. Since the primary focus is on the samurai in film, perhaps that's the best place to begin by asking . . .

What Is a Samurai Film?

To provide the widest possible scope, the definition of "samurai film" has been kept deliberately loosey-goosey. Basically, for the purposes of this book, the minimum requirements are these:

1. The film has samurai in it.
2. There is sword fighting.
3. It takes place during one of the designated historical periods (see **Historical Setting** below).

This may upset genre purists out there. Sorry 'bout that. The purpose of this book is to turn people on to great films without getting too bogged down with tedious genre distinctions. And nobody gets more meticulous classifying and categorizing film genres than the Japanese. Here's a taste:

Japanese filmmakers and audiences traditionally designate two primary genres from which all other genres derive:

1954 Toho

The magnificent
Seven Samurai

Jidai-geki (period film) and gendai-geki (contemporary film). From here, things subdivide further. For example, within gen-dai-geki there are movies specifically about the trials and trib-ulations of mothers, called haha-mono (mother story). There is also the tsuma-mono (wife film). And although a wife can be a mother, haha-mono and tsuma-mono are very different indeed. Then there are "salaryman" comedies, home dramas, you name it—all aspects of modern life get their own distinct film genre. (This highly specialized genre scheme also applies to manga, or Japanese comics, but that's another story.)

Within jidai-geki there is chambara (sword film), but not all jidai-geki are chambara. Hiroshi Inagaki's Samurai Trilogy, for example, is considered jidai-geki but not chambara. *Destiny's Son* is definitely chambara, as well as jidai-geki. Some Japanese film scholars tend to sneer at chambara, using it as a term of derision (usually for films they don't like). You could say one of the themes of this book is "Chambara rocks!"

Films featuring Zatoichi, the blind swordsman, are technically matatabi-eiga (wandering yakuza films). This should not be confused with ninkyo-eiga (chivalry films), which involve yakuza, but in a more recent historical period (from 1868 to the beginning of World War II). However Zatoichi films have so much in common with the samurai film (they are both jidai-geki and chambara) that to leave them out of the discussion would be too glaring an omission. By the same token, many samurai film fans would probably reject inclusion of the film *Daimajin,* claiming that it is really a kaiju-eiga (giant monster film). This is true, but it is also jidai-geki, and there's enough swordplay and political intrigue (not to mention a giant guy in samurai armor) to qualify as a samurai film.

So enough with the taxonomy. The question you really should be asking is . . .

What Is a Samurai?

The Samurai is a figure grounded in historical realities but embellished by oral traditions, isolated in an unfamiliar past, and elevated through repeated representations in art to the level of myth. Separating the actuality from the mists of legends is, if possible at all, no simple task. (Alain Silver, *The Samurai Film*)

Well, let's go through the standard line: Samurai were the elite warrior class in Japan from roughly the eleventh century to the mid-nineteenth century. Not unlike their European counterparts, the chivalric knights, these proud warriors followed a code of honor (Bushido), served their feudal lords (daimyo), and fought battles to advance and defend the interests of their clans.

The sword was considered the soul of the samurai, and prowess in swordsmanship was of utmost importance. More accomplished samurai developed their own schools, handing down their sacred sword techniques from generation to generation. It wasn't uncommon for a samurai to introduce himself by telling you his name followed by his sword school. This typically happened right before a swordfight and was possibly the last thing you ever heard. In film, the samurai is often seen admiring the skill of a superior swordsman, even choking out

Shintaro Katsu in Kojiki Taisho

"Magnificent!" or "Superb!" before dying on his opponent's blade.

It's impossible for a foreigner to fully grasp the historical and cultural importance of the sword in Japanese history. In no other country is it more traditionally revered. At the age of 15 the young samurai male was considered a man and was allowed to don the katana (long sword) and wakizashi (short sword). The two-sword tradition (daisho) was established by legendary swordsman Musashi Miyamoto in the early seventeenth century. The katana was over two feet long and is what people commonly consider a "samurai sword." The wakizashi was between one and two feet. Master swordsmiths dating back to the tenth century jealously guarded the secrets of their forging and tempering techniques. The master crafts-man's personal inscription on the nakago (base of the sword covered by the hilt) assured the samurai that his was among the finest swords in Japan (as well as the entire world).

Along with the sword, the other defining element of the samurai was the code of Bushido. Central to Bushido was the concept of giri, or obligation. This obligation was first and foremost to the daimyo, but it extended to the clan as well. The samurai was prepared to die at a moment's notice for the sake of giri and was encouraged to keep death foremost in his mind at all times. His mind was steeped in the existential immediacy of Zen Buddhism, wherein life is considered an il-lusion and death merely the leave-taking of this insubstantial, floating world. By considering each day his last, the samu-rai was able to live life more fully, act more boldly, and keep things in true perspective.

The so-called Bushido code, ironically, was never codified. No one actually started writing about it until the seventeenth century, after its tenets had been established and followed for centuries. Beyond the saddle of giri, Bushido also stressed the importance of honor (or "face") and what to do if you lost it. This often involved the Japanese ritual of sep-puku (known informally as harakiri). Seppuku, a self-disem-boweling ceremony, was used for a variety of personal and political purposes and employed its own specialized termi-nology. Samurai retainers might follow their lord into death

Tonya no Sakefune by Kyoden

(junshi); a samurai might use seppuku as a form of protest to rebuke an unjust lord (kanshi); a samurai committing a transgression of the law might be allowed to perform seppuku if his behavior was shown to have conformed to the Bushido code (sokutsushi). Seppuku was always considered preferable to the humiliation of execution. The formal ritual required a kaishakunin (second) to behead the samurai once he had cut his belly open with the tanto blade (somewhat shorter than the wakizashi, under 12 inches). This was done as a courtesy to end the man's suffering from what could only have been an excruciating wound.

However, seppuku was not always the only way to go in face-saving. Vengeance was often a remedy for the loss of face in the murder of a family member, teacher, friend, or lord. The vendetta (kataki-uchi) had its own codes and rituals, among which was the requirement that the head of the offender be severed and placed on the grave of the avenged. Revenge is a standard plot-mover in the samurai drama, as indeed it is in the drama of all nations from time immemorial. Classic revenge tales like that of the Soga Brothers (twelfth century) and the Loyal 47 Ronin (eighteenth century) were portrayed in film as early as 1908 and have been samurai film favorites ever since.

As Alain Silver states above, there is a mythic element to all this that should be considered when speculating about the historical samurai. Truth is, people are people, and the number of samurai who actually lived up to the Zen superman ideal put forth by Bushido was no doubt in the minority. Samurai were of the privileged class in the society and in all likelihood behaved as badly as any other privileged class in any other society. There was probably a higher degree of self-discipline, though, a hallmark of Japanese culture, and due to the Shinto/Buddhist (as opposed to Judeo-Christian) spiritual underpinning, attitudes regarding life and death were different (more frank, perhaps).

The scheme of giri defined service to the lord as the samurai's raison d'etre. What then became of the samurai who found himself no longer in such service, through banishment by (or dissolution of) his clan? He became a ronin, literally "wave

Minamoto no Yoshi-
tsune *by Kiyohiro
Torii*

man," a man tossed on the waves of fortune, cut loose from the society in which he had formerly reigned supreme. Trained in martial arts, some formed schools; well educated, some became teachers of the fine arts; some fell on hard times and had to stoop to manual labor (look for these poor wretches making umbrellas and selling noodles in *Sword of Doom* and *Ronin-gai*); and many became swords for hire. This last group predominates in samurai film. They might be honorable men such as the ronin in *Seven Samurai* or scheming rogues like Sanjuro in *Yojimbo.* Some became assassins (*Tenchu!, Lone Wolf and Cub*). And some were just plain nuts (*Secret of the Urn*).

The ronin became a potent symbol in the 1960s, representing the outcast, the misfit, the forgotten man of society, a resonant theme in a decade of burgeoning social awareness. However, tales of ronin date back to the earliest Japanese films, their plight providing the meat of many a gripping drama. In a conformist society like Japan, a story of a man who goes his own way, facing down the uncertainties of life outside the system, is particularly compelling and possesses a perennial appeal.

Historical Setting

The samurai films we'll be looking at were made by Japanese people for Japanese people, and as such were not always forthcoming with what I would call "cultural context"—the historical backdrop and circumstances surrounding the drama at hand. Every Japanese school kid knows all about the figures, events, and historical periods that shape the samurai drama, but since the culture is so homogenous and insular, it can be harder for Western audiences to grasp the significance and relevance of what's going on at any given moment. Therefore, a little understanding of the historical underpinnings of the films goes a long way. The vast majority of samurai films take place during one of two historical periods, the Sengoku and the Tokugawa.

Sengoku-jidai (Sengoku pierod or Warring States period): This was an extended period of mass chaos and civil wars that stretched from 1478 to 1603. During this period, many of the stronger regional daimyo became bloody warlords, launching

Samurai full helmet with moustache

endless campaigns against one another. The Ashikaga line of shoguns that had ruled since the mid-fourteenth century were by now terribly weakened by corruption and excess, leaving the warlords to ravage and plunder the land and generally go picnicking upon one another.

This hellish time of turmoil, marked by perpetual war, starvation, peasant revolts, and bloodthirsty bandits, provides a rich canvas upon which many a samurai drama is painted. Here we find the likes of Shingen Takeda and Nobunaga Oda, great warlords bent on total domination of Japan. This is the time of great battles, of thousands of armored samurai on horse and tens of thousands on foot engaged in gruesome combat. Most of director Akira Kurosawa's samurai films are set during this period. If you're interested in the glory days of the samurai warrior, this is your period.

The Sengoku-jidai effectively ended in 1600 at the Battle of Sekigahara. It is here that we first meet legendary swordsman Musashi Miyamoto, the subject of scores of samurai films including the Samurai Trilogy (see the reviews section). By 1603 the victor of Sekigahara and new shogun, Ieyasu Tokugawa, had established what would prove to be the strongest and most enduring period of enforced peace and isolation in Japan's history, the Tokugawa Shogunate.

Tokugawa-jidai or **Edo-jidai** (Tokugawa or Edo period): Stretching from 1603 to 1868 (265 years and 15 Tokugawa shoguns in all), the Tokugawa period was a time in which a newly unified Japan was ruled with an iron fist by what was essentially a military dictatorship. Ieyasu Tokugawa established meticulous guidelines that codified every facet of daily life. The Japanese people were divided into four classes (samurai, farmers, artisans, and merchants), and these classes were separated, physically as well as socially (farmers in rural villages, samurai in castle towns and cities). The samurai were the ruling class, occupying the top 10% of the population.

However, since this was a time of external isolation and internal peace, there were no wars for the samurai to fight. Also, the Tokugwawa clan, in a bid to both maintain its power and feather its own nest, was notorious for dissolving rival clans for the slightest offense, real or imagined. This usually

Amida Waterfall on Kiso Road *by Hokusai*

involved ordering the rival clan's daimyo to commit seppuku. One result of this was the creation of ronin. Lots of ronin. Very pissed-off ronin. Add to this an ever-increasing corruption in the government, and you begin to get an idea of the pressure cooker the Edo period gradually became.

Samurai were continually faced with tests to their giri. The lucky ones, the ones who managed to keep their posts as clan retainers, were constantly embroiled in unsavory scenarios brought about by internecine clan disputes, shogunate treachery or both. The unlucky ones, the ronin, were faced with the more dire problem of simple survival and the quest to regain what they'd lost. They were left to scrape out some stark existence, usually with the blade of their swords.

The tension generated by the samurai's attempt to maintain his pride and purpose under the crushing weight of the Tokugawa bakufu (military government) led to what's known as the giri/ninjo conflict. Ninjo is the term for human feelings, sympathy, conscience, the voice within that tells you what is right; when this comes into conflict with giri, the samurai's obligation to lord and clan, that's when the trouble starts. This was a period when a lord might demand a retainer behead his wife to prove his loyalty. Think of the dramatic possibilities of such a situation. The giri/ninjo conflict arises again and again in samurai drama.

Tokugawa society crystalized into a mask of cultural refinement and aesthetic perfection; this mask hid the scheming face of corruption that lurked in the corridors of power. Over time, the combination of social stagnation, moral turpitude, and the excesses of the Tokugawa clan weakened the bakufu, so much so that when the U.S. sent warships in 1854 for a little gunboat diplomacy to open up trade, the Tokugawa regime rapidly splintered into factions and fell in upon itself. The last gasp of the period, roughly 1854 to 1868, is known as the Bakumatsu period and was marked by bloody assassinations and political intrigue unlike anything seen before. Factional plotting and political murder became so widespread that the shogunate instituted bands of ronin for public protection, the Shinchogumi in Edo (the city was renamed Tokyo after 1868) and the Shinsengumi in Kyoto, the imperial capital. The Shin-

Inume Pass in Kai Province *by Hokusai*

sengumi is another subject of numerous films, two of which are reviewed in this book.

The Tokugawa period ended in 1868 with the dissolution of the shogunate and the rise to supreme power of the Emperor Meiji. This was known as the Meiji Restoration and it ushered in rampant industrial acceleration, leaving behind the old ways in favor of a new, modernized society to rival those of the West. Not many samurai films are set in the Meiji period (as the Meiji regime abolished most aspects of samurai culture), but there are a few, such as *Lady Snowblood* (reviewed here).

Nature

Perhaps no country on earth has a deeper cultural reverence for nature than Japan. Shinto, Japan's ancient pre-Buddhist religion, has as its central focus the spirituality of the natural world. With the arrival of Buddhism in the seventh century, contemplation of nature carried over to become a central facet of the contemplative life of the Buddhist monk.

The Japanese have traditionally turned to nature for retreat and respite from the intense pressures of society. The minimalist poetic form of the haiku is based on immediate, transcendental impressions of nature; the art of ikebana (flower arrangement), bonsai (miniature trees), and Japanese architecture itself, integrating the garden as a central feature of the dwelling, all reflect this awareness of the importance of nature and the need to incorporate some aspect of it into one's daily life.

Therefore, it's no surprise that the natural world is perpetually present in the samurai film. Even in the bloodiest sword films, one is struck by the beauty of the settings. A sword duel on an idyllic beach at dawn, a massacre in gently falling snow, murder and betrayal in a sunny glade, these confluences stem from an artistic tradition that has long dominated the visual landscape of Japanese film. Forest, ocean, river, mountain, sand and surf, wind and flower, one is never far from some vision of natural beauty. This tends to elevate the experience of the samurai film, as well as place the human drama in a larger context. Sometimes the trees stand in mute witness to the bloody folly of men and their swords. At other times the wind and rain whip the scene into a frenzy to match the desperate battle of, say, a handful of ronin fighting an army of bandits.

Nature imagery is more often than not used symbolically to provide subtext. This symbolism is sometimes lost on Western viewers; it is an encoded language of metaphor familiar to every Japanese filmgoer, but we in the West need to be aware that a shot of a river can be referring to the impermanence of life, or falling cherry blossoms might symbolize the fleeting nature of youth or the suddenness of death. Seasonal shifts indicate change, and often point out development or decay in characters and their relationships to one another. Weather always means something: rain can signal the onset of a plot development or simply add emphasis.

One complex, water-based symbol that pops up periodically in the films discussed here is that of an old mill next to a river with a big water wheel driving the machinery within (usually pounding equipment for grain). Keep an eye out for the water mill in *Seven Samurai*—what does it symbolize? Perhaps agrarian harmony with nature? Its destruction by bandits then takes on a deeper significance. In other films, such as *Sword of Doom* and *Lady Snowblood,* the pounding, grinding machinery of the mill reinforces the brutal act of rape, thus pointing out something unnatural; the mill becomes an aberration.

In any case, aside from making these films more pleasing to the eye, the nature imagery that fills them is usually there to tell us something. Just being aware of this fact adds another fascinating dimension to the experience of watching a samurai film.

2

The Samurai Film Genre

The fact that the samurai film is defined by a specific film genre is not a bad thing. Cinema snobs tend to hold genre films in low regard. Critics and culture vultures look on them as inferior works with cookie-cutter characters and plots, manufactured to quell the teeming masses with mindless boredom-killing entertainment. While this can indeed be the case, nevertheless genres tend to evolve, usually to a point where they ultimately transcend themselves; a filmmaker comes along and subverts the genre, turns it on its head, inside out, or combines it with other genres to create something totally new. Since the audience is already familiar with the expectations dictated by the genre, the new forms are that much more compelling because we're all in on it. Genres make well-worn tracks, and when we go flying off them, we are sent hurtling into the unknown.

In general what makes the samurai film genre so compelling, aside from the sword action, is its capacity for philosophy, politics, and complex states of mind, all wrapped up in the beauty and stunning simplicity of the Japanese aesthetic. Where else can one observe heated sword fights accompanied by cool musings on the nature of existence? Whether played out in nature or immaculate architectural settings, the stories are infused with a worldly wisdom rarely seen in genre entertainment, crediting the audience with a greater intelligence

1954 Toho

Takashi Shimura lets his bow do the talking in Seven Samurai

and capacity for conflicting thoughts and emotions than it tends to get from formulaic Hollywood fare.

By the mid-'60s the samurai genre had become a hybrid, incorporating elements of the U.S. western, spaghetti western, film noir, political thriller, psychological thriller, swashbuckler, action, adventure, romance, gangster, even supernatural, and giant monster genres. For samurai films, the '60s represents a Golden Age, when the genre did indeed morph into something very special and unique, creating a variety of new forms. Before the '60s, the samurai film held to certain preconceptions about what a samurai was and, by extension, what Japanese society was. Even the innovative films Akira Kurosawa made in the 1950s still upheld fundamental notions regarding the noble samurai, a man of ethics, fighting the good fight. But the '60s was a time of cultural and political change, not just in the U.S. and Europe, but worldwide, and very much so in Japan. Something was in the air, and filmmakers began to seriously question the societal assumptions underlying "the samurai" (as well as their own everyday lives).

This questioning enters the frame in the figure of the lone ronin. Although no stranger to the traditional samurai film, this new '60s version is often poor and disheveled, always cynical, and usually somewhat contradictory: out for himself, he helps others; hating the hypocrisy of the samurai system, he nevertheless embraces its core values. In effect the ronin feels betrayed by something that is his very essence. As a result, he drinks too much, he smells bad, he hits people up for money, maybe he kills for it: all big samurai no-nos. And yet he is more a samurai than the bowing, conformist, back-stabbing, ass-kissing, pate-shaving topknots he sees around him.

In 1961 Akira Kurosawa gave the world *Yojimbo,* essentially codifying the cynical ronin figure. It wasn't long before filmmakers like Masaki Kobayashi and Hideo Gosha took full advantage of this new icon of rage and disillusionment to really stick it to the system, both the Bushido code of the Tokugawa period and the social milieu of contemporary Japanese society. There was a growing radicalism during the 1960s, as well as a decline at the box office (due to the rise of television). As a result there emerged new trends, new approaches, and new directors taking chances and bending the rules to give audiences something they couldn't get on the small screen. All these elements combined to create some of the most astounding films ever made in any era, genre, or nation. For this reason, samurai films of the 1960s make up the majority of the films discussed in this book.

All this is not to say that there aren't specific genre conventions that samurai films share. Some of these would be:

1. There is a hero and he is most likely a swordsman.
2. He is a samurai, ex-samurai (ronin), or yakuza and is motivated by:
   (a) revenge
   (b) loyalty
   (c) self-interest
   (d) protection of innocents
   (e) a combination of two or more of the above.
3. He has a mission.
4. He has an enemy (most likely accompanied by a lot of swordsmen).

5. There will be a series of swordfights involving many assailants.
6. He will face his enemy (who will most likely be accompanied by a lot of swordsmen).
7. Unless there's a sequel, he'll probably die.

Bear in mind, however, that these are merely the bare bones, the absolute minimum requirements. Just watch a string of Zatoichi films to witness endless variations on these basic components. The genre is also porous enough to allow for cross-pollination with other genres and cultures. For example, the original source material for *Yojimbo* was a Dashiell Hammett novel, *Red Harvest,* and *Yojimbo* itself was remade as the spaghetti western classic, *A Fistful of Dollars. Seven Samurai* was remade as *The Magnificent Seven,* and *The Hidden Fortress* provided the core concepts that led to *Star Wars.* So the genre is flexible to say the least.

This Is Not Hollywood

If you're new to samurai films (or Japanese films in general) there are a few adjustments you'll have to make in the way you normally watch movies. Don't worry, they're not painful, and you'll find that a little effort will open up a whole world of insanely great cinematic experiences you can enjoy for years to come.

First off, the subtitles. We've all heard the complaint, "If I wanted to read, I wouldn't have gone to the movies," etc. But unless you're functionally illiterate, there's no reason why you can't do both. Reading subtitles is something you get used to like anything else, and soon you'll find you don't even notice them (unless they go by too fast). After all, you're a thrill seeker, right? You've come here looking for something different, something wild, something wholly other. Listening to some idiotic, dubbed version of a samurai film (or any other foreign film) just isn't going to cut it. You've got to experience the real deal, you need to hear these guys go off in Japanese. There's simply nothing else like it.

Next, there's the issue of Japanese names. For one thing, they can be very long and somewhat daunting when you read them on the screen. Actually, they're not that hard to pronounce once you realize that the Japanese language is syllabic—it isn't spoken and written in letters like English, but in whole syllables, known collectively as the gojuon (the 50 sounds). So when reading a long Japanese name like Tomisaburo Wakayama, just break it down to consonant/vowel pairs like this: TO-MI-SA-BU-RO, get it? Then, WA-KA-YA-MA. While viewing a film, use the pause button until you get the hang of this. If you're in a theater, well, just roll with it.

Japanese names also differ in that the surname commonly comes first, then the given name. So in Japan, the actor's name above would be Wakayama Tomisaburo. In this book I utilize the convention of surname last so that the names come a little easier to Western readers. But bear in mind when reading subtitles that very often the subtitler does not observe this convention, and the name will appear "backward." Some subtitlers do observe the convention, which can make things confusing, but it's nothing to worry about. Once you're ten minutes into a film, you'll know which way to go.

Then there's the issue of the down ending. Things rarely end well for the protagonists in samurai films, there's just no two ways about it. This is due in part to a principle of Japanese aesthetics known as "mono no aware," literally "sadness of things," the savoring of the exquisite pain and grief of mortality. Mono no aware runs through many film genres and the samurai film is one of them. It might seem perverse, this pleasure-taking in the painful passing away of life in art, but one often finds an intertwining of pain and pleasure in the drama and literature of Japan.

The down ending is also a reflection of a stark, unflinching attitude toward life common to the culture of Japan. Where Hollywood mollycoddles the audience with happy endings, the hero overcoming impossible odds to ride off into the sunset with his best gal by his side, the Japanese are much more realistic. Nine times out of ten, when you go up against the system or a superior foe, you're going to lose. Far more important to the Japanese moviegoer is what author Ivan Morris terms "the nobility of failure," the fighting spirit of the doomed

Tatsuya Nakadai tests the wind direction in Kagemusha

1980 Toho

hero who struggles on, even in the face of certain death. This is also, as it turns out, the essence of the Bushido code, revealing just how much this martial ethic has remained a vital facet of the culture.

One other reason for the doomed hero in samurai drama is a political one: a samurai who fights against the system and dies is no longer a threat to the system. This is perhaps a cynical take, implying that the Japanese are so deeply authoritarian in their social orientation that authors would deliberately kill off any offending heroic figures, but there's some truth to it. If the hero goes down fighting the good fight, he's satisfied Bushido, and won't rock the boat by doing something so awkward as continuing to exist, a thorn in the side of entrenched power. Everybody wins!

The good news for samurai film fans in the West is the level of quality of what's on offer. Toho isn't going to release just any old B-film, they're going to whip out their best stuff like *Chushingura, Seven Samurai,* and *Samurai Rebellion.* All that subtitling, video transfer, and packaging costs money, and the companies marketing these films, in order to assure sales, make sure you get the cream of the crop. Beyond this commerce-based filtering, however, it should be noted that Japanese films in general tend to adhere to a fairly high quality standard (unless we're talking about sweaty guys in rubber suits . . .).

Consistent quality in Japanese films also extends to films in a sequence, like the Zatoichi series. In Hollywood, sequels tend to suck, and each one sucks worse than the previous one. But you can watch Zatoichi after Zatoichi and each one is great. This is because the filmmakers knew their stuff. They had a unified vision and exhibited less ego than their Hollywood counterparts. The contract directors at Daiei Studios actually took turns making the Zatoichi films, but outside of occasional stylistic differences, you'd never know it—they are seamless in a way that no Hollywood sequel ever is.

There is one caveat, however, namely that the first film in a series is often not as good as the second. This is true of Lone Wolf and Cub, Sleepy Eyes of Death, and Zatoichi. For some reason the first film in each of these series feels like the writers and directors were still grappling with the characters and exposition. By the second film, though, they've got it down—unencumbered by having to stop and give background, the second film in each series moves. Therefore, it's often a good idea when approaching a new series to watch the second film first, then go back and see the first one. This way you can hit the ground running and get the back story later.

The Big Five

Just as Hollywood had its Big Five movie studios in the '30s (Warners, Fox, Paramount, MGM, and RKO), so Tokyo had its own Big Five in the post–World War II period: Toho, Daiei, Shochiku, Toei, and Nikkatsu. Here's the breakdown:

Toho

Formed in 1933 as P.C.L. (Photo Chemical Laboratories), Toho is the Japanese studio best known to U.S. audiences not for its samurai films (of which it can boast more than a few masterpieces) but for a certain giant lizard. Toho was the home of directors Akira Kurosawa, Mikio Naruse, Kihachi Okamoto, Hiroshi Inagaki, and Ishiro Honda, close personal friend of Kurosawa and the man who gave us Godzilla. Famous Toho faces include Toshiro Mifune, Tatsuya Nakadai, Takashi Shimura, Minoru Chiaki, Daisuke Kato, Kamatari Fujiwara, Bokuzen Hidari, Yoshio Tsuchiya, Eijiro Tono, and Isao Kimura.

During World War II Toho did well, but in 1946 two labor disputes resulted in a number of top stars forming the Flag Group of Ten and leaving to form Shin Toho (New Toho), an idealistic venture that failed after a dozen years. Throughout the '50s and '60s Toho produced a steady stream of great films including all of Kurosawa's best work. Toho also distributed pictures produced by Mifune Pictures, Toshiro Mifune's production company, as well as Katsu Productions, the outfit owned by Shintaro "Zatoichi" Katsu.

Toho's successful distribution deals, combined with regular showings of its films in Toho-owned theaters in the U.S. (such as the Toho LaBrea in Los Angeles), made an indelible mark on American pop culture. Godzilla continues to cast a long shadow, unfortunately obscuring Toho's great samurai output. Nevertheless Toho samurai titles available today on VHS/ DVD far outnumber those from other members of the Big Five.

Daiei

Daiei was formed in 1942 as part of a wartime effort to merge the ten then-existing studios (Toho, Shochiku, Nikkatsu, Shinko, Koa, Daito, Nan-o, Tokyo Hassei, Otaguro, and Takarazuka) into two large ones. Masaichi Nagata, then head of Shinko, came up with the idea of a third studio (formed from Shinko, Nikkatsu, and Daito) called Dai-Nihon Eiga (Greater Japan Motion Pictures) or Daiei (big picture) for short. Nagata of course became the head of the new studio, raising suspicions that he had bribed the Information Office. He was arrested, but released after 50 days without being officially charged. He continued to produce films at Daiei until 1980.

Directors who called Daiei home include Kenji Mizoguchi, Kon Ichikawa, Tokuzo Tanaka, Kenji Misumi, Kazuo Ikehiro, Kazuo Mori, and Kimiyoshi Yasuda. Putting asses in seats for Daiei were Raizo Ichikawa, Shintaro Katsu, Tomisaburo Wakayama, as well as a colorful collection of contract players.

During the '60s Daiei made great chambara. The Zatoichi series (26 films starring Katsu) and the Sleepy Eyes of Death series (12 films starring Ichikawa) are some of the best samurai fare you'll ever see, and this was just a fraction of the movies Daiei churned out during that fabulous decade. Daiei also experimented with genre-blending, combining chambara with ghosts and giant monsters (see *Yokai Monsters* and *Daimajin* in the reviews section). Speaking of giant monsters, Masaichi Nagata introduced titanic turtle Gamera in 1965 to compete with Toho's Godzilla franchise, adding a new reptilian face to the kaiju pantheon.

Sadly, Daiei went out of business in the early '70s. But the studio's contribution to the samurai genre was incalculable, providing a wealth of titles for us to discover and enjoy for years to come.

Shochiku

The Shochiku company started out at the turn of the twentieth century as a theatrical outfit, owning Kabuki troupes and theaters. The company's founders were two former theater peanut vendors, Matsujiro Shirai and Takejiro Otani. Noticing the impact of D. W. Griffith's *Intolerance,* they decided to get into the moving picture game and started producing pictures in the '20s. Shochiku went on to become, alongside Toho, the biggest, most consistently successful of the Big Five. A bona fide entertainment mega-company, Shochiku's offerings include theater chains and video retail outlets.

A prestige outfit, Shochiku was the home of legendary directors Yasujiro Ozu, Nagisa Oshima, and Kenji Mizoguchi (who left for Daiei in the early '50s), as well as samurai film auteurs Hideo Gosha and Masaki Kobayashi. Although Shochiku's U.S. distribution doesn't come close to thatof Toho or Daiei, the half dozen Shochiku titles covered in this book are among the best the samurai genre has to offer, including *Harakiri, Tenchu!,* and *Hunter in the Dark.*

Toei

Toei (a contraction of Tokyo Eiga) was established in 1952 and immediately became a powerhouse, producing exciting, inexpensive jidai-geki. Following Shochiku's lead, Toei ramped up production to provide both halves of double bills (traditionally shared by two different studios), resulting in increased revenues and stock price.

During the '60s and '70s, the studio churned out hundreds of yakuza pictures, becoming highly influential in the genre. In the '80s, Toei moved into children's film and television, producing anime titles and the infamous "Mighty Morphin' Power Rangers." Toei has continued to thrive to the present and remains an entertainment industry force to be reckoned with. Sadly, Toei's distribution in the U.S. has been minimal, leaving samurai and yakuza enthusiasts at the mercy of bootleggers and shady foreign distributors.

Action directors Kinji Fukasaku and Teruo Ishii called Toei home, as did action man Shinichi "Sonny" Chiba, yakuza stars Ken Takakura and Koji Tsuruta, and chambara legend Kinnosuke Nakamura (later known as Kinnosuke Yorozuya).

Chiba and Nakamura star side by side in Fukasaku's 1978 samurai megaproduction, *Shogun's Samurai* (see review).

Nikkatsu

Of all the films reviewed in this book, none are from Nikkatsu. This is due to a combination of the studio's choice of genre output and a lack of any distribution scheme in the U.S. (outside of the odd release by American Cinematheque).

Nikkatsu is short for Nippon Katsudo Shashin (Japan Cinematograph Company) established in 1912, the oldest of the Big Five. During the '20s, Nikkatsu made a name for itself by actually making films about real people, the trials and tribulations of the poor and disenfranchised which came to be known as the "Nikkatsu Style" (as other studios wouldn't touch such topics).

In the early '30s Nikkatsu stumbled badly with unsuccessful sound-on-disc experiments, and, with the coming of World War II, the studio was absorbed into the newly formed Daiei. Nikkatsu did not resume production until the '50s, specializing in "Nikkatsu Action"—action/yakuza/western/spy films catering to the youth market. Their output was prolific and successful throughout the '50s and '60s, producing some 60 to 80 features annually and claiming half the top-grossing titles released domestically. The '70s proved more difficult, and in 1971 Nikkatsu switched over to producing "pink" films (softcore porno) exclusively, which they marketed as "roman porno" (short for "romantic porno").

House directors for Nikkatsu included Seijun Suzuki, Yasuharu Hasebe, and Noboru Tanaka. Among their top stars were Jo Shishido, Akira Kobayashi, Tetsuya Watari, and Ruriko Asaoka.

3

The Artists

The great films of the samurai genre are obviously the result of the hard work of thousands of people. Writers, editors, producers, actors, directors, cameramen, cinematographers, and designers all deserve praise that could fill volumes. The following short list of sketches comprises some of the heavy hitters, figures whose talents broke new ground and provided a depth and richness to the genre seen neither before nor since.

Akira Kurosawa (1910–1998)

His name translates as "bright black valley," an accurate description of the landscape that most intrigued him: the human soul. By far the most well-known Japanese director in the West, Akira Kurosawa introduced Japanese film to the world. A gifted artist who blazed a trail for his contemporaries, Kurosawa broke all the molds and provided the world with an incredible legacy of creative innovation in light and sound. He is the doorway through which most of us discover the cinema of Japan and, very likely, the samurai film.

Kurosawa started out writing scripts and became an assistant director for Toho in 1936 (back when it was still Photo Chemical Laboratories). He rose rapidly through the ranks, becoming a director in record time. By the 1950s he was a force to be reckoned with, a cinema titan of limitless energy

1980 Toho

A bad day to forget your umbrella: Kurosawa on the set of Seven Samurai

Kurosawa: A towering figure in Japanese film

and creative vision. Kurosawa could do it all: contemporary drama, psychological thriller, jidai-geki, arthouse, martial arts, chambara, tear-jerker, action, comedy, shakai-mono (social awareness story), crime drama, war epic, even propaganda films (during World War II).

Nicknamed "Tenno" (The Emperor), Akira Kurosawa was a stern taskmaster and an uncompromising visionary. But he was also a maverick, accused by many a countryman of making "un-Japanese" films. There's no doubt that he was more aware of and influenced by Western culture than his fellow directors: he adapted Shakespeare and Dostoyevsky and was a disciple of John Ford. These influences, however, never overshadowed his own firmly rooted cultural orientation. Nevertheless, after *Rashomon* won the coveted Grand Prix at the Venice International Film Festival in 1951, bringing praise from Western critics and audiences, Kurosawa was lambasted by critics at home. The rationale was that if foreigners could get a handle on his film, it must lack some intrinsic Japanese quality that would otherwise have repelled and confounded them. His detractors concluded that it was mere novelty and exoticism that attracted the foreigners. Kurosawa was enraged by this critical undermining of his work and protested vociferously.

Soon enough, however, Kurosawa was recognized, at home and abroad, as a world-class filmmaker, a master to take his place alongside Welles, Kubrick, Fellini, Renoir, and Bergman. At the height of his powers he produced a string of masterpieces unparalleled in the their humanism and cinematic invention: *Drunken Angel* (1948), *Stray Dog* (1949), *Rashomon* (1950), *Ikiru* (1952), *Seven Samurai* (1954), *Throne of Blood* (1957), *The Lower Depths* (1957), *The Hidden Fortress* (1958), *The Bad Sleep Well* (1960), *Yojimbo* (1961), *Sanjuro* (1962), *High and Low* (1963), and *Red Beard* (1965). After a slump in the '70s, he returned to form with the visually stunning *Kagemusha* (1980), *Ran* (1985), and *Dreams* (1990).

Masaki Kobayashi (1916–1996)

If the samurai genre has a social conscience, Masaki Kobayashi is it. His samurai films were intensely anti-feudal and his humanism was different from Kurosawa's: more political, more passionate, displaying a hatred for corrupt state power and the abuses it commits. Kobayashi frankly admitted that "[all my films were] concerned with resisting entrenched power. That's what *Harakiri* is about, of course, and [*Samurai*] *Rebellion* as well. I suppose I've always challenged authority. This has been true of my own life, including my life in the military" (Linda Hoaglund, "A Conversation with Kobayashi Masaki," *Positions 2-2*, 1994, p. 393).

A student of philosophy and art history, Kobayashi eventually left school to join Shochiku in 1941. Eight months later, he found himself in Manchuria with a rifle in his hands. He was against the war, hated the army, and refused promotion, remaining a private until his capture by the Americans in the southern Ryukyu Islands in 1945. He was a P.O.W. for a year before returning to Shochiku, where he resumed his career. Kobayashi funneled all the horror and frustration of his wartime experiences into the epic World War II trilogy *The Human Condition* (1959–1961), three films that traced the progress of a pacifist caught in circumstances similar to those faced by the filmmaker himself. The films made a star out of their leading man, Tatsuya Nakadai, and confirmed Kobayashi's genius. The first film, *Human Condition I: No Greater Love* (1959), won the San Giorgio prize at the Venice Film Festival in 1960.

Kobayashi only made 22 films in his career, due largely to his politically subversive, anti-authoritarian subject matter—Shochiku, the most conservative of the majors, eventually let him go and he worked for a time at Toho. Yet he graced these studios with one samurai masterpiece each, *Harakiri* (1962) and *Samurai Rebellion* (1967) respectively. You won't find better depictions of the true nature of Bushido anywhere, certainly not in the comparatively traditional, nostalgic work of Kurosawa. Kobayashi's mastery of cinematic form can also be witnessed, in a more purely formalist state, in the collected ghost stories that make up *Kwaidan* (1964).

Kobayashi's style is methodically paced, Kubrickian, executed with crystalline clarity. That he was not able to make more films in his career is testament to the triumph of the entrenched power he fought so hard against. Little wonder, then, that Japanese film so often contains such pessimistic fatalism.

Just look at Kobayashi and the message is clear: fight the system and you're going to lose.

Hideo Gosha (1929–1992)

From childhood, Hideo Gosha loved chambara. Little did young Hideo's parents realize that he would grow up to become one of the genre's greatest directors. Following a stint in the navy and a business degree from Meiji University, Gosha joined Nippon Television in 1953 as a reporter. In 1957 he moved to the newly founded Fuji Television and rose to the position of producer and director, creating successful action and chambara shows throughout the '50s. One show, *Three Outlaw Samurai,* featured the exploits of a Three Musketeers–style band of ronin. Impressed with his work on the show, Shochiku offered Gosha the chance to adapt it into a feature film in 1964. This became Gosha's screen debut, a simultaneous homage to and updating of several Akira Kurosawa films.

From there, Gosha went from strength to strength with a string of fantastic chambara pictures, each better than the one before: *Sword of the Beast* (1965), *The Secret of the Urn* (1966), *Samurai Wolf I* (1966), *Samurai Wolf II* (1966), *Goyokin* (1969), and *Tenchu!* (1969). *Goyokin* and *Tenchu!* were both big at the box office and represent the peak of Gosha's career. With the onset of the '70s, Gosha turned his attention to yakuza, yet most of these films were still period sword films such as *The Wolves* (1972), *Bandits vs. Samurai Squadron* (1978), and *Hunter in the Dark* (1979).

Gosha's contribution to the samurai genre was twofold: a febrile vitality combined with a frank realism. His days in TV honed his sense of timing, making for more compact scenes that move at a faster pace; at the same time the violence of his sword fights is at times shockingly brutal, with rending, ripping sound effects and fountains of blood. The graphic violence of Gosha's films never crosses over into exploitation—it simply explodes, much like violence does in real life, creating a shocking, disorienting chaos that's often over before we even realize what's happened.

Like Kurosawa, Gosha tends to probe the souls of his characters but with the political savvy and pessimism of Kobayashi. This makes him an intriguing hybrid and a filmmaker worth searching out. Unfortunately, Hideo Gosha's films are hard to find in the U.S.; although famous in Japan, Gosha is still virtually unknown in the West. This, combined with Shochiku's significant lack of overseas distribution, means you really have to hunt down his work.

Note: Beware of poor quality DVDs of Gosha fims. There are a number of them out there like *The Wolves, Hunter in the Dark,* and *Bandits vs. Samurai Squadron.* We can only hope that in time there will be a critical reevaluation and more works of this fine filmmaker will be made available in pristine digital transfer.

Shinobu Hashimoto (1917–)

What can you say about a screenwriter whose first script was *Rashomon?* Shinobu Hashimoto is the man behind some of the most important, intense, groundbreaking samurai films in the genre. He wrote scripts for all the top directors, the most for Akira Kurosawa (himself a superior screenwriter), from whom Hashimoto learned his craft. With Kurosawa he wrote *Rashomon* (1950), *Ikiru* (1952), *Seven Samurai* (1954), *Record of a Living Being* (1955), *Throne of Blood* (1957), *The Hidden Fortress* (1958), *The Bad Sleep Well* (1960), and *Dodes'ka-den* (1970). Reflecting on first meeting Hashimoto, Kurosawa remarked, "He seemed to have substance, and I took a liking to him" (Akira Kurosawa, *Something Like an Autobiography*, p. 181).

However, not every script Hashimoto wrote with Kurosawa came easily. The script for *Seven Samurai* was troubled at the outset because, as Hashimoto explained, "We wanted to write a screenplay about a single samurai. We decided to show one day in a samurai's life, from the time he woke up, prayed with incense, spent time with his family, went to the castle and so on. At one point during the day he would make some kind of mistake, and at the end of the story he would commit seppuku" (Stuart Galbraith IV, *The Emperor and the Wolf*, p. 170). After three months work, this storyline was abandoned for the band-of-ronin-fighting-bandits plot we all know and love, but Hashimoto saved the research he'd put in on the first draft, using it years later for *Harakiri* (1962), directed by Masaki Kobayashi. Hashimoto would go on to write *Samurai Rebellion* (1967) for Kobayashi as well.

For director Kihachi Okamoto he wrote *Samurai Assassin* (1965) and *Sword of Doom* (1966), two films so dense with historical detail he might have overdone it on the research. They nevertheless represent the height of that director's output. In 1969, a "banner year" for Hashimoto, he wrote *Tenchu!* (1969) for Hideo Gosha and *Samurai Banners* (1969) for Hiroshi Inagaki. Both films stand out in each director's oeuvre.

As noted above, Hashimoto had a tendency at times to overpack his scripts with characters and historical detail, but this is only a hindrance when one tries to absorb all the details in a single viewing. Fortunately, we live in the twenty-first century and can obtain our own copies of these films and watch them repeatedly at our leisure. In this way, the compact art of Shinobu Hashimoto's scripts can be savored and explored. That's the essence of art: its capacity for revisitation. With Hashimoto, revisitation isn't just rewarding, it's mandatory!

Toshiro Mifune (1920–1997)

The most influential Japanese actor of the twentieth century was undoubtedly Toshiro Mifune. The impact of *Rashomon* in 1950 was largely due to his electrifying performance. He starred in 16 of Akira Kurosawa's films, arguably the best in the director's canon. Mifune exhibited a range and intensity never before witnessed by Japanese audiences. Kurosawa himself was astounded: "Mifune had a kind of talent I had never encountered before in the Japanese film world," writes Kurosawa in his autobiography, *Something Like an Autobiography.* "It was, above all, the speed with which he expressed himself that was astounding. . . . The speed of his movements was such that he said in a single action what took ordinary actors three separate movements to express. He put forth everything directly and boldly, and his sense of timing was the keenest I had ever seen in a Japanese actor. And yet with all his quickness he also had surprisingly fine sensibilities. . . . I'm a person who is rarely impressed by actors, but in the case of Mifune I was completely overwhelmed" (Akira Kurosawa, *Something Like an Autobiography*, p. 161). Mifune's profes-

Toshiro Mifune in the 1950s

Mifune, the elder statesman

sional relationship with Kurosawa stands alongside the great actor/director pairings that include Von Sydow/Bergman, Wayne/Ford, Ryu/Ozu, Mastroianni/Fellini, and De Niro/Scorsese.

Born in Manchuria to Japanese parents, Mifune entered the army during World War II and served as a photographer. Even then he was aware of the power of the camera: he took photos of himself posing by fighter planes and sent them home to his family, claiming he was a flyer. After the war he found himself in Tokyo, penniless and in need of work. A friend of his was working as a cameraman at Toho and advised him to try out for the New Faces competition Toho regularly held to audition new talent. If he got his foot in the door as an actor, his friend reasoned, he could eventually transition over to the camera crew.

The audition was a disaster. Mifune resented being treated like a monkey, being ordered to act out this and that. When told to act drunk, he let out his anger and told the men assembled what he thought of them. They weren't impressed, but the ferocity of his rage fascinated a certain tall man standing in the back, one Akira Kurosawa. The rest is film history.

Toshiro Mifune went on to appear in 126 films and 17 TV movies. His versatility lent itself to a wide range of roles, allowing him to effectively portray a peasant or a lord, stern businessman or desperate criminal, severe samurai or clod-hopping clown. Of his own talent he said, "I'm not always great in pictures, but I'm always true to the Japanese spirit" (Stuart Galbraith IV, *The Emperor and the Wolf*, p. 6). This could be summed up as a kind of quiet strength, a resilient resignation that lay beneath the surface of the characters he played.

Tatsuya Nakadai (1930–)

Discovered working as a retail clerk by director Masaki Kobayashi, Tatsuya Nakadai went on to rival Toshiro Mifune as the greatest Japanese actor of the '60s samurai scene. They appeared together in a number of legendary samurai films like *Yojimbo* (1961) and *Samurai Rebellion* (1967). But Nakadai had an altogether different screen presence. Trained as a stage actor, he was lithe and supple, a snake to Mifune's stray dog.

Tatsuya Nakadai as Shingen Takeda in Kagemusha

Throughout his career he communicated a seething intensity through his large, glassy, low-lidded eyes that could convey menace, soul-searching sincerity, or complete ambiguity.

Tatsuya Nakadai first appeared onscreen in Akira Kurosawa's *Seven Samurai* (1954), as a walk-on samurai, an uncredited two seconds of screen time (it would be half a dozen years later before he worked with The Emperor again). Soon thereafter, he began his partnership with Kobayashi, appearing in *Black River* (1956), a film concerning criminal conduct on U.S. bases in Japan.

Nakadai in a pensive moment

Mr. Suave, Tatsuya Nakadai

Nakadai appeared in numerous films throughout the '50s including director Kon Ichikawa's *Conflagration* (1958), as a club-footed womanizer alongside Raizo Ichikawa's sociopathic monk, and *The Key* (1959), a kinky black comedy. But the role that brought him international acclaim was that of Kaji, the pacifist in Masaki Kobayashi's nine-hour, three-part war epic, *The Human Condition* (1959–1961). At this point Kurosawa gave him a second look and cast him as the psychotic yakuza Unosuke in *Yojimbo* (1961) opposite Toshiro Mifune. He would return to work with Kurosawa in *Sanjuro* (1962), *High and Low* (1963), *Kagemusha* (1980), and *Ran* (1985).

Throughout the '60s and '70s Nakadai was in so many great films it's almost ridiculous. With Masaki Kobayashi he went on make *Harakiri* (1962), *Kwaidan* (1964), *Samurai Rebellion* (1967), and *Inn of Evil* (1971). He starred in the Hideo Gosha pictures *Cash Calls Hell* (1966), *Goyokin* (1969), *Tenchu!* (1969), *The Wolves* (1972), *Bandits vs. Samurai Squadron* (1978), and *Hunter in the Dark* (1979). He starred in *Sword of Doom* (1966) and *Kill!* (1968) for Kihachi Okamoto. He shot *The Face of Another* (1966) with Hiroshi Teshigahara, *Kojiro* (1967) with Hiroshi Inagaki, *Buraikan* (1970) with Masahiro Shinoda, and *The Ambitious* (1970) with Daisuke Ito. Nakadai even appeared in a Zatoichi film, *Zatoichi—The Festival of Fire* (1970).

Now in his 70s, Tatsuya Nakadai is still going strong, a living legend of the Japanese stage and screen. He is truly a mesmerizing talent whose performances one can watch again and again.

Shintaro Katsu (1931–1997)

While known in the West only as Zatoichi, in Japan Shintaro Katsu was a superstar who appeared in over 100 feature films. So active was Katsu during the '60s that while filming the Zatoichi series (26 films, 1962–1989), he starred simultaneously in two other film series, Yakuza Soldier (9 films, 1965–1972) and Bad Reputation (aka Tough Guy, 16 films, 1961–1974). His boundless energy, amazing swordplay, and compelling mixture of warmth and lethality captivated Japanese audiences. They couldn't get enough of him. His husky

Shintaro Katsu bites off more than he can chew

Tough guy Katsu

Young Katsu with topknot

frame, gruff voice, and blunt manner stood in stark contrast to the usual slick pretty-boy matinee idol, making him a kind of anti-idol, but in the end his charm and personal magnetism won over the crowds.

Katsu was born Toshio Okumura into a family of Kabuki performers specializing in the traditional music and dance form Nagauta. Young Toshio and his big brother Masaru (later to become Tomisaburo Wakayama) were trained from childhood in Nagauta music (singing accompanied by shamisen). By age 20, Toshio became successor to his father, taking the name Katsutaro Kineya. In 1954, Katsutaro and his family toured the U.S., where he had a pivotal encounter with James Dean. Upon his return to Japan, the star-struck Katsutaro headed straight to Daiei Studios. In 1955 he appeared in *A Girl Isn't Allowed to Love* as Shintaro Katsu.

Katsu's big breakthrough came with his performance in *Samurai Vendetta* (1959) opposite then-reigning Daiei samurai star Raizo Ichikawa. The following year's *Agent Shiranui* (1960) saw Katsu starring for the first time as a blind masseur, although quite a different character from Zatoichi. In this film, Katsu's character murders and impersonates his master, a blind masseur of high rank. Based on the strength of Katsu's performance and popular response, the first Zatoichi film was released in 1962. By the mid-'60s, the Zatoichi series had become a phenomenon. Other studios tried to cash in on the blind sword-slinger craze, such as Shochiku, with their short-lived Crimson Bat series, featuring a blind swordswoman, Oichi (Yoko Matsuyama).

By the early '70s, Katsu had formed his own production company (Katsu Productions, what else?) and produced the Lone Wolf and Cub series (featuring his brother Tomisaburo Wakayama), as well as half a dozen Zatoichis and a new vehicle for himself, *The Razor*. By 1974, however, his film career was effectively over. He spent more and more of his time indulging his love of booze, women, tobacco, and pot (at one point getting himself busted in Hawaii for marijuana possession). He returned to make four films from 1988 to 1990, but by then his hard-partying lifestyle and mounting debts had caught up with him. Fortunately for us he left a rich film legacy behind and we can only hope more of his films will be released in the future.

Tomisaburo Wakayama (1929–1992)

Wakayama in stunning ensemble

Older brother of Shintaro Katsu, Tomisaburo Wakayama was the superior martial artist and a more ferocious screen presence. Not that he couldn't be funny and charming like his brother: check out one of his Wicked Priest films for the more antic side of the usually scowling Wakayama. Because of his imposing persona, he was often cast as heavies opposite Raizo Ichikawa and brother Katsu in Daiei chambara pictures of the '60s. He is best known in the West for his portrayal of Ogami Itto in the six Lone Wolf and Cub or "Baby Cart" films (1972–1974).

Wakayama began martial arts training in his early teens, his love of judo gradually overtaking his dedication to the family Kabuki troupe. He eventually left the theater to become a judo instructor, but wound up entering the film industry instead, appearing in his first film at roughly the same time as his brother (the mid-'50s). During his early career, his fascination with martial arts expanded, and soon he was mastering the sword skills of iaido and kendo, becoming the most formidable screen swordsman in chambara. He also augmented his sword and judo chops with bo-jutsu and shorinji kenpo.

Throughout the '60s Wakayama never failed to light up the samurai screen, making notable contributions to the Sleepy Eyes of Death, Zatoichi, and Shinobi no Mono (Ninja) series as well as countless other features. During the late '60s and early '70s he transitioned into the ultra-violent yakuza genre. Toward the end of a long and varied career, a 60-year-old Wakayama appeared as an aging yakuza boss in the Michael Douglas vehicle *Black Rain* (1989), delivering a haunting speech about the inky precipitation resulting from the U.S. atomic bomb blast at Hiroshima. He died of a heart attack three years later.

Raizo Ichikawa (1931–1969)

Considered the James Dean of Japanese cinema, the cool, charismatic Raizo Ichikawa was Daiei's bona fide superstar, rivaled in popularity only by Shintaro Katsu. To insure packed

Raizo Ichikawa: "You talkin' to me?"

Young Ichikawa in his argyle period

houses, theaters routinely booked double features of one star each, their divergent personae creating the perfectly balanced double bill. Katsu's affable earthiness offset Ichikawa's mysterious, wraithlike presence; Katsu's garrulous gambler contrasted with Ichikawa's cynical samurai; and where Katsu was a candid canine, Ichikawa proved the formidable feline.

Born Kichiya Ota in Kyoto, Ichikawa was adopted by the Kabuki actor Kudanji Ichikawa and given the name Yoshio Takeuchi. By age 20 he was an established Kabuki performer, playing such prestigious houses as the Osaka Kabukiza under the name Raizo Ichikawa. A few years later he made his screen debut for Daiei in *The Great White Tiger Platoon* (1954). Even at this early stage Ichikawa received the full star treatment: he would arrive at the studio each day by limousine, while fellow thespian Katsu had to take the bus!

In addition to samurai films, Ichikawa also appeared in prestige pictures for Kenji Mizoguchi (*Tales of the Taira Clan,* 1955) and Kon Ichikawa (*Conflagration,* 1958), the latter based on the novel by Yukio Mishima. His best-known series in the West are the Sleepy Eyes of Death films (12 pictures, 1963–1969) and the Ninja saga (7 pictures, 1962–1966). The Ninja films are particularly worth seeing for anyone interested in the origins of this sub-genre, as they were the first (and still the best) ever made. The ninja action and choreography were supervised by real-life ninja masters Masaki Hatsumi and Toshitsugu Takamatsu, so what you're seeing, while somewhat cinematically spiced up, are the real movements, stances, leaps, and shuriken-flinging of the original shinobi. Very cool.

Tragically, Ichikawa died just before his 38th birthday from rectal cancer. This untimely death and his matinee idol good looks have prompted the James Dean comparisons, but the big difference between the two stars is that upon his death, Dean had made three films. Ichikawa, in his short career, made over 100. Talk about your Japanese work ethic!

Tetsuro Tamba (1922–)

The ubiquitous Tetsuro Tamba (sometimes credited as Tetsuro Tanba) is one of those actors who seems to have been in everything. How has he done it? His secret, by his own ad-

Tetsuro "Never
Turns Down a Role"
Tamba

Tamba: A living
legend

mission: he's never turned down a role. This philosophy has gained him appearances in upward of 300 films, including some of the best of the samurai genre. As the cruel and sadistic Omodaka he fought Tatsuya Nakadai in *Harakiri* (1962); he was Shiba the heroic ronin in *Three Outlaw Samurai* (1964); and in *Shogun's Samurai* (1978) he is the mysterious master swordsman Genshinsai, the only man who'd dare challenge the mighty Munenori Yagyu.

Born Shozaburo Tanba into a noble family as old as Japan itself, the young Tetsuro enjoyed a life of luxury among elites. In 1951, he won a New Faces competition at Shin Toho, kicking off a long and varied career. From Shin Toho he moved on to shoot pictures for Toho, Toei, and Shochiku. While he often played heavies, his range was such that he could really pull off any role, from a kind-hearted samurai to a wicked yakuza thug to even Tiger Tanaka, the head of the Japanese secret police in the James Bond vehicle *You Only Live Twice* (1967). As with other journeymen actors such as Klaus Kinski or Michael Caine, the roles Tamba took were not always under the strictest quality control, but this never stopped him from putting in a class performance.

During the '80s, Tamba became something of a cult figure as a result of his writings (and movie projects based upon them) concerning what he termed "Dai Reikai" (great spirit world), a teaching he developed to help those approaching decrepitude and death (like himself) find peace and acceptance. One film concerns a fellow who dies in a car accident, wanders about in the world of the dead, and finally comes back to life. Dai Reikai became a phenomenon in Japan, helping to ease scores of followers into that good night. However, all this death talk hasn't slowed Tamba down one bit, and he continues to make film after film, recently appearing as the grandfather in Takashi Miike's musical black comedy *The Happiness of the Katakuris* (2001) and as the uptight uncle in the moving rural samurai drama *The Twilight Samurai* (2002). Perhaps he really does know something we don't know . . . ?

Kurosawa-gumi

"Gumi" means group or gang. The Kurosawa-gumi is a term coined for the stock company of players that routinely showed up in Akira Kurosawa's pictures during the '50s and '60s. They include Toshiro Mifune, Takashi Shimura, Tatsuya Nakadai, Kamatari Fujiwara, Bokuzen Hidari, Isuzu Yamada, Minoru Chiaki, Eijiro Tono, Susumu Fujita, Yoshio Tsuchiya, Yunosuke Ito, Isao Kimura, Daisuke Kato, and Kyoko Kagawa.

The Kurosawa-gumi were an elite group of consummate professionals—they had to be. To pass muster with Kurosawa was no easy feat: many an actor was chewed up and spat out by The Emperor. You had to stay on your toes, know your chops, hit your mark, and be ready to comply with the most impossible demands. In *Rashomon,* for example, Machiko Kyo was forced to stare at the sun without blinking, and in *Throne of Blood* Isuzu Yamada had to keep her face as frozen as a Noh mask. During the shooting of *Yojimbo,* Tatsuya Nakadai was told not to blink while firing his gun (while holding it up very close to his eye). No deviation would be tolerated. It was intense, sometimes nerve-wracking, but the results are there on the screen: perfection.

Below is a chart showing how Kurosawa cast various Kurosawa-gumi members in the six samurai features from his Mifune period (1948–1965).

The Kurosawa-gumi

	Rashomon	Seven Samurai	Throne of Blood	The Hidden Fortress	Yojimbo	Sanjuro
Toshiro Mifune	Tajomaru	Kikuchiyo	Washizu	Makabe	Sanjuro	Sanjuro
Takashi Shimura	Woodcutter	Kambei	Odagura	Nagakura	Tokuemon	Kurofuji
Kamatari Fujiwara		Manzo		Matashichi	Tazaemon	Takebayashi
Minoru Chiaki	Priest	Heihachi	Miki	Tahei		
Yoshio Tsuchiya		Rikichi	Samurai		Kohei	Samurai
Daisuke Kato	Policeman	Shichiroji				Inokichi
Isuzu Yamada			Asaji			Orin

Seeing the Films

The good news about the films discussed in this book is that they're available to the public. I didn't go to some university film archive and write about a bunch of films you'll never see. These films, in addition to being the cream of the crop, are all 100% acquirable—you will be able to rent and/or purchase all of them. Keep in mind that you will do so with varying degrees of difficulty—in the case of roughly 90% of these films, you can pick up a new copy immediately, online or elsewhere. The rest are a little more problematic, either because they're out of print or only available through a third-party collector. Each review is appended with an availability rating: "Easy," "Tricky," or "Tough." Here's what each classification means:

Easy

One-click done. You can get it from Amazon.com, HKFlix. com, or any number of other online retailers. Some you may find in a Borders or Barnes & Noble, like Kurosawa titles and Zatoichi, but not as many as the online stores. In any case, we're talking pretty much instant gratification.

Tricky

These are films that get a limited video release or no release at all. In some cases they're out of print but you can still find

1969 Toho

The bigger the star, the bigger the helmet: Toshiro Mifune and the cast of Samurai Banners

used copies for sale online. I've found a lot of out-of-print titles through Amazon.com, using their Amazon Marketplace feature (individuals and third party businesses that sell through Amazon). Also, there are independent distributors that provide subtitled copies of rare and hard-to-find films from whom you can make purchases directly online (a list is available on The Ninja Dojo website at http://www.ninjadojo. com). Also, if you live in one of the bigger cities, there should be a Japanese or Asian-oriented retailer in your area.

Tough

Some of these films are just plain tough to get. You have to keep scouring the web, checking back periodically on eBay, Amazon, or wherever else these things pop up. I acquired several out-of-print videotapes from AnimEigo's Sleepy Eyes of

Death series this way, waiting months until I found a used copy for sale. It's hard, but rewarding. Don't give up. If you look long and hard enough, your persistence will pay off!

As for renting samurai films, the bigger the city you're in, the better your chances. Out in the sticks, it's unlikely you'll find a copy of *Chushingura* or *Kwaidan,* even though they're easy to buy online. But in college towns and bigger cities, particularly those with a large Asian community, you'll find you can even rent rare titles, bootlegs, whatever. So demographics has a lot to do with what's available to you. Bear in mind there are also online rental outfits like Greencine.com and Netflix.com which you can use wherever, so if you're in an isolated location these services might be just the ticket.

And then there's the big screen. Colleges and arthouses are a great resource for foreign films, and Japanese films are right in there, although how many samurai films you'll see is another question. More often the Japanese film fare at these theaters winds up being either the academy-approved stuff (Ozu, Mizoguchi, Kurosawa) or contemporary film—not much sword action. Don't get me wrong, there's nothing wrong with that, but this is a book about sword films; you're going to get a lot more flashing blades and bloody revenge on video and DVD. However, don't let that stop you from going to arthouse and college theaters and exploring other types of Japanese film. You'll most likely find that samurai films are a doorway to a wider experience of Japanese film and foreign film in general.

Using the Handbook

Stray Dogs & Lone Wolves is designed as a companion, a faithful guide and reference as you discover the great works of this vital film genre. It provides historical background, cultural insights, production anecdotes, actor and director bios, and detailed plot synopses (although I never give away an ending).

The book also features a combined glossary and cross-index, creating a one-stop shop for all questions samurai. You can look up actors, films, terminology, even specific words and phrases often heard in the films like "yosh" (so be it), "baka" (fool), and "so ka" (is that so?). Throughout the review section, many of these names and terms have been printed in **bold text**, your cue to check the cross-index at the back for more information. This provides instant enlightenment for those inevitable questions that arise while viewing samurai movies.

The book also features vital, never-before-in-English actor/character attributions. This last feature is invaluable in the pursuit of what I like to call "samurai spotting." Just as bird watchers identify and name birds and train spotters identify and name trains, samurai spotters like to identify and name actors in samurai films. ("Hey, isn't that the guy who played the one-eyed ronin in *Hunter in the Dark?*") The samurai genre is filled with great actors, and getting to know these artists and spot them as they appear again and again is one of the hidden pleasures of watching these films.

One thing to bear in mind regarding the English titles for Japanese films: there are often more than one; depending on the scope and location of distribution, they can pick up quite a few alternative titles. For example, Tomisaburo Wakayama's "Wicked Priest" series is alternatively known as "Killer Priest," "Priest Killer," and "Heinous Priest"—it depends on who's doing the translating. I've endeavored to choose the most commonly used, default English title for each of the films (as well as supplying its original Japanese title), so between the two you should have what you need to track it down.

As mentioned earlier, Japanese people commonly state their names as surname/given name. In this book I've opted for the Western form: Toshiro Mifune and not Mifune Toshiro. Occasionally there is a character in a film whose name is so iconic in its Japanese form (such as Ogami Itto in the Lone Wolf and Cub series, or Nemuri Kyoshiro in the Sleepy Eyes of Death series) that I use that form instead. Another point: the romanization of character names is not entirely consistent. ("Romanization" refers to the way Japanese words are rendered into the 26-letter English alphabet.) Different film distributors use different romanization schemes: one film might have a character labeled "Gonzo" and another might have a "Gonzou," even though it's the exact same name). When writing about the characters in the films, I favored the way their names were spelled on the screen, regardless of how they are romanized. I hope this will not cause undue confusion.

Part II
The Films

5

The '50s

Rashomon

Rashomon

1950, Daiei

DIRECTOR: Akira
Kurosawa

CAST: Toshiro Mifune,
Machiko Kyo,
Masayuki Mori,
Takashi Shimura,
Minoru Chiaki,
Kichijiro Ueda,
Fumiko Honma,
Daisuke Kato

AVAILABILITY: Easy

COMMENT: DVD from
Criterion Collection

Rashomon is among the finest films ever made, right up there with *The Seventh Seal, Grand Illusion, The Third Man, L'Avventura,* and *Citizen Kane.* It is also a samurai film, proving the genre can accommodate a masterpiece of world cinema (see also **Harakiri**, **Kwaidan**, and **Seven Samurai**).

Rashomon is a puzzle piece. Nobody, not even the writer and director, really knows what happens in it, for it concerns truth and the way the light of truth reflects and refracts through the mind of a human being. The story is simple: a samurai, his wife, and a bandit encounter one another in the forest, one of them winds up dead, and a woodsman happens upon the scene at some point. These are the only "facts" of which we can be sure. Beyond that, we have only their individual, conflicting reports, which they relate, both to a local magistrate and, second hand, to a cynical commoner. The magistrate is never shown, he is only a first-person presence (the camera) to whom the principle characters give their accounts. The magistrate is, in fact, a stand-in for the audience, allowing us to hear the wildly divergent testimonies and reach our own decision.

There is so much going on in this film that to attempt a treatment is to get caught up in the enigma that it presents, an

*The venerable Ta-
kashi Shimura*

impenetrable conundrum that has confounded and delighted filmgoers for over half a century. It is based upon two short stories, "In a Grove" and "Rashomon," both by renowned author Ryunosuke Akutagawa (1892–1927). The latter tale provides the frame story within which the former is played out. "Rashomon" was the name for the southern gate of Kyoto, a massive structure typical of the Heian period (794–1184) with huge pillars and the capacity to house a garrison. It is here, beneath the crumbling ruins of the gate, that the woodcutter (**Takashi Shimura**), the commoner (**Kichijiro Ueda**), and a priest (**Minoru Chiaki**) gather, sheltering from a torrential downpour. The priest and the woodcutter have just attended a murder inquest, and describe to the commoner the testimonies of the bandit Tajomaru (**Toshiro Mifune**), a samurai (Masayuki Mori), and his wife (**Machiko Kyo**). The samurai happens to be the murdered man, so his story is told by a medium (Fumiko Honma). A statement is also given by the policeman (**Daisuke Kato**) who apprehended Tajomaru.

What follows is a confounding journey through the deluded psyches of the various deponents, as well as that of the woodcutter, who has his own story to tell (contradicting the other contradictory accounts). Director Akira Kurosawa himself had this to say about *Rashomon*: "Human beings are unable to be honest with themselves about themselves. They cannot talk about themselves without embellishing. This script portrays such human beings—the kind who cannot survive without lies to make them feel they are better people than they really are" (Akira Kurosawa, *Something Like an Autobiography*, p. 183).

The script was a collaboration between Kurosawa and a 32-year-old beginner named **Shinobu Hashimoto**. Their partnership would be a long and fruitful one, lasting 20 years and producing eight Kurosawa classics including **Seven Samurai, Throne of Blood,** and **The Hidden Fortress**. The script is noteworthy not only for the things people say, but for the long stretches wherein nothing is said at all. The influence of silent film is strong in *Rashomon,* as it was on a young Akira Kurosawa, who never forgot the valuable lessons it taught him, namely the power of the human face and form to communicate every possible emotion and mental state. He was fortunate in assembling a first-rate cast capable of meeting the demands of these long, silent sequences.

The look of *Rashomon* is like no other film in the Kurosawa canon, due to the genius of its director of photography, **Kazuo Miyagawa**. Miyagawa played Greg Toland to Kurosawa's Orson Welles, the two men challenging each other to greater and greater heights of invention. Just look at the elaborate tracking shots of the woodcutter as he walks through the forest in the beginning of the film; note the way the shadows of leaves play across the faces of the principal characters, a meticulously crafted effect involving large mirrors to reflect the sunlight and hand-manipulated leafy branches; observe at any moment the striking chiaroscuro; and witness the face of the sun, filmed here for the first time, shining down through the trees, something no cinematographer had dared try before. This is not just great filmmaking, it's a pivotal moment in cinema history.

During shooting, Akira Kurosawa was displeased with the rain; it didn't look dense enough, so he had black ink mixed with the water, which was sprayed from fire engines. The effect works: the rain is an oppressive deluge that perpetually pours over the massive gate. The blasted, ravaged state of the structure disguised structural problems, as Kurosawa explains: "What we built as a set was gigantic. It was so immense that a complete roof would have buckled the support pillars. Using the artistic device of dilapidation as an excuse, we constructed only half a roof and were able to get away with our measurements" (*Something Like an Autobiography*, Akira Kurosawa, p. 181).

Rashomon won the Grand Prix at the Venice International Film Festival in 1951, the first Japanese film to do so. This exposed it to a wider world audience and opened the door for many Japanese films to follow. In addition, it won the Academy Award for Best Foreign Language Film for 1951.

Gate of Hell

Jigokumon

1953, Daiei

DIRECTOR: Teinosuke Kinugasa

CAST: Kazuo Hasegawa, Machiko Kyo, Isao Yamagata

AVAILABILITY: Easy

COMMENT: VHS from Home Vision Entertainment

Think samurai are just cold, dispassionate retainers, living only to serve the will of their lord? Think a samurai would never let his lust pull him down into the fires of hell? Think again.

This early '50s entry from **Daiei**, while not strictly a sword film, is nevertheless important for the samurai film enthusiast: it gives us a glimpse into the hoary past of medieval Japan, to the early years of the samurai and the world of **Bushido**—most samurai movies are set during the **Edo period**. It's remarkable to see how consistent samurai culture remained over the centuries. Dramatically, *Gate of Hell* shows us what happens when the tenets of Bushido are abandoned for the sake of carnal lust. Unfortunately for all involved, it doesn't end well. . . .

The year is 1159 and a rebel uprising has broken out in the imperial capital of Kyoto. Clan loyalist Moritoh Endo (Kazuo Hasegawa) makes a daring rescue of a woman he thinks is the Empress, only to learn that he has in fact saved a kagemusha (double), a beautiful lady-in-waiting named Kesa (the lovely and talented **Machiko Kyo**). He is smitten, and when asked later by his daimyo to name a reward for his bravery, he requests Kesa's hand in marriage. Moritoh is informed that she is already married to another samurai, Wataru Watanabe (**Isao Yamagata**), and that he cannot have her. This sets Moritoh off; he becomes a man obsessed, a samurai stalker. His character disintegrates before our eyes, and it's not long before he's stomping on a koto (Japanese harp), kicking a dog, and challenging everyone around him to a duel!

Ask Takuan, the Know-It-All Priest

Q: I noticed in *Gate of Hell* that Kesa's Aunt Sawa has black teeth. I see this occasionally in other samurai flicks as well. What's going on? Did they have really bad oral hygene?

A: No no, it was not her toothbrush that ruined Sawa's smile, it was the practice of ohaguro, a ridiculous fashion in ancient Japan. Acidic dyes were applied to the teeth, permanently blackening them. This bizarre manifestation of vanity was very popular in Sawa's day and continued to go in and out of style for centuries. By the Edo period it was much less fashionable, and only employed by old-fashioned married women.

Soon all of Kyoto knows that Moritoh is in love with another man's wife. And he'll do anything to get her. He tries challenging her husband to a horse race, perhaps to humiliate him, or as a pretext for further personal conflict. The husband, a mild-mannered man with a long, soulful face and kind expression, seems to let Moritoh win, so as not to exacerbate the situation. Of course this only enrages Moritoh more. Tension mounts as Moritoh begins to threaten Kesa's family members, and finally Kesa herself. He eventually coerces her into helping him set up the circumstances of her husband's murder. As mentioned above, things don't end well.

Visually, *Gate of Hell* is a knockout, presented with a stately grandeur, a sweeping play of deeply saturated technicolor blues and reds, and featuring Kesa consistently in stunning kimono of gold or orange. These are important colors symbolically. Orange is a sacred color in the Shinto religion and underscores Kesa's purity of spirit; gold is used to represent her precious qualities, making her seem like a radiant angel. The filmmaker plays with a bit of Montague/Capulet color dichotomy as well, often dressing Moritoh in blue, particularly during the horse-racing sequence, when he goes against the "red team," his rival Wataru riding in a striking crimson tunic. (**Akira Kurosawa** would later utilize the same red/blue/yellow scheme to great effect in his King Lear spectacular, *Ran*.)

A note of warning to action fans: *Gate of Hell* is not heavy on action. There is some fighting with rebel forces in the beginning, but the remainder of the film is more about escalating inner tension, mental and emotional deterioration, and a kind of "he knows you're alone" dread. In a way, *Gate of Hell* has more in common with contemporary psychological thrillers of the '90s, where the most threatening aspect of the story is one very unbalanced man. Moritoh's sexual obsession is played like a spell or a curse, so suddenly and completely does it overtake him. The man he becomes is an inversion of the righteous samurai, a man completely unhinged by his own lust.

In 1954, *Gate of Hell* won the Grand Prize at the Cannes Film Festival, and the Academy Award for Best Foreign Language Film.

Seven Samurai

Shichinin no samurai

1954, Toho

DIRECTOR: Akira
Kurosawa.

CAST: Toshiro Mifune,
Takashi Shimura,
Yoshio Inaba, Seiji
Miyaguchi, Minoru
Chiaki, Daisuke Kato,
Isao Kimura, Keiko
Tsushima, Kamatari
Fujiwara, Bokuzen
Hidari, Yoshio
Tsuchiya, Eijiro Tono,
Isao Yamagata, Yoshio
Kosugai, Kokuten
Kodo, Tatsuya
Nakadai

AVAILABILITY: Easy

COMMENT: DVD from
Criterion Collection

1954 Toho

Seven Samurai

Seven ronin defend a village from bandits. Some of them die.
The end. What's the big deal? Well, somewhere along the way
your life is changed.

For those watching *Seven Samurai* for the first time,
there is more than likely an expectation of dour, frowning,
humorless Japanese men of honor ready to die fighting for the
Bushido code, etc. What a revelation then, to find oneself in
the company of gentle, noble, laughing men who embody a
humanity and decency far beyond the archetypal Hollywood
action hero. Make no mistake, however, these guys are deadly
serious when it comes to battle; they're kick-ass warriors, far
beyond the expectations of the wretched farmers who hire
them. They radiate a cool Zen serenity that stays with you
long after the film has ended.

Here's the rundown on the eponymous ronin:

KAMBEI (**Takashi Shimura**)—He's the leader, older and
wiser, a battle-savvy veteran of many wars whose very presence engenders awe and respect. He would, of course, be the
last to agree with this assessment: "You embarrass me. You're
overestimating me. Listen, I'm not a man with any special
skill. But I've had plenty of experience in battles, losing battles, all of them. In short, that's all I am." Don't you believe it,
that's just his self-deprecating manner. He's magnificent.

KATSUHIRO (**Isao Kimura**)—The youngster, and as such
the stand-in for the audience. It's all new to him (and us), and
his performance is all the more impressive considering that
Isao Kimura was 31 years old at the time; you'd never know
he was more than 17 or 18. We meet Katsuhiro early on, as he
witnesses Kambei disarm and dispatch a thief (**Eijiro Tono**)
who has kidnapped a seven-year-old boy. Filled with admira-
tion, he begs Kambei to take him as a disciple. Kambei refuses
him repeatedly, but the youth's tenacity eventually wears him
down. Katsuhiro's in.

KIKUCHIYO (**Toshiro Mifune**)—The wild one. Kikuchiyo is
similar to the bandit Tajomaru in **Rashomon**, exhibiting the
same over-the-top histrionics, wild faces, and generally un-
washed itchiness. But he's not a bandit, he's a farmboy who's

Kambei

1954 Toho

Heihachi

1954 Toho

Kyuzo

1954 Toho

run away to become a samurai. He's got a huge nodachi (outsized battle sword). He's got pomp and swagger. He's even got a pedigree showing his name and lineage, which he uses to prove to Kambei that he is a true samurai. Only problem is, the document states his year of birth as "the second year of Tensho" (1574). Kambei and the others burst out laughing, as this would make Kikuchiyo 13 years old. (This detail also reveals a continuity error in the film: The opening exposition card after the credits states that the story takes place in the early 16th century, whereas Kikuchiyo's document places the action in 1587.)

GOROBEI (**Yoshio Inaba**)—The smiling samurai. Like Kambei, he's seen a few battles, and becomes Kambei's de facto lieutenant. When we first meet Gorobei, Kambei is auditioning samurai for the upcoming battle with the bandits. Kambei has instructed Katsuhiro to hide behind the door with a large tree branch and whack the samurai over the head as they enter. This is a test. Their first candidate (**Isao Yamagata**) catches the club, but turns down the gig. But Gorobei stops before even entering, grins, and says, "Please! No jokes." Kambei beams, and Gorobei joins them. As the samurai who smiles the most, Yoshio Inaba's performance is all the more impressive when you realize that on the set he was miserable most of the time. Director **Akira Kurosawa**, for no particular reason, had singled him out for abuse, making him the whipping boy of the shoot. Kurosawa often did this, not a flattering aspect of his character. They didn't call him The Emperor for nothing.

SHICHIROJI (**Daisuke Kato**)—This chubby, bald samurai was Kambei's right-hand man in many a campaign, and the two are immensely pleased and somewhat shocked to see each other again. Shichiroji acts as Chief Operating Officer to Kambei's Chief Executive Officer (if such corporate analogies can be drawn). Knowing his former commander's mind, he instinctively sets about executing the procedural aspects of Kambei's battle plans. Unfortunately, Daisuke Kato is underutilized in the film. A beloved comedic character actor of the day (see his hilariously bestial Inokichi in *Yojimbo*), he doesn't have much to do here beyond boss farmers around in

Gorobei

1954 Toho

Kikuchiyo

1954 Toho

Katsuhiro

1954 Toho

preparation for the decisive confrontation with the bandits. Once the battle is underway, though, he fights valiantly.

HEIHACHI (**Minoru Chiaki**)—Gorobei happens upon this cheerful fellow chopping wood to pay for his meal at a local tavern. Heihachi candidly admits that his swordsmanship is second rate, but his frank, good-natured character instantly endears him to the group. "Good company in adversity," says Gorobei. It's refreshing in this setting to find someone valued for more than merely his skill set. Casting Minoru Chiaki in this role was a stroke of genius, as the actor's real-life personality was not far off from that of Heihachi, imparting added verisimilitude to his performance.

KYUZO (Seiji Miyaguchi)—The master swordsman. The role, originally intended for Mifune, is carried off so expertly, you'd never know that Miyaguchi had never handled a sword before. Clearly the theater-trained actor knew how to prepare for a role. His performance is dead-on, the epitome of the Bushido ideal: focused clarity of mind and spirit, a samurai at one with his sword, ready to die in an instant. Kyuzo has the fewest lines in the picture, but he doesn't need them. He's a man of action, so cool that on an ambush mission he almost falls asleep waiting for a group of bandits. Upon their arrival, however, he's eliminated two before we even know what's happened. Over the course of the film he gains the undying idol-worship of Katsuhiro, who tells him in a fit of excitement, "You are really great! I've always wanted to tell you that!"

Then of course there are the farmers. These men carry most of the emotional tension of the film. There's Rikichi (**Yoshio Tsuchiya**), the young farmer whose intense hatred of the bandits and frantic anxiety over the village's fate stem from a secret shame. Manzo (**Kamatari Fujiwara**) is a nasty piece of work, an oyaji not above killing samurai on the run and stripping their armor. He has a daughter (Keiko Tsushima) whose chastity is his unhealthy obsession. There's also stand-up dude Mosuke (Yoshio Kosugai) and the Grandad (Kokuten Kodo), the village elder who initially suggests hiring the samurai.

When Kikuchiyo finds Manzo's stash of samurai armor, it creates the first serious rift between the farmers and the samurai. The normally easy-going Heihachi says, "I'd like to

Shichiroji

kill every farmer in this village." Kikuchiyo, who knows all about farmers, sets them straight: "A fine idea! Hey, you, what do you all think of farmers? Saints? Bah! They're foxy beasts! They say: 'We've no rice, we've no wheat, we've got nothing!' But they have. They have everything! Dig under the floors! Or search the barns! You'll find plenty! Rice, salt, beans, sake! Hah! Ahhahah! Look into the canyons—hidden farms! They pose as saints but are full of lies! If they smell a battle, they hunt the defeated! Listen, farmers are stingy, foxy, blubbering, mean, stupid, and murderous." Somehow this speech diffuses the situation. It's as if the realization that the farmers aren't merely helpless victims creates some grudging respect among the ronin. Later, on the eve before the big battle, Kikuchiyo's words prove true as the farmers provide one hell of a party, with rice cakes and sake all around.

No discussion of the farmers is complete without mentioning Yohei (**Bokuzen Hidari**). For many, Yohei is the star of the show, a rubber-faced old man for whom every minute of life is a trial and conundrum. He is a tragedy mask in a kimono, the sad sack's sad sack who steals every scene. Bokuzen Hidari was playing these befuddled old men long before he became one himself, and continued thereafter, a Japanese film institution. Yohei is forever infuriating Kikuchiyo, providing

Character Actor Hall of Fame

Bokuzen Hidari (1894—1971)

Lovable, hapless old sad sack Bokuzen Hidari (real name Ichiro Mikashima) was a popular character actor with a face that bespoke of never-ending grief and befuddlement. The corners of his mouth regularly pulled downward, his eyes wincing, he is instantly recognizable and was so beloved that his talents were always in demand. He began playing his trademark sad old milquetoast in middle age, and grew into the part over the years; toward the end of his career, as an old man in his seventies, studio heads would half-jokingly urge their directors to shoot his scenes quickly before he dropped dead. Hidari's performances weren't limited to samurai films. A frequent member of the Kurosawa-gumi, he appeared in modern dramas such as *Ikiru,* turning in a marvelous performance as timid clerk turned sake-fueled tiger! (Ironically, he was a tee-totaler). He also made a brief but memorable appearance in the first Gamera film, and played the near-deaf fireworks maker in *Zatoichi's Flashing Sword.* He had a large part in *The Lower Depths* as a wise old man in a flophouse. But his finest hour is as plucky peasant Yohei in *Seven Samurai.* His comic business with Toshiro Mifune, his bravery in battle, and that face all transform a minor role into a remarkably rounded and unforgettable character.

1954 Toho

Kikuchiyo's fraudulent pedigree is exposed in Seven Samurai

superb comic moments, such as when a frustrated Kikuchiyo roars, "Yohei! What's wrong with your face!" He also proves to be a brave fighter; he is the first to spear a bandit, his contorted countenance frozen with fear.

Seven Samurai also marks the screen debut of **Tatsuya Nakadai**. It's just a walk-on; he plays the first of many ronin the farmers see when searching for protectors, and his appearance is just a couple of seconds as he walks across the screen. According to Nakadai, Kurosawa was displeased with his movements, yelling, "That's not how a samurai walks!" The director worked with him for hours to get just the right poise and stride, until he was satisfied. He must have seen potential in the 19-year-old actor; any other director would have simply gotten someone else. It's a tribute to Kurosawa's eye for talent—Nakadai went on to become one of the great screen legends of the '60s and '70s (see more of him in ***Samurai Rebellion, Yojimbo, Harakiri, Sanjuro, Kwaidan, Kagemusha,*** and ***Sword of Doom***).

It's important to note the distinction between the ronin in

1954 Toho

Kikuchiyo shows 'em what he's made of in Seven Samurai

Seven Samurai with the more alienated and misanthropic variety that came along in the '60s. In comparison, the samurai here are quasi-mystical, Zen supermen, almost angelic in their spiritual supremacy over the earthy farmers and bestial bandits. This is due in part to Kurosawa's own idolization of the samurai, himself a descendant of samurai lineage. It also happened to be 1954 and social commentary in jidai-geki wasn't yet in vogue. But even in the '60s Kurosawa was not one to question the underlying contradictions of Bushido and samurai culture. While a moralist, Kurosawa tended to avoid political critiques; his films never explore the anti-feudal themes present in the works of **Hideo Gosha** or **Masaki Kobayashi**. He manages this by setting most of his samurai films in the **Sengoku period**, a time before the rigid social engineering of the **Tokugawa period**. The Sengoku period was a time of war and chaos, more wide-open and better suited to Kurosawa's liberal-humanist mindset and morality-tale plotlines.

Shot on location for **Toho** Studios, *Seven Samurai* was the most expensive Japanese film ever made, costing ¥210,000,000 (some $560,000). This was at least five times the average film budget. It was also the longest, running 207 minutes, roughly three and a half hours. Add to this the studio's other two big features for 1954, **Hiroshi Inagaki**'s *Samurai 1: Musashi Miyamoto* and Ishiro Honda's new monster movie, *Godzilla*, and you can bet it was white knuckle time at Toho. Fortunately all three films were big successes, guaranteeing more work for the filmmakers. It's a shame that more people in the West have seen *Godzilla* than the other two films combined.

In discussing artistic achievements of the caliber of *Seven Samurai*, one can only scratch the surface. The fact is that Akira Kurosawa and a cast and crew of hundreds went to a lot of trouble to tell their story themselves, and their work is the final word; in the end, all that need be said is right up there on the screen. If you haven't seen *Seven Samurai*, see it. If you have, see it again. In any case, you'll be amazed at how fast three and a half hours can fly by.

Samurai 1: Musashi Miyamoto

Miyamoto Musashi

1954, Toho

DIRECTOR: Hiroshi Inagaki

CAST: Toshiro Mifune, Rentaro Mikuni, Kuroemon Onoe, Kaoru Yachigusa, Mariko Okada, Mitsuko Mito, Eiko Miyoshi

AVAILABILITY: Easy

COMMENT: DVD from Criterion Collection

The story of Japan's greatest swordsman, **Musashi Miyamoto** (1584–1645), is given a lavish, *Gone With the Wind*–style treatment here by Toho's resident epic-maker, Hiroshi Inagaki. The film, adapted from a play based on the popular novel by renowned author Eiji Yoshikawa (1892–1962), is a classic example of the traditional, nostalgic jidai-geki. Filmed in color, it has a decidedly MGM feel, telling the life story of the great Musashi over the course of three films, cumulatively known in the West as the "Samurai Trilogy." Although Musashi Miyamoto has been the subject of countless films dating back to the silent era, this 1954 version is the best known in the West, cementing in the minds of millions the association between the title character and its star, **Toshiro Mifune**.

The year 1954 was a big one for Toshiro Mifune. In addition to *Samurai 1* and **Seven Samurai**, he made an additional four pictures for Toho. *Samurai 1* was another vehicle, like *Seven Samurai* and **Rashomon**, that allowed his natural physicality free rein, resulting in a lead character that virtually leaps off the screen. Running, jumping, climbing trees, beating ass, he is a force of nature, a hurricane, an earthquake! Never before had Japanese audiences seen such a dynamic, energetic, quintessentially masculine presence. But it was not just macho chest-beating that made Mifune great; he had range, and could change up in an instant. Compare the wild animal he portrays in the beginning of the film with the chastened, refined fledgling samurai at the end. These are tough transitions, yet played off with a surety and natural ease that were his trademarks.

When we meet the young man who will become the samurai known as Musashi Miyamoto, he is still an untamed youth, Takezo Shinmen, an orphan living on his own, shunned by the people of Miyamoto village. It is the eve of the Battle of Sekigahara (1600), the final, decisive conflict that ushered in the dawn of the **Tokugawa period**. Takezo and his best friend Matahachi Honiden (**Rentaro Mikuni**) decide to run off and join the battle, hoping for fame, honor, and position. Too bad they're on the wrong side, and only manage to survive by playing dead among the corpses scattered across the battlefield. They take refuge in a house, the abode of mother-and-daughter scavenger team Oko (**Mitsuko Mito**) and Akemi (**Mariko Okada**). Oko and Akemi live at the whim of local bandits who eventually show up to take the ladies' hidden booty.

The brigands are in for a big surprise. Takezo, wielding his trademark bokuto (wooden sword), comes charging out, breaking bones and busting skulls left and right. The fact that he uses the bokuto to maim and bludgeon his enemies to death, a method far more brutal than the elegant slice of a samurai sword, works as a symbol of his still-unrefined power, sheer and total as it is. Oko gets very turned on by Takezo's performance, and later tries to seduce him; he's frightened and confused by her advances, and resists, going to sleep outside. Oko, scorned, tells Matahachi and Akemi that it was Takezo who attacked her, and that he won't be back. The three of them head for Kyoto.

Takezo meanwhile returns to Miyamoto to assure Matahachi's mean old mother Osugi (**Eiko Miyoshi**) that Matahachi's not dead, but he encounters a roadblock and winds up braining a few guards, thus initiating a manhunt. Takuan the

1954 Toho

Shooting Samurai 1: Musashi Miyamoto

know-it-all priest (**Kuroemon Onoe**) and Otsu (**Kaoru Yachigusa**), Matahachi's faithful fiancée, finally do what hordes of villagers and soldiers couldn't: they go for a hike in the mountains and capture Takezo—all it took was a little millet porridge and Otsu's flute playing. Next thing you know Takezo is bound and dangling 30 feet in the air from a giant cryptomeria tree in the temple compound. Otsu feels terrible about all this, and decides to literally take matters into her own hands (lowering Takezo is no mean feat and the rope rips them up pretty badly). On the run, Otsu's love for Takezo blossoms. He is recaptured by Takuan and held captive in Himeji Castle (a magnificent fortress that stands, whole and undamaged, to this day). Here at Himeji, locked up for three years with a bunch of books, Takezo takes the first steps toward becoming a full-fledged samurai (with the help of cruel-to-be-kind Takuan), setting the stage for *Samurai 2: Duel at Ichijoji Temple.*

While watching *Samurai 1: Musashi Miyamoto,* note the use of color. American filmmakers at the time were intrigued by the naturalistic approach to color in Japanese films, which varied dramatically from the bright, garish hues that filled Hollywood Technicolor features of the '40s and '50s. Reverence for nature (a central theme in samurai films) dictated that the natural greens and browns of the forest take precedence in the location shots that dominate much of this first film (the action is restricted more to sets in parts two and three). The Japanese aesthetic dictated that color be used to enhance the dramatic aspects of the story, not just call attention to itself as a technological innovation. Just as Japanese woodblock prints of the mid-1800s profoundly affected the French Impressionists, so mid-twentieth-century Japanese cinematographers influenced their Hollywood counterparts.

It's worth mentioning that **Rentaro Mikuni**, here playing Takezo's troubled friend Matahachi, starred as Musashi Miyamoto himself the same year in a **Toei**-released version (*Miyamoto Musashi,* directed by Yasuo Kohata). In this rarely seen interpretation, the title character is a slovenly, bestial rogue, an early precursor to the cynical anti-heroic ronin that would come to dominate the samurai genre a decade later. This Musashi rapes and robs and generally spews his contempt for the world. Ironically, this image of the historical Musashi might not be too far from the truth; despite his later conversion to Zen Buddhism and his talents for wood carving, painting, and writing (he authored *The Book of Five Rings,* 1643), a man born into the **Sengoku period**, survivor of Sekigahara and more than 60 sword duels, had to be one tough son-of-a-bitch and perhaps not as nice as Toshiro Mifune.

Samurai 1: Musashi Miyamoto was the second most expensive film ever made in Japan after *Seven Samurai,* costing $500,000, a princely sum for Japanese films of the day. No worries, though: it was a big hit, securing a U.S. release (the fourth Japanese feature to do so after *Rashomon,* Mizoguchi's *Ugetsu,* and *Gate of Hell*). The film's success in the U.S. was helped greatly by the efforts of American actor William Holden, who spent time on the set, lobbied behind the scenes in Hollywood, and even provided narration and editing services for the U.S. version. Holden's enthusiasm for the project helped secure the picture an honorary Academy Award in 1955.

Some will no doubt find *Samurai 1: Musashi Miyamoto* somewhat corny and sentimental, and there's nothing wrong with that. That's the kind of film it is. Hiroshi Inagaki knew what he was about; he was no anti-feudalist, just a specialist in entertaining, tear-jerking period dramas. Nevertheless, here he delivers a gripping film about the growth and development of a remarkable man that will certainly leave you anxious to see what happens in parts two and three.

Samurai 2: Duel at Ichijoji Temple

Zoku Miyamoto Musashi: Ichijoji no ketto

Toho, 1955

DIRECTOR: Hiroshi Inagaki

CAST: Toshiro Mifune, Koji Tsuruta, Mariko Okada, Kaoru Yachigusa, Mitsuko Mito, Daisuke Kato, Akihiko Hirata, Yu Fujiki, Michiyo Kogure, Eijiro Tono, Kuroemon Onoe

AVAILABILITY: Easy

COMMENT: DVD from Criterion Collection

I became wiser. And greedier. I suffered between my love of you and of my sword. And far have I traveled. To speak the truth now, I prefer my sword to you.

Harsh words, but if you watch his face, Musashi (**Toshiro Mifune**) is pretty broken up. Baring one's soul is never easy for the Japanese, and a hundred times harder for this macho super-swordsman. Clearly he and Otsu (**Kaoru Yachigusa**) aren't going to get together this time around. We'll look forward to the last film for love to triumph. In the meantime, there are lots of guys that need killing.

Duel at Ichijoji Temple should really be called "Ambush at Ichijoji Temple" because that's what it amounts to. The man Musashi's supposed to have the duel with, sword sensei Seijuro Yoshioka (**Akihiko Hirata**), doesn't show up until after 80 members of the Yoshioka sword school have already tried to save him the trouble by jumping Musashi at the appointed hour. They are, of course, unsuccessful, and most of them wind up face down in a sticky rice paddy. Not that Seijuro wanted their help; although something of a low-life, having raped and confined Akemi (**Mariko Okada**), he's no coward. He's infuriated by the meddling of his sycophantic lieutenant Toji (**Daisuke Kato**), big brother Denshichiro (Yu Fujiki), and the rest of his sword school. He wants to face Musashi. The good name of Yoshioka is at stake. He's ready to fight. Good thing for him he's ready to die. . . .

This being the middle film in a preplanned trilogy, things are less constrained by the pressures of exposition (like in the first film) and resolution (as in the third), so there's a whole lot of room to run around, meet people, do things, have adventures, and develop character. We encounter pretty-boy swordslinger Kojiro Sasaki (**Koji Tsuruta**), the beautiful courtesan Yoshino (Michiyo Kogure), spunky orphan kid Jotaro (Kenjin Iida), and old Baiken (**Eijiro Tono**), master of the kusarigama. Baiken's deadly sickle and chain weapon takes Musashi by surprise, prompting the swordsman to use his now-famous double sword technique, the Nito-ryu.

Unfortunately, Musashi's character stays as flat as a pancake. He's trying to rein in his wild side, but that leaves just a morose man whose expressions and reactions run the gamut from merely uncomfortable to completely depressed. People are drawn to him, but can't help telling him what's wrong with him, which keeps him in a perpetual state of anxiety. After watching Musashi vanquish Baiken, a toothless old monk chides: "You won the fight, but you lost as a samurai. . . . You are really strong, but you're not mentally relaxed. That means you

Ask Takuan, the Know-It-All Priest

Q: I'm fascinated by the samurai hairdo (bald head with ponytail lying on top). What's it called?

A: This is known as the topknot, the name referring to the "ponytail" as you say. The top of the head is shaved, the remaining hair is grown long, and gathered in a knot at the back of the head. It is then waxed and set lying forward across the top of the man's shaved pate. The fashion dates back to the late Heian period (twelfth century) and developed out of the necessity to cool hot heads (literally).

The helmets worn as part of a samurai's armor were very hot, an uncomfortable and sweaty affair made all the worse by an abundance of hair. To alleviate this problem, two solutions: (1) a small ventilation hole in the top of the helmet, and (2) the topknot hairstyle. Since only samurai wore their hair this way, the topknot became associated with them. Over the centuries, as the samurai's stature in society grew, the topknot eventually became popular with men everywhere in Japan, regardless of their social standing.

As part of the reforms of the Meiji Restoration, the topknot was banned, and thereafter only Kabuki performers and sumo wrestlers wore their hair in this fashion.

Samurai 2: Duel at Ichijoji Temple

Akemi begs Musashi to stay with her in Samurai 2: Duel at Ichijoji Temple

may win in a match but you are not yet a true samurai. You'll always remain just a tough man." Later Yoshino tries to come on to Musashi, but he just broods. Yoshino: "You can hardly call yourself a mighty samurai if you can't conquer a courtesan."

Elsewhere, Akemi and Otsu meet and discover they're both in love with the same man. Akemi is streetwise and claims Musashi is her fiancé (a lie), which upsets poor Otsu so much that she decides to become a nun. Takuan the know-it-all priest (**Kuroemon Onoe**) is about to cut off all her long, silky black hair when she reconsiders, her heart still drawn to Musashi.

Then there is the ultra-cool Kojiro Sasaki, the one swordsman evenly matched with Musashi. Their showdown will climax the third film, but he starts showing up more and more throughout this second installment, allowing for important character development. He's Musashi's opposite number. Where Musashi is a big, muscular he-man, Kojiro is slender, sleek, catlike ("He looks like an actor rather than a swordsman," a sword-polisher tells Musashi). Where Musashi is awkward with the ladies, Kojiro has no such difficulties. Kojiro is hip, sophisticated, far removed from Musashi's country bumpkin. But he recognizes talent when he sees it. During an early ambush attempt on Musashi by Toji and the Yoshioka boys, Kojiro appears out of nowhere and tells Toji, "He's too skillful for you. Stop and plan it out again." This advice enrages Toji, who draws on Kojiro. Toji's topknot is off in an instant, Kojiro having wielded his extra-long daito which he jokingly calls "Clothes Rod."

Kojiro was as famous as Musashi Miyamoto in their day. In 1967 **Hiroshi Inagaki** made *Kojiro,* a film focusing on Kojiro Sasaki's side of things. This film features **Tatsuya Nakadai** as Musashi Miyamoto, but we see very little of him until the big duel at the end. When we finally do happen upon him, Nakadai's Musashi is still fairly brutal and wild, perhaps to offset Kojiro's sophistication. This film is hard to find, but highly recommended for anyone interested in this great Japanese saga of swords and samurai.

In the meantime, on to the final chapter of Inagaki's mighty trilogy, *Samurai 3: Duel on Ganryu Island.*

Samurai 3: Duel on Ganryu Island

Miyamoto Musashi kanketsuhen Ketto Ganryujima

Toho, 1956

DIRECTOR: Hiroshi Inagaki

CAST: Toshiro Mifune, Koji Tsuruta, Kaoru Yachigusa, Mariko Okada, Kichijiro Ueda, Minoru Chiaki, Daisuke Kato, Takashi Shimura, Kokuten Kodo

AVAILABILITY: Easy

COMMENT: DVD from Criterion Collection

The pinnacle of the Musashi Miyamoto saga is the duel between Musashi and equally legendary swordsman Kojiro Sasaki on Ganryu Island in western Japan. Director **Hiroshi Inagaki** gives dapper bon vivant Sasaki (played in fey fashion by future yakuza icon **Koji Tsuruta**) ample screen time (introducing him early in the second film) and the swordsman fairly dominates this third installment. Inagaki couldn't get enough of Kojiro Sasaki, even giving him his own film treatment in 1967's *Kojiro*. Sasaki is a magnificent foil for Miyamoto—he is predatory panther to **Toshiro Mifune**'s lone wolf. He also harbors an obsession for Musashi that verges on the homoerotic. Poor Otsu, she thought her only rival was Akemi!

But Kojiro Sasaki is first and foremost a careerist. He appears in the first scene of the film standing by a magnificent 100-foot waterfall, its spray creating a rainbow. But he doesn't notice this scene of stunning natural beauty; he's driven by his ambition, and tells his sword all about it: "'Clothes Rod' my poor sword, your owner, such a fencer, is still unrecognized despite his great skill. His dream remains unattained! Blind fools!" In his rage he demonstrates his Swallow Turn Swing by neatly halving a swallow with Clothes Rod. Akemi (**Mariko Okada**) is there and laments the poor bird. As for Kojiro, she tells him, "You scare me. You horrify me."

We learn that Musashi Miyamoto has had some 60 matches by now, and his bearing is decidedly nobler, his gaze tranquil, his gait stately—all signs of the true samurai he has become. He has a run-in with Agon (**Kichijiro Ueda**), a wild, rotund monk with a spear and an attitude. Yet as Agon charges, Musashi merely grasps the weapon, holding it fast, thus rendering the hulking prelate helpless. The brutish monk's elder turns out to be Nikkan (Kokuten Kodo), the same old toothless priest that castigated Musashi in the second film for not being "mentally relaxed," and hence just a "tough man." Now he praises Musashi: "I remembered your old self in priest Agon. I marvel at your perfection."

Later, in Edo, Kojiro kills four members of a sword school, and Musashi "Mr. Nice Guy" Miyamoto winds up burying

1956 Toho

Samurai 3: Duel on
Ganryu Island

them. In the graveyard the two swordsmen meet. "I've always wanted to meet you," gushes Kojiro like a schoolgirl. He challenges Musashi to a duel and they agree to a time and place, but while waiting for Musashi to show up, Kojiro gets a letter. "I have decided to leave on a journey. Let me please postpone the promised match for a year. When we meet again, I will be quite ready to vie with you. Musashi Miyamoto." Clearly neither Musashi nor director Inagaki is rushing toward this conflict, in fact the storyline necessitates keeping the eponymous duel until the very last minute.

Along the way, Musashi helps farmers fight bandits and makes wood carvings of Buddhist deities; Akemi faces off with Otsu (**Kaoru Yachigusa**); and the low-life Toji (**Daisuke Kato**) reappears, forcing Akemi to betray her beloved Musashi. There's also an amusing scene in which Musashi frightens a group of ruffians by picking flies out of the air with chopsticks. Not as impressive as **Zatoichi**'s fly-slicing technique, but hilarious all the same.

The final duel between Musashi and Kojiro is magnificently executed on the beach of Ganryu Island at dawn. Seemingly in real-time, the orange sun gradually rises over the head of Musashi as he stalks along the water's edge, ankle deep in the waves, the ferocious image of samurai perfection. He wisely keeps the ocean at his back, ensuring that the first rays of the rising sun will provide just the right blinding advantage in the duel. Whether this strategy pays off, well, you'll just have to see for yourself.

In addition to being the most balanced, best realized of the three films, *Samurai 3: Duel on Ganryu Island* also serves as a **Rashomon** reunion of sorts. Five of the eight people in *Rashomon* also show up in *Samurai 3*. Kichijiro Ueda, here playing the explosive priest Agon, appeared in *Rashomon* as the commoner; **Minoru Chiaki**, the boatman that ferries Musashi to Ganryu Island for his final showdown, was the priest; Daisuke Kato, the scheming Toji, was the policeman; **Takashi Shimura**, here in a criminally minor role as a court official, was the woodsman; and of course Toshiro Mifune, Musashi Miyamoto, was the unforgettable bandit Tajomaru.

Musashi Miyamoto remains a towering figure in Japanese

culture to the present day. In 2003, I had the pleasure of visiting Himeji Castle, where Takuan lured and captured Miyamoto at the end of *Samurai 1: Musashi Miyamoto.* I'd quite forgotten this detail until I noticed in the gift shop the traditional likeness of the famous swordsman on a box of cookies. Suddenly it all came flooding back. I held up the box and asked simply, "Miyamoto Musashi?" The ladies behind the counter giggled and nodded and I beamed, proud of my knowledge of Japanese culture (learned from samurai films, of course). As I sat eating green tea ice cream outside, one of the ladies came out and handed me a gift. It was one of the cookies. There, in the center of the cookie, Musashi Miyamoto glared fiercely up at me. I wondered what the talented artist and Zen swordsman would have thought of his likeness on such a souvenir confection. Then I ate it.

Throne of Blood

Kumonosu-jo

1957, Toho

DIRECTOR: Akira Kurosawa

CAST: Toshiro Mifune, Isuzu Yamada, Minoru Chiaki, Chieko Naniwa, Hiroshi Tachikawa

AVAILABILITY: Easy

COMMENT: DVD from Criterion Collection

If you tread the path of demons, tread it in the most cruel, most hideous manner. If you build a mountain of corpses, build it to the sky. If you shed blood, let it run like a river.

This timeless advice is dispensed by an evil she-ghost, the Japanese counterpart to the three witches in this reworking of Shakespeare's *Macbeth.* Medieval Scotland has become **Sengoku period** Japan, and Macbeth himself is now General Taketori Washizu (a perpetually grimacing **Toshiro Mifune**). The ghost foretells of Washizu's rise to power, and the prediction comes to overshadow his mind and the mind of his wife, Lady Asaji Washizu (**Isuzu Yamada**), until it becomes a self-fulfilling prophecy. Much bloodletting ensues.

The play translates perfectly (castles, warriors, treachery, murder, madness) with the exception of the aforementioned "weird sisters." "The story is understandable enough," Kurosawa observed, "but the Japanese tend to think differently

Throne of Blood

1957 Toho

Throne of Blood

1957 Toho

about such things as witches and ghosts" (Donald Richie, *The Films of Akira Kurosawa*, p. 117.) Kurosawa knew that Japanese culture, rooted as it is in nature worship, sees witches and sorcerers in a more neutral light. Hence the conversion of three "heretical" Anglo-Saxon figures into one malignant Japanese ghost. She sits at a spinning wheel in the forest, bathed in white light. "Men are vain mortals," she says, "life is but a thread—a leash, at which men strain and yelp, a stalk on which ambition blooms and withers." Her voice is deep, seemingly a man's voice. Now and then a syllable is doubled by another, deeper voice out of nowhere. The effect is uniquely unsettling.

When Washizu balks at the ghost's prediction that he will first become master of North Mansion, then lord of Cobweb Castle (the English translation of Kumonosu-jo, the film's original title), she laughs. "You mortals! Your behavior is very mystifying. You want something, but act as if you do not want it." He wants it alright. Yoshiaki Miki (**Minoru Chiaki**), Washizu's friend and fellow general, is told that his luck "turns slower, but lasts longer" than Washizu's, and that his son will eventually become master of Kumonosu-jo. A clue is given at the outset about the relative characters of the two men: as they ride through the forest, each has a flag mounted on his back, displaying his regimental crest. Washizu's is a giant centipede, all twisted with long legs and antennae (read crawling, subterranean, verminous). Miki's is a rabbit (read leaping, fertile, life-affirming). This is a stylistic innovation not in Shakespeare, yet it encodes things handily.

Throne of Blood is a film almost perpetually shrouded in mist and fog. It has a dreamlike quality; we feel it and so do the characters. "I feel as though I'm asleep and dreaming," Washizu tells Miki after the two have had their encounter with the prognosticating ghost. They ride their horses through fog so thick they seem to appear and disappear into a vapor wall of white, symbolizing the miasma of the spirit's curse. (Later, Lady Asaji makes a similar stylistic foray, albeit into the blackness of a dark doorway, the latter perhaps symbolizing her own perfidious soul.)

We first meet Lady Asaji in her new digs at North Mansion. She and Washizu are sitting in a large, wood-paneled room with nothing in it. This can be seen to represent the emptiness they feel, the hollow victory in light of the greater prize they covet. Lady Asaji starts right in, pushing her somewhat less bloody-minded husband in the direction of her ambitions. These can only be realized through the assassination of Lord Tsuzuki (**Hiroshi Tachikawa**), whom Washizu serves. Here, the English Renaissance horror of killing a king is perfectly mirrored by the unthinkable transgression of **Bushido** in the act of murdering one's lord. And, like Lady Macbeth before her, Lady Asaji doesn't care two straws about it. "Without ambition, a man is not a man," she tells her still-hesitant husband.

They commit the act, they descend into madness, things get ugly. Along the way we get a lot of nice touches: Miki's horse goes wild prior to his murder; Miki shows up at the feast Lord Washizu is holding in his honor, incandescent and dead as a doornail; Cobweb Castle guards, acting as a theatrical chorus (a standard Kurosawa device), discuss how Miki's son got away and how the castle's foundations are rotting and all the rats have left. These elements are present in *Macbeth* and might have been glossed over by a lesser director; Kurosawa knew the upheaval of nature at the killing of the lord was one aspect of the original play that would dovetail perfectly with his cinematic interpretation.

Much has been made of the **Noh** influence on this film. It is primarily the two female figures, the ghost and Lady Asaji, who represent this aesthetic. During the filming, Kurosawa handed Isuzu Yamada a Deigan mask (used for female spirits in Noh dramas). As Ms. Yamada relates in the 2001 documentary *Kurosawa*, the director instructed her, "Don't ever blink—you are a Noh mask." Yamada, a talented stage and screen veteran, followed her director's mandate to the letter. It is her performance that draws most heavily from the Noh, her poised, masked mannerisms intensifying her sinister purpose and providing contrast to the heightened theatricality of Mifune's performance. His face, too, seems to resemble a Noh mask, the Shikami, a demon spirit suffused with agitation and rage. Rarely does it leave his countenance, even from the first frame.

Throne of Blood is the first film in Kurosawa's oeuvre to feature samurai armies, knights on horses, forts, the whole array of elements and images that would figure largely in his later Sengoku-period war films, **Kagemusha** and *Ran*. As in *Ran*, *Throne of Blood's* exteriors were filmed on Mt. Fuji, hence the black, volcanic sand and rugged terrain. Of the three films, *Throne of Blood* is the most balanced and realized. Indeed, it stands apart in Kurosawa's canon, a singular gem with its own unique style and emotional dynamic. In this way it can be compared to **Rashomon**: a one-off masterpiece, unlike anything else in the catalog of Kurosawa classics. Watch many times.

The Hidden Fortress

Kakushi toride no san akunin

Toho, 1958

DIRECTOR: Akira Kurosawa

CAST: Toshiro Mifune, Minoru Chiaki, Kamatari Fujiwara, Misa Uehara, Susumu Fujita

AVAILABILITY: Easy

COMMENT: DVD from Criterion Collection

The Treasure of the Sierra Madre meets *Star Wars* (minus the spaceships) in **Warring States period** Japan. More on this later. . . .

There's a lot going on in *The Hidden Fortress:* action, suspense, gold fever, a peasant revolt, a spear duel, a fire festival, mounted samurai in sword combat, forced labor, a beautiful princess, greed, a cunning general, betrayal, intrigue, and at the center of it all two luckless, pathetic peasants. **Akira Kurosawa** had just made two very down films (**Throne of Blood** and *The Lower Depths*) and was ready for a bit of a romp. The result was *The Hidden Fortress,* the most fun-loving, straightahead samurai adventure in his oeuvre.

The story revolves around Tahei (**Minoru Chiaki**) and Matashichi (sometimes listed as "Matakishi," played by **Kamatari Fujiwara**), two constantly bickering peasants caught up in the chaos of a provincial war. Akizuki Province is currently occupied by the victorious Yamana forces. However, Akizuki's princess Yuki (Misa Uehara) and all of Akizuki's gold reserves have vanished. There is a reward for the princess, and the starving Tahei and Matashichi decide this would be a good way to make some quick dough (they have, of course, no idea where she is). They do manage to stumble upon some of the

Akizuki gold, ingeniously hidden inside pieces of firewood. (Ironically, they'd just escaped a forced labor dig in Akizuki Castle looking for the same gold.)

No sooner do the two bungling buddies make their find than a mysterious stranger appears. He follows them menacingly, then finally sits down at their campfire. He has a piece of gold too. They take him for a mercenary and he recruits them to help him find the rest of the gold, promising them a cut. He is in fact General Rokurota Makabe (**Toshiro Mifune**), a legendary Akizuki samurai. His goal is to move the gold and the princess (both secured in the hidden fortress) to safety in neighboring Hayakawa Province. Unfortunately the only way to get there is through the enemy Yamana territory. He convinces the punchy pair that the princess is his mute girlfriend, and after making them dig for a few days in the hot sun, reveals the cache of gold. It's time to go.

From here the movie becomes a road picture of sorts. Makabe uses the gold to control Tahei and Matashichi, and though they attempt to run off with it periodically, Makabe manages to stay on top of the situation and keep one step ahead of his pursuers. This often involves giving the two peasants heart failure by treating the gold (hidden in large bundles of sticks) in cavalier fashion to elude detection, a hide-in-plain-sight strategy.

Eventually the group find themselves at a traditional Jap-

Character Actor Hall of Fame

Kamatari Fujiwara (1905–1985)

Among the most expressive faces in Japanese cinema, Kamatari Fujiwara's specialty was middle-aged angst. The causes for said discomfiture could range anywhere from the concerns of a toadying civil servant (*Ikiru*) to a father's anxiety over a blossoming daughter (*Seven Samurai*) to the suicidal tendencies of a cornered salaryman (*The Bad Sleep Well*). Fujiwara did his best work as a member of the Kurosawa-gumi (as these examples attest), but appeared in numerous films for other directors including *Sword of Doom* (Kihachi Okamoto), *Chushingura* (Hiroshi Inagaki), *Double Suicide* (Masahiro Shinoda), and *The Funeral* (Juzo Itami). His standout performance is undoubtedly that of Matashichi, one half of the deliriously dopey and avaricious duo at the center of *The Hidden Fortress*. Together with comic foil Minoru Chiaki (as Tahei), Fujiwara presents a character almost completely without any redeeming features, yet we're behind him 100 percent. Caught as he is in the vicissitudes of war, we feel for his plight, and while we might not identify with his particular brand of craven scheming, we applaud his efforts and are gratified when he eventually prevails.

The Hidden Fortress

1958 Toho

anese fire festival. Tahei and Matashichi lose their minds as Makabe, suspecting they've been spotted, tells them to throw the gold-filled sticks into a giant bonfire as the peasants sing:

> The life of a man
> Burn it with the fire
> The life of an insect
> Throw it into the fire
> Ponder and you'll see
> The world is dark
> And this floating world is a dream
> Burn with abandon.

The Buddhist theme of the song contrasts with the two peasants' gold fever, emphasizing it all the more. This is just one of a dozen thrilling, heart-stopping moments in *The Hidden Fortress,* a roaring, never-gets-old actioner that finds Toshiro Mifune taking a more supporting role as straight man to the comical capers of Chiaki and Fujiwara.

The Hidden Fortress was the last film Kurosawa shot for Toho as an employee; Toho, ever nervous about the free-spending director, forced him to form his own production company and, in turn, take on part of the cost of future productions. It is also Kurosawa's first widescreen film, and he utilizes the oblong frame with intuitive perfection. Whether its open vistas and mountain ranges, or subtle mise-en-scène depicting dynamics between characters, Kurosawa masterfully manipulates the screen elements within this new, broader range.

The part of the plucky princess was a casting nightmare. Kurosawa saw some 200 actresses, but none would do. He finally put out a call to the Toho theater chain, requesting that theater employees keep their eyes peeled for the special young face he sought. This approach paid off with the discovery of 20-year-old Misa Uehara, who plays the role of the fierce girl raised as a boy. When Mifunes's character informs her that his sister, her kagemusha, has died in her place, she castigates him for his cold samurai manner, "Your nobility that doesn't even shed a tear when you've killed your sister!" She storms out, and subsequently blubs away, her anguished tears flowing from the real-life pressure of the shoot. Her career only lasted a few years, but her performance here is excellent and has stood the test of time.

As to the *Star Wars* issue mentioned at the outset of this review, it's widely known that George Lucas appropriated several key elements of *The Hidden Fortress* for his space saga. Tahei and Matashichi became R2-D2 and C-3PO, the tough princess stayed a tough princess, her male protector splintered into several male leads, and the whole issue of moving through dangerous territory on a mission is utilized as well. The first and last scenes of the film figure largely in *Star Wars,* as does the choice to focus on the two underlings. And let's not forget the Japanese influence on costumes and a little thing called a light saber (read samurai sword). Just add a healthy dose of Frank Herbert's *Dune,* and the recipe is complete. (To his credit, George Lucas would later return the favor, helping put together a production deal with 20th Century Fox for Kurosawa's 1980 feature, **Kagemusha**.)

The Hidden Fortress was a big box office hit for Kurosawa, the biggest since **Seven Samurai** and only to be surpassed by **Yojimbo**. In addition, it was a critical success, garnering the director the Tokyo Blue Ribbon Prize, International Film Critics Prize, and a Silver Bear at the Berlin International Film Festival.

6

The Early '60s

Yojimbo

Yojimbo

1961, Toho

DIRECTOR: Akira Kurosawa

CAST: Toshiro Mifune, Tatsuya Nakadai, Isuzu Yamada, Kyu Sazanka, Daisuke Kato, Seizaburo Kawazu, Eijiro Tono, Kamatari Fujiwara, Takashi Shimura, Hiroshi Tachikawa

AVAILABILITY: Easy

COMMENT: DVD from Criterion Collection

Iconic.

With *Yojimbo,* the alienated, sardonic ronin antihero was indelibly inked into the pages of samurai film history. A smash success upon its release in 1961, *Yojimbo,* and its lead character, Sanjuro (**Toshiro Mifune**), would reinvigorate the landscape of samurai films for the remainder of the '60s; from this fertile soil would spring a wide range of lone wolf swordsmen with bad attitudes, from the sleek sophistication of *Sleepy Eyes of Death*'s Nemuri Kyoshiro to the disheveled debauchery of Shinkai, the *Wicked Priest*. Before long, even blind masseurs were getting into the act!

Yojimbo also marked the reunion of director **Akira Kurosawa** and cinematographer **Kazuo Miyagawa**, who together, a decade before, had blown the Western world's mind with their 1950 masterpiece, *Rashomon*. Miyagawa was the perfect foil for Kurosawa. With his camera he brilliantly interpreted Kurosawa's rich, complex set-ups through the use of deep-focus photography (a technique wherein everything in the background and foreground stays in perfect focus). This allows Gonji the tavern-keeper (**Eijiro Tono**) to explain the layout and power dynamics of his shabby little town for Sanjuro (and us) by simply opening various shuttered windows; within each aperture a complete mini-scene plays out in puppet pantomime, individuals broken into sub-sections by the window's wooden slats. It's a brilliant device, allowing for tight, compact storytelling within a few short shots.

When we first encounter Sanjuro, we're staring at his back. He shrugs his shoulders and scratches his head. He does this a lot—he's very tense and itchy. Also, when he's thinking, he pulls his hand out of his kimono sleeve, bringing it up to the neckline of the garment to rub his chin. The body language says he's surreptitious, guarded, cunning. The move is a visual cue to the audience that he's pondering, he's working something out.

At a fork in the road, Sanjuro throws a stick in the air and heads off in the direction it points. He passes a farmer and his son, in mid-altercation: "Who wants a long life eating porridge?" asks the yakuza-wannabe son, storming off to town. The father complains to his wife, "The smell of blood brings the hungry dogs," as his eye falls on Sanjuro.

Sanjuro enters the dusty, wild west–style town (basically one big, wide boulevard for showdowns). The camera cuts to a host of Felliniesque characters, yakuza grotesques, and pallid prostitutes, framed in windows (the window motif again) as they watch his approach. He is greeted by a stray dog carrying a severed human hand, an image that sets the violent/absurdist tone of the film.

Sanjuro soon learns from Gonji how it is. Two yakuza bosses, allied with merchants, are squaring off:

VS	
Seibei—yakuza boss, owns the brothel **(Seizaburo Kawazu)**	Ushitora—yakuza boss **(Kyu Sazanka)**
Orin—Seibei's wife, brothel madame **(Isuzu Yamada)**	Inokichi—Ushitora's stupid brother **(Daisuke Kato)**
Yoichiro—Seibei's son **(Hiroshi Tachikawa)**	Unosuke—Ushitora's smart brother **(Tatsuya Nakadai)**
Tazaemon—silk merchant **(Kamatari Fujiwara)**	Tokuemon—sake brewer **(Takashi Shimura)**

Caught in the middle is a small peasant family, as well as Gonji, the gruff yet kind-hearted tavern keeper who befriends Sanjuro. Gonji spends most of his time lecturing Sanjuro about how killing is wrong—he is the moral center of the movie and, understandably, in a state of perpetual anxiety. "I'll cause some trouble and pay you," Sanjuro tells him. "In this town I'll get paid for killing. And this town is full of men who are better off dead."

From here we move through a series of plot twists, each leaving Sanjuro more enriched, until things suddenly turn nasty and our antihero finds himself a prisoner of Ushitora, lying on the floor of the sake brewery in a bloody heap. Will he prevail? Sure, but he's going to need some time off. . . .

Integral to the impact and originality of *Yojimbo* is the score by longtime Kurosawa collaborator **Masaru Sato**. It is percussive and playful, full of blaring horns and unusual arrangements. Sato's much-beloved harpsichord is here, years before the instrument would come to dominate pop music and the soundtracks of the late-'60s. The score is clearly influenced by the antic sophistication of Henry Mancini, a fact openly acknowledged by Sato, who called him "one of my favorite composers" (Stuart Galbraith IV, *The Emperor and the Wolf,* p. 303.)

Character Actor Hall of Fame

Anyone who's seen Sergio Leone's 1964 classic spaghetti western *A Fistful of Dollars* will find striking similarities with *Yojimbo,* as the former is a shot-for-shot remake of the latter.

Eijiro Tono (1907–1997)

Incredibly prolific character actor Eijiro Tono's career spanned five decades during which he appeared in upward of 200 films. He is probably best known to samurai film fans as Gonji the kindly curmudgeon who befriends Toshiro Mifune's ronin character in *Yojimbo.* But Tono is one of those actors who, once you start looking for him, starts popping up all over the place. He's old Baiken, the kusarigama-wielding opponent of Musashi Miyamoto at the beginning of *Samurai 2: Duel at Ichijoji Temple.* He's the kidnapping thief who is handily dispatched by Takashi Shimura in *Seven Samurai.* He is the avuncular Kisoya in *Samurai Assassin.* Eijiro Tono worked with the great directors of Japanese cinema including Kurosawa and Ozu; the latter used him frequently, casting him as benevolent drunkards in contemporary family dramas *Good Morning* and *Tokyo Story.* Other memorable period pieces featuring Eijiro Tono include Senkichi Taniguchi's *The Gambling Samurai,* Kurosawa's *The Lower Depths* and *Red Beard,* and Zatoichi films like *Samaritan Zatoichi* and *Zatoichi the Outlaw.*

When *A Fistful of Dollars* was released, Leone received a letter from Kurosawa. It began, "Signor Leone—I have just had the chance to see your film. It is a very fine film, but it is my film." Apparently, the Italian film's producers had sought remake rights, never got them, but went ahead with the film anyway. Lawsuits followed, culminating with Kurosawa being awarded 15% of worldwide receipts.

Ironically, despite this litigation over creative rights, Kurosawa himself seems to have lifted something from another film during the making of *Yojimbo*. In the scene where Sanjuro faces Unosuke, a smiling sociopath with a pistol, he throws a knife and incapacitates the gunman. This same scene was used in *The Magnificent Seven,* John Sturges' 1960 remake of Kurosawa's own **Seven Samurai!** Perhaps Kurosawa felt that, in light of this artistic concatenation, it was OK, perhaps even his right, to take a souvenir. It's a harmless appropriation, and a nice touch.

If you are new to samurai films, this is probably the best film to start with. Epics like *Seven Samurai* and **Hiroshi Inagaki**'s Samurai Trilogy are great when you're ready, but start with *Yojimbo*. It is a pivotal film in the genre, an initiation rite that will bring you firmly into the fold of the samurai film fan.

Abayo!

Sanjuro

Tsubaki Sanjuro

1962, Toho

DIRECTOR: Akira Kurosawa

CAST: Toshiro Mifune, Tatsuya Nakadai, Yuzo Kayama, Akihiko Hirata, Kunie Tanaka, Reiko Dan, Yoshio Tsuchiya

AVAILABILITY: Easy

This follow-up to **Yojimbo** features the granddaddy of all chambara blood spurts. Actually, the effect is not so much a spurt as a blown fire hydrant. The special effects technician was so nervous about pleasing the notoriously short-tempered **Akira Kurosawa** that he cranked up the pressure beyond what good taste and personal safety might dictate. The effect is magnificent—The Emperor was overjoyed.

"Sanjuro" means "thirty years old." This was the name Mifune's itchy, bearded ronin character gave in *Yojimbo* as well, although his surname in that picture was Kuwabatake (mulberry field). Here, it's Tsubaki (camellia). Both names come

COMMENT: DVD from
Criterion Collection

Sanjuro

1962 Toho, Kurasawa Productions

from whatever his eyes light on at that particular moment. The message is that as a ronin, he no longer has an identity.

Where *Yojimbo* saw our hero mucking about in the demi-monde of yakuza skullduggery, here he's mixing with the upper classes, and seems decidedly uncomfortable most of the time. He falls in with nine young, inexperienced samurai clansmen led by Toho matinee idol **Yuzo Kayama**. Also among the ranks of the unnamed nine are **Akihiko Hirata**, **Kunie Tanaka**, and **Yoshio Tsuchiya**. The samurai have uncovered corruption in the han (it's never specified—a MacGuffin), and think the chamberlain is behind it. They have gone to the superintendent with their story, and are very pleased with themselves indeed, when they discover a sleepy Sanjuro in the back room of the old Shinto shrine where they've gathered. He's overheard their story and tells them they've got it all wrong. Just from listening, he's figured out the backstory, that in fact the chamberlain is the good guy and the superintendent is the bad guy. He proves his theory by pointing out the window, where a large contingent of the superintendent's men have gathered, surrounding them. Sanjuro hides all the young dudes and sets about slicing the superintendent's men like potatoes. Finally their leader, Hanbei Muroto (**Tatsuya Nakadai**), breaks things up and, impressed by his sword work, offers Sanjuro a job.

The rest of the film is a series of plot twists that keep Sanjuro and his nine charges running around in circles, trying to rescue the kidnapped chamberlain, his wife, his daughter, and various members of their own team who get captured along the way. It is a romp, trampling all the conventions of traditional jidai-geki and reinforcing the new cynical ronin paradigm launched in *Yojimbo*. This character type will come to dominate the whole samurai genre by the end of the '60s.

Sanjuro is also a study in mise-en-scène (placement within the frame). Kurosawa was a master of mise-en-scène and this movie is a particular example of his genius. Since so many scenes in the film contain ten people (Sanjuro and the nine young samurai), he has a ball arranging Mifune and the others in a multitude of geometric patterns, layers, strategic groupings, you name it. And the blocking is so meticulous that at any given moment all ten characters are visible in the frame.

At times the throng parts to reveal other characters or plot elements, creating a human curtain effect. In one scene Mifune is sneaking through some bushes in a squatting position, followed by the other nine, forming a human centipede. He comments on this with irritation (the original line was, "You're following me like a trail of goldfish dung," but, sadly, was changed). Try keeping ten people out of each other's way, as well as the way of the camera, in a tight space, and you begin to appreciate the amount of rehearsal that must have gone into each scene.

There's a lot of humorous bickering going on in *Sanjuro*. The young hotheads always want to act, usually to do the wrong thing, and their mentor, Sanjuro, has to set them straight. Sometimes he just gets sick of them: "Go ahead then. Who cares?" He's never less than frank: "You disgust me. Stupidity is dangerous." But he never abandons them and does all the killing for them as well. One spectacular scene shows him wiping out 20 swordsmen in 40 seconds.

Camellias play a strategic role in the film, and it's interesting to note as you're watching that the camellias in the film aren't real. They were actually made from the petals of the sakaki plant, which photographs better. It is an example of Kurosawa's meticulous attention to detail.

Sanjuro is a film you can watch over and over again. It is deceptively simple, yet one can pull something new out of it with each viewing. It really never gets old. I suppose that's the definition of a classic.

Abayo!

Ask Takuan, the Know-It-All Priest

Q: What's the difference between a chamberlain and a superintendent?

A: These terms are used a lot in the world of the samurai, so it's good to keep them straight. The chamberlain (karo) is second only to the lord (daimyo) of the clan. During the Tokugawa period, the shogun required daimyo to spend every other year in Edo, so that he could keep an eye on them and keep them shuffling back and forth, a form of passive harassment. For the time the lord was in Edo, the chamberlain administered affairs in the han.

The superintendent or intendant (daikan) was a representative of the shogunate posted in the han. Serving as a regional administrator, the intendant was in charge of overseeing public works and collecting taxes for Edo.

Harakiri

Seppuku

1962, Shochiku

DIRECTOR: Masaki
Kobayashi

CAST: Tatsuya Nakadai,
Akira Ishihama,
Tetsuro Tamba,
Rentaro Mikuni

AVAILABILITY: Easy

COMMENT: VHS
from Home Vision
Entertainment

An empty suit of samurai armor. This image opens and closes *Harakiri*, signaling to hip moviegoers that this is a *symbol*. This symbol also occurs in **Tenchu!**, where it represents the samurai of old, an active warrior in battle, fighting for his daimyo—the pre-**Tokugawa-period** samurai before he was reduced to a wandering vagabond ronin. Here in *Harakiri*, while it has that connotation, the focus is more on its emptiness. For *Harakiri* is, more than anything else, a scathing, devastating indictment of the hollowness and hypocrisy of **Bushido**, the Way of the Warrior.

Harakiri takes place in 1630, early in the Tokugawa period. Hanshiro Tsugumo (**Tatsuya Nakadai**), a middle-aged ronin, has become one of the first victims of the shogunate's campaign against the daimyo, losing his position when his clan was abolished some ten years earlier. He appears at the compound of the Iyi clan, and tells the clan elder, Kageyu Saito (**Rentaro Mikuni**), that he can no longer go on in dire poverty and wishes to die honorably by harakiri. He requests the use of a corner of the compound to do so. Before granting Tsugumo's request, however, the elder relates an account of another ronin who recently appeared at the Iyi residence with a similar story. There follows a series of flashbacks.

According to the elder, the young ronin, Motome Chijiiwa (Akira Ishihama), appeared to be faking his request for harakiri in order to garner sympathy and a handout; his swords were of bamboo (a sign that he'd pawned his real ones) and so could not actually be used for the disemboweling ceremony. When word of this gets to Hikokuro Omodaka (**Tetsuro Tamba**), a cruel and imperious Iyi retainer, things take a horrible turn, as Omodaka forces the hapless young ronin to go through with the ceremony . . . with his own bamboo wakizashi (short sword). What follows is almost unwatchable. Suffice to say, Chijiiwa manages to perform the excruciating ritual to the satisfaction of the sadistic Omodaka, who has volunteered to be his kaishakunin. Finally, after some torturous lingering, Omodaka delivers the fatal blow, beheading Chijiiwa.

The elder finishes his tale, and implies that a similar fate awaits Tsugumo if he has come with similar intentions. Tsugumo assures the elder his blades are real, as is his resolve. As he kneels in the courtyard, his wakizashi before him, Tsugumo requests Omodaka for his kaishakunin. When told that Omodaka is out sick, the elder, by now in awe of Tsugumo's force of will, sends for Omodaka anyway. As they wait, Tsugumo relates his own tale. He begins by admitting that Chijiiwa "was a lad of some slight acquaintance." This admission, along with his request for Omodaka, is our first clue that there is far more to Tsugumo than merely a ragged ronin looking for a place to die. From here the picture shifts gears, becoming a revenge tragedy of Shakespearean proportions.

At the heart of *Harakiri* is the conflict between **giri** (the duty to Bushido) and **ninjo** (human feelings, compassion, conscience). It isn't hard to tell which side the filmmaker comes down on. Director **Masaki Kobayashi** was bitterly critical of the Japanese martial tradition, whether in the samurai system or the modern Japanese army (see his Human Condition trilogy). His thesis is always that such militarist systems are inhuman and hide their inhumanity behind noble-sounding rules and codes that are ultimately hollow and hypocritical. In *Harakiri,* not only does Tsugumo expose the treachery that led to Chijiiwa's death, but he castigates the rotten core of a system that would tolerate such a heinous act. "Our samurai honor merely glosses the surface," Tsugumo tells the elder. Unfortunately, when all is said and done, his actions are covered up, again pointing up the craven, cover-your-ass cowardice of the Warrior's Way.

Ask Takuan, the Know-It-All Priest

Q: Can you explain this whole harakiri ritual? Is it the same as seppuku?

A: "Hara" means belly and "kiri" means cut. The same two kanji (Chinese characters) are reversed to form "seppuku," the latter being the more formal term. In the full ritual, the samurai would cut his belly and then immediately have his head cut off by the kaishakunin, or "second," to alleviate his suffering. During the Tokugawa period, the shogun and his family set about reducing the number of daimyo, to eliminate possible challenges to shogunate authority as well as to pick up the loot. This meant lots of lords committing seppuku, for crimes real or imagined, and the dissolution of their clans. Often the retainers of a lord would follow him into death by committing seppuku themselves.

Shinobu Hashimoto wrote the script, and would later use some of the same devices in **Samurai Assassin***:* there is the ronin at odds with the system, the scribe who acts as narrator and winds up wiping unpleasant details from the official record, as well as the extensive and innovative use of flashbacks. However, in the hands of Masaki Kobayashi, Hashimoto's material has a totally different feel. While *Samurai Assassin's* director, **Kihachi Okamoto**, at times seems to rush through the fine points to get to the sword fights, Kobayashi is meditative, brooding, creating an aura of menace and impending doom that descends inexorably, like the crushing hand of fate. Where the grand finale sword battle in *Samurai Assassin* is vicious and chaotic, *Harakiri's* is almost balletic, a dance of death. Okamoto's is the art of action; Kobayashi's is the action of art.

Kobayashi's style is complemented brilliantly by Tatsuya Nakadai's performance. Only 30 years old here, Nakadai communicates the world-weary yet poised persona of the mature samurai. A man of character and conviction, a veteran of the civil wars, his tragic fate and destitute circumstances have not broken his spirit, nor will they hinder his quest for revenge. All of this comes across in waves of searing screen heat from this master-class performer. Also worthy of note is Rentaro Mikuni as the elder, Kageyu Saito. While he toes the Bushido line to the end, his face tells another tale, that of his own giri/ ninjo conflict. He sees quite clearly what is happening, and his character is never in doubt, yet he is so invested in the system that he is incapable of doing the right thing. It is a complex performance, carried off with a sad-eyed gravitas.

Like the harakiri ritual itself, this movie hurts, it's painful. It penetrates you in your gut. It leaves you feeling disillusioned, as if everything around you has shifted slightly. It is the action of Kobayashi's art, and it cuts deep.

Harakiri won the Special Jury Prize at the 1963 Cannes Film Festival.

The Tale of Zatoichi

Zatoichi monogatari

1962, Daiei

DIRECTOR: Kenji Misumi

CAST: Shintaro Katsu, Shigeru Amachi, Masayo Banri, Ryuzo Shimada

AVAILABILITY: Easy

COMMENT: DVD from Home Vision Entertainment

In 1962, **Daiei Studios** released the first of what would become the most successful chambara series in the history of Japanese cinema. Although compared with later films in the series, *The Tale of Zatoichi* is a little rambling (there are too many subplots and extraneous characters that tend to detract from the central story), it is nevertheless a fine film that gets the ball rolling to great effect. Starring the incomparable, irrepressible **Shinaro Katsu** as Zatoichi the blind swordsman/masseur, the film is so entertaining, even your mom will like it (mine did). There is enough action, intrigue, character development, and sheer emotion to hook just about anyone.

Zatoichi's day gig is giving massages, which he does only sporadically because his sideline, gambling, pays much more. Being a gambler makes him a member of the yakuza, a centuries-old organized crime underworld that continues to play a role in Japanese society to this day. He is also an expert swordsman, with an almost supernatural ability. One might think that, being blind, he is faced with an insurmountable handicap, especially for a gambling swordsman. But it is his very blindness, along with his indomitable spirit, that gives

Ask Takuan, the Know-It-All Priest

Q: I know this is a foolish question, but what's the difference between a samurai and a yakuza?

A: There are no foolish questions, foolish one, only fools (laughs).

The early Tokugawa period was a time of intense social organization. Ieyasu Tokugawa, the first shogun, divided the people into rigid classes, and the vagabonds of the day like the gamblers (bakuto) and the peddlers (tekiya) began to organize themselves as well, forming what would eventually become the yakuza. The name derives from Oicho-kabu, a card game popular with gamblers. The object was to reach 19. Ya (8), ku (9), za (3) makes 20, a loser. So while the samurai enjoyed their status at the top of the society, the yakuza dwelled in the shadows, never to show their faces in the light of day.

The yakuza developed elaborate forms of custom and ritual not unlike the samurai to identify one another and show that they knew how to behave within their respective social worlds. Corrupt samurai would often hire yakuza to do unsavory jobs or demand payoffs from yakuza bosses. So perhaps they weren't so different after all?

1962 Dalei

The Tale of Zato-ichi: *Ichi kisses his one true love, his sword*

1962 Dalei

Ichi tries to dis-suade Tane's ad-vances in The Tale of Zatoichivances.

him the edge in the fight. He has no sight to distract him, you see, and his other senses are so amazingly acute, he winds up having a great advantage over the scores of sighted swords-men that he regularly cuts to pieces in each film.

The opening scene of *The Tale of Zatoichi* finds Ichi pay-ing a call on a local yakuza boss, Sukegoro (**Eijiro Yanagi**). The boss has seen what Zatoichi can do with the sword he keeps concealed in his cane, and wants him for an upcom-ing war with a rival gang. However, the rival gang, run by Boss Shigezo (Ryuzo Shimada), also has an ace in the hole, an honorable and skilled yet consumptive ronin named Hirate (**Shigeru Amachi**).

Of course Hirate and Zatoichi become fast friends, which makes for problems later on. Also, both bosses are schem-ing wretches, as are their men, and Zatoichi has to straighten them all out. Not to mention the beautiful girl, Tane (**Masayo Banri**), who falls for our hero. It's not giving anything away to say that there is a huge sword battle at the end; this is the con-vention in all chambara films, and in Zatoichi pictures they are always exciting, crazed, and brilliantly staged.

If it's your first time watching *The Tale of Zatoichi,* you might be a little thrown by the names of the respective bosses, towns, and who works for whom. If so, here's the deal:

	VS	
Towns	Sasagawa	Iioka
Bosses	Shigezo	Sukegoro
Swordsmen	Hirate	Zatoichi

It's important to see this first film of the series, as it pro-vides valuable exposition, such as the scene where Zatoichi tells his story, how he had been a regular masseur until three years before, when he started sword training. He had taken abuse from the seeing world long enough and was determined never to be looked down upon again. He illustrates his skill by throwing a candle in the air and chopping it in half—longways. And both halves are still burning when they hit the tatami. Af-ter that, the gang members give him a somewhat wider berth.

Both this film and its sequel, ***Return of Masseur Ichi***, are in black and white. The remaining 24 films in the series are in color.

The Tale of Zatoichi Continues

Zoku Zatoichi monogatari

1962, Daiei

DIRECTOR: Kazuo Mori

CAST: Shintaro Katsu, Tomisaburo Wakayama, Masayo Banri, Sonosuke Sawamura, Eijiro Yanagi

AVAILABILITY: Easy

COMMENT: DVD from Home Vision Entertainment

Such was the class system in feudal Japan that a person like Zatoichi, a blind masseur, was considered "hinin"—literally "non-man," an outcast, with no rights under law. Add to this the samurai's right of "kirisutegomen," the legal right to kill a man of lower rank, and you start to see why a figure such as Zatoichi would have been so unusual. His life wasn't worth the straw sandals he stood in, and yet he carried, indeed *demanded,* the rights and dignity of a human being. And here, in the second film of the series, he continues to demand those rights, at the point of his concealed cane sword if need be.

Zatoichi (**Shintaro Katsu**) is hired to massage the lord of the Kuroda clan, a creepy, giggling fellow who is quite obviously insane, even to the blind masseur. Zatoichi does his best with the crazy daimyo, and it's funny and embarrassing to watch. Desperate to keep their lord's condition a secret, several retainers set out to silence the masseur afterward; they don't know who they're up against. To them, he is merely hinin, and they have the right of kirisutegomen, so what's the problem? They soon find out, a little late of course, as the lightning blade has flashed and is back in the cane before their bodies hit the ground.

Realizing they're in over their heads, the Kuroda samurai contract with a local yakuza boss, Kanbei (**Sonosuke Sawa-**

Ask Takuan, the Know-It-All Priest

Q: Why does Zatoichi have that white cloth wrapped around his midriff? Is it a girdle?

A: No, cretinous one, it is not a girdle. It is a sarashi that he wears, a long strip of white cotton, and he does not wear it out of vanity. Well perhaps he is modest, but the reason swordsmen normally wore the sarashi was to provide an extra measure of protection against sword cuts. Of course it would only protect against a glancing blow, but any advantage in sword combat is welcome.

The Tale of Zatoichi Continues

The Tale of Zatoichi Continues: *Ichi chats with wicked one-armed swordsman Yoshiro*

mura), who in turn contacts another yakuza boss, one Sukegoro (**Eijiro Yanagi**), whom we recall from the first film. We also see Tane (**Masayo Banri**), Zatoichi's old flame, now engaged to a carpenter. Her heart races when she hears that Zatoichi is back in town to visit the grave of Hirate, the noble samurai he killed in the prior installment.

But wait, there's more: A mysterious one-armed swordsman keeps crossing paths with Zatoichi. He says little, but radiates menace with the slightest gesture. This character, Yoshiro, is portrayed by **Tomisaburo Wakayama**, Shintaro Katsu's real-life older brother. It's tempting to imagine a backstage sibling rivalry coming through in their performances. (Given their respective career trajectories, it's perfectly plausible that Tomisaburo Wakayama could have been venting some angst during their fight scenes.) But they were both such consummate professionals, it's impossible to tell. In any case, Yoshiro and Zatoichi are on a collision course, and when they finally face each other, brace yourselves for one of the great moments in chambara.

It seems Yoshiro was once a member of Sukegoro's gang, but has since been a very bad boy indeed, going on a robbing, raping, killing spree of his own with a young apprentice. Sukegoro is less than pleased to see him, and gives him his walking papers. Now Yoshiro's *really* pissed! Most fans know Tomisaburo Wakayama from his role as Ogami Itto in the **Lone Wolf and Cub** films of the early 1970s, but he was a samurai film legend long before he embodied that character. Ironically, compared with the Ogami Itto of the popular "Lone Wolf and Cub" manga (upon which the films were based), he's somewhat past it, looking overweight and more than a little shopworn. But here, in 1962, he's lean and mean, a one-armed fighting machine!

The pace and plotting of *The Tale of Zatoichi Continues* are tighter than in the first film and the tension mounts steadily, inexorably, as one by one, every character and group winds up pursuing Zatoichi: the Kuroda clan, Kanbei's gang, Sukegoro's gang, Yoshiro, even Tane! The film features the first of many *huge* sword battles, with Ichi taking on 50 or 60 guys at once. Shintaro Katsu displays his talent for swift movements

*Ichi defends against
multiple assailants*

that hide the choreography; his unlucky adversaries always seem genuinely stunned, and pause magnificently before hitting the dirt. This tableau of death is a standard feature in samurai films—it's as if the filmmaker is freezing the moment so that we may savor it.

Fans of Masayo Banri, who plays the lovely Tane, will get one more chance to see her in the fourth installment, *Masseur Ichi the Fugitive.* Those hankering for more Tomisaburo Wakayama will have to wait for #6, *Masseur Ichi and a Chest of Gold.*

Destiny's Son

Kiru

Daiei, 1962

DIRECTOR: Kenji Misumi

CAST: Raizo Ichikawa, Eijiro Yanagi, Yoshio Inaba, Masayo Banri, Shiho Fujimura, Shigeru Amachi, Junichiro Narita

AVAILABILITY: Tricky

COMMENT: Available as an import or through third-party collectors and independent distributors

What would you do if the man you thought was your father was brutally murdered and with his last dying breath he told you (1) you were adopted, (2) your real father beheaded your mother, (3) dad did it for love, and (4) it was mom's final wish? Sure gives a whole new meaning to "head over heels in love"!

These are the kinds of things young Shingo Takakura (**Raizo Ichikawa**) must cope with in *Destiny's Son.* "Kiru," the Japanese title of the film, has a lot of meanings including to kill, murder, cut, chop, behead, carve, saw, sever, shear, slice, strip, fell, etc., indicating the linguistic association in Japanese between death and the sword. However the meaning we're looking for here is "behead," for the beheading of Shingo's mother is a recurring image. We don't actually see her head fly off; it's not that kind of film. We just see her kneeling by an old, dead tree in a clearing, looking up at her husband poised above her with his sword, a gentle smile passing between them, then the sword swiping across the frame, the sun behind.

Shingo's mother, Fujiko (**Shiho Fujimura**), was formerly a lady-in-waiting in the Iida clan. Lord Iida had a mistress who held power over him, and this worried the chamberlain so much that he secretly directed Fujiko to stab the lord's mistress to death. We observe this murder under the opening

The great Raizo Ichikawa

credits. Needless to say, this doesn't go down well with Lord Iida, who sentences Fujiko to death. Lady Iida takes pity on her and asks the chamberlain to save her. The chamberlain tasks Sohji Tada (**Shigeru Amachi**), a Nagaoka samurai, to rescue Fujiko, hide out with her somewhere, and have a baby, the idea being that motherhood would increase the chance of Lord Iida's forgiveness.

Well, no such luck. After a happy year and the birth of their son, the two are apprehended and Fujiko is once again sentenced to death. But no Iida clansman is willing to do the beheading. Nevermind; Sohji Tada volunteers, and as it happens it's what she wants as well. As Shuemon Takakura, Shingo's adopted father, tells him, "She would be happy if she were killed by the man she loved." The chamberlain brings the baby Shingo to Takakura who raises him as his own. With this last detail, Takakura expires. Shingo's sister has also been slain, and the first thing Shingo does upon gaining his composure is wreak bloody revenge on the heinous perpetrators, fellow samurai clansmen Ikebe (**Yoshio Inaba**) and his son. Then he sets out on the road to live the life of the ronin.

Shingo seeks out his biological father, now a monk living deep in the forest. Dad shows Shingo Fujiko's grave, they share a tearful moment, and then Shingo's off on his ronin path. At an inn along the way he encounters Mondo Tadokoro (Junichiro Narita) and his sister (**Masayo Banri**), who are on the run from the government for murdering some corrupt officials (Narita and Banri also appear in the fourth **Zatoichi** film, *Zatoichi the Fugitive*). Tadokoro asks Shingo to protect his sister, as the inn is being surrounded by swordsmen as they speak. Although Shingo tries to restrain her, Tadokoro's beautiful sister runs to save her brother by stripping to distract the government goons (just like Keiko Awaji did in *Secret of the Urn*). The swordsmen slice first and ask questions later. The image of blood running down her supple naked body haunts Shingo long after he escapes the fracas.

Eventually Shingo lands a job as yojimbo for shogunate minister Matsudaira (**Eijiro Yanagi**). By now it's 1861, the middle of the **Bakumatsu** period, and the **Mito Tengu** is raging—not a good time to be a shogunate yojimbo. But Shingo is preternaturally gifted with a sword, dispatching a dozen men in as many seconds. He's up to the challenge. Or is he?

The feel of *Destiny's Son* is like a haiku. Lyrical, minimalist, it is a beautiful film infused with the Japanese aesthetic qualities of tranquility, introspection, and reverence for nature. There are gentle moments and smiling faces. People use few words. Early on, upon returning from a trip, the local lord asks Shingo, "So what did you do?" "Not much, just looked around." "What did you see?" "Just fields and mountains." "Fields and mountains. That's wonderful!" A deep Zen calm surrounds and interpenetrates the people and settings of the film; even the violence and treachery are subsumed in it, making these elements somehow more and less disturbing simultaneously.

The theme of family is also very strong in the picture. Father/son, brother/sister, mother/father, these relationships are central to the story, primarily in terms of loss: sons losing fathers, brothers losing sisters, fathers losing sons, etc. Such loss is the tragic underpinning of the picture as well as the prime mover of the plot.

Destiny's Son is only around 70 minutes or so, but what a revelation it is. Whether you're a Raizo Ichikawa fan or you're interested in Musashi Miyamoto's ideal of the fusion of Zen and sword, or if you just want to see a really good film, see this one.

(NOTE: This film is not to be confused with **Kihachi Okamoto**'s 1968 film *Kiru,* marketed in the U.S. as *Kill!*)

Chushingura

Chushingura—Hana no maki yuki no maki

Toho, 1962

DIRECTOR: Hiroshi Inagaki

The Chushingura is the national epic of Japan, a true story of bravery and revenge that has been filmed over 200 times. It is the compelling testament of the Loyal 47 Ronin of the Asano clan and their vendetta against the wicked Lord Kira, the man responsible for the death of their lord. It is such a centerpiece of traditional Japanese heroic storytelling, it's hard to overstate its cultural importance, much less the degree to which it per-

CAST: Koshiro Matsumoto, Yuzo Kayama, Chusha Ichikawa, Tatsuya Mihashi, Toshiro Mifune, Seizaburo Kawazu, Takashi Shimura, Daisuke Kato, Keiju Kobayashi, Yoshio Tsuchiya, Kamatari Fujiwara

AVAILABILITY: Easy

COMMENT: DVD from Image Entertainment; copied onto disk from videotape—subtitles burned into screen, therefore not a pristine transfer, but passable

meates the samurai genre. In a way, it's the ultimate samurai tale, full of noble, self-sacrificing warriors for whom **Bushido** is all; they defy the shogun himself to avenge their lord, knowing full well they will all face the penalty of **seppuku**.

This 1962 production remains the finest, longest (207 minutes), and most comprehensive film adaptation of the Loyal 47 Ronin saga. **Toho Studios**, to mark their 30th anniversary, went all out, producing half a dozen special features in 1962; Chushingura was the centerpiece of these, receiving a princely budget and helmed by **Hiroshi Inagaki**, Toho's own David Lean of jidai-geki. His style was traditional, perhaps even old-fashioned compared to mavericks like **Akira Kurosawa** and **Masaki Kobayashi**, yet in this film all of his talents are perfectly suited to the material—Inagaki delivers a 3 ½ hour film that keeps you glued to the screen from beginning to end.

Although the core plot (like *Seven Samurai*) is ridiculously simple, *Chushingura* is nevertheless a sprawling saga containing myriad subplots, all revolving around the courageous Asano samurai, the women who love them, their families, their drinking buddies, the townspeople of Ako (seat of the Asano clan), as well as the despicable Lord Kira, his retainers and yojimbo, imperial envoys, spies, geisha, and the working class and power elite of Edo.

The year is 1701. The trouble all starts when the high-minded Lord Asano (**Yuzo Kayama**), in charge of reception for the annual delegation of imperial envoys to Edo, refuses to bribe his superior, Lord Kira (Chusha Ichikawa), the Grand Master of Ceremonies. Kira is a craven, weasely character, prone to proclaiming his despicableness à la *Richard III.* He says things like "With lust and greed as my values, I intend to live a long life" and "The reason I studied to become Grand Master of Ceremonies was to avoid the samurai duty to die at the slightest provocation. Samurai all look very stupid to me." Chusha Ichikawa gives an exaggerated, antic performance full of funny faces, silly walks, and bizarre, tortured line reads. Lord Asano, on the other hand, is played with nobility and bottled rage by Toho heartthrob Yuzo Kayama (who starred the same year in *Sanjuro*). Even though it was traditional to bribe one's superiors, Asano refuses to offer such tribute to Lord Kira, stating simply, "I don't like bribery. I hate it. It's the cause of corruption in the government, isn't it? As long as he teaches me, I will honor Lord Kira and treat him with due respect."

Poor Lord Asano doesn't know what he's in for. Kira treats him like garbage, withholding instruction and insulting him openly and maliciously. It doesn't help that Asano is something of a young hothead, but observing the abuse he endures from Kira, we in the audience are reaching for our swords just as Asano does—he can't take it anymore. He gets in a couple of glancing blows, but is restrained by castle guards before he can do any real damage. Meanwhile, Kira crawls away, squealing like a stuck pig.

The penalty for drawing one's sword in the shogun's palace is seppuku, and that's the sentence leveled on young Asano. Before he takes his leave, observing the falling cherry blossoms, he writes a poem:

> Sadder than blossoms
> Swept off by the wind
> A life torn away
> In the fullness of spring.

Ask Takuan, the Know-It-All Priest

Asano's clan is dissolved and his chamberlain, Kuranosuke Oishi (**Koshiro Matsumoto**), is ordered to surrender Ako Castle. The clan samurai are all for defending the castle against the shogun's forces, to go down fighting and join their lord in death, but Oishi has other plans. What follows are two long years of plotting, stalling, and deception as Oishi attempts to eliminate all suspicion of the Ako men's secret intention to

Q: Why do samurai tie a cord or sash across their backs when going into battle? It makes a big X on their backs. Is it ceremonial?

A: Foolish one, every moment of life is ceremonial on some level. However, you are inquiring about tasuki gake, the act of tying the cord (tasuki) used to tuck up the sleeves of a kimono. As you no doubt have noticed, Japanese fashion has always leaned toward big, puffy sleeves—they make good pockets! But in the heat of sword battle, those baggy cloth flaps tend to get in the way, and having them tied up tight with the tasuki can mean the difference between life and death.

Night Attack of the 47 Ronin *by Kuniyoshi*

Victoria & Albert Museum

1954 Toei

Koshiro Matsumoto as Kuranosuke Oishi in Chushingura

wreak revenge on Lord Kira. Oishi even goes so far as to live in a brothel for awhile, feigning a dissolute life (what a guy!). During this period many subplots unfold concerning the loves, lusts, and allegiances of the Loyal 47 Ronin. Oishi eventually fools everyone except Gemba Tawaraboshi (**Toshiro Mifune**), a ronin and mighty master of the Hozoin lance. Tawaraboshi deliberately puts about the rumor that he is working as a yojimbo for Kira, just to see if the Asano samurai will come after him; when they do, his suspicion is confirmed and he decides to help them. What follows is the inevitable. . . .

If there is a weakness to *Chushingura,* it is the sheer volume of characters and subplots, many of which, even at 3 ½ hours, get only a passing scene or two and little to distinguish them to Western viewers. For the Japanese audience of the day, these were all well-known figures requiring only a cameo appearance. This was also the case for the actors who performed them, a star-strewn cast of Toho's heavy hitters. Keep an eye out for **Seizaburo Kawazu**, **Takashi Shimura**, **Daisuke Kato**, **Keiju Kobayashi**, **Yoshio Tsuchiya**, and **Kamatari Fujiwara** (blink and you'll miss him!)

As mentioned earlier, there have been scores of film adaptations of the Chushingura story, dating back to the silent days. It has been filmed so many times that some filmmakers have gone to extremes to get a new spin on the tale. In 1958 Daiei came out with *Samurai Vendetta,* a blending of the Chushigura and Tange Sazen stories starring **Shintaro Katsu** and **Raizo Ichikawa** (for more on Tange Sazen, see *Secret of the Urn*); in 1960, Toho released *Salaryman Chushingura,* placing the events in a corporate setting (with feudal lords replaced by company presidents to hilarious effect); as late as 1994, director **Kinji Fukasaku** made *Crest of Betrayal,* combining the stories of the Loyal 47 Ronin and the equally famous supernatural revenge drama Ghost of Yotsuya.

Inagaki's *Chushingura* is traditional, nostalgic jidai-geki at its best. It's a foundational film, like *Seven Samurai* and *Harakiri,* a must-see addition to your samurai film experience. It may not have the blood of a **Lone Wolf and Cub** or the sexiness of a **Sleepy Eyes of Death**, but one thing it does have is Bushido. It is Bushido to the core.

New Tale of Zatoichi

Shin Zatoichi monogatari

1963, Daiei

DIRECTOR: Tokuzo Tanaka

CAST: Shintaro Katsu, Mikiko Tsubouchi, Seizaburo Kawazu

AVAILABILITY: Easy

COMMENT: DVD from Home Vision Entertainment

The third installment of the Zatoichi series and the first in color, *New Tale of Zatoichi* marks a turning point for the character and franchise as well. Instead of a balls-out chambara action picture, this film is a moody, complex character study, indicating a willingness on the part of **Daiei** to slow down, take some time, and render a realized, three-dimensional Ichi. At this point they know they've got a hit on their hands, and they want to seal the deal by creating a truly rounded character that will appeal to audiences for years to come.

For one thing, our hero is sporting a brand new matinee idol hairdo (as opposed to the crewcut in the first film). For another, he sings! Admittedly, this is no symphonic Elvis moment, but rather a subdued number about being a blind man, sung to his own accompaniment on shamisen (a kind of square Japanese banjo). **Shintaro Katsu**'s father had been a Kabuki performer, training his children in the traditional forms of **Nagauta** singing and instrumentation, and Katsu had the chops. However, he doesn't do much chopping in this movie, only killing a dozen guys or so. He's sworn off the sword, you see. But wait, let's back up a little.

We know something is up with Zatoichi at the outset of the movie when, after dispatching three attackers, he begins to weep. All this killing is taking its toll. He heads for Shimodate, the town where he trained to be a swordsman. He's joined on the road by an old friend, and in the evening they stop at a flop house where Ichi sings his song, charming the destitute masses huddled around him. Suddenly a gang of bandits rushes in to rob the wretched people. Zatoichi keeps cool, not wanting to cause trouble for his friends, but he already knows who the bandits are—"I hear there's a gang of thieves, Tengu from Mito or something like that, running around lately. Is that you?" The bandits blow him off, but the next day he shows up at the local yakuza boss's place. He knows who the men are, and forces them to cough up.

He looks up his old sword sensei, Banno (**Seizaburo Kawazu**), whom we learn is in with the **Mito Tengu**. Historically, this is the same group of loyalist rebels that staged the

*Shintaro Katsu:
Superstar*

assassination in **Samurai Assassin**. They're also mentioned in **Sword of Doom**. This is a few years later, however, and they're on the run from the law and have fallen to robbing peasants. Their connection with the yakuza isn't made clear in the picture.

Meanwhile, sensei's young sister, Yayoi (Mikiko Tsubouchi), has eyes for Ichi, figuratively speaking, and for the first time, he returns a woman's affections—he'd avoided getting involved with Tane, the love interest in the first two films. Yayoi proposes to him and he accepts. This scene provides more insight into his character. He's tortured by conflicting feelings of love and unworthiness, which he expresses poignantly. He speaks of being a criminal, a killer, a cripple, as well as revealing his far-from-virgin status with the ladies: "These women I've bought with money. And not just five or ten of them!" He vows to change his life, leave the yakuza, and abandon the way of the sword.

This doesn't last, of course. Suffice to say events conspire against him, forcing him to slay. Along the way we learn other things about Zatoichi, like details about his blindness. When Yayoi tells him the moon looks nice, he replies, "When I'm told the moon is beautiful, it floats inside my own eyes too. I can still see the image of Shimodate in my mind, lit by the moonlight, back when I could still see." Ah ha, so he wasn't blind from birth. What robbed him of his sight? We aren't told. In another scene, Ichi is giving a massage, and can tell by feeling the man's upper musculature that he's an accomplished swordsman. This kind of knowledge comes in handy for a blind masseur who will surely have to face the fellow later on.

What is perhaps most striking about *New Tale of Zatoichi* is the look of the film. Director Tokuzo Tanaka and cinematographer Chishi Makiura enhance the psychological drama with moody, noir lighting on the set. Many faces are in half-shadow, indicating conflict and things hidden. In addition, there are extreme close-ups, deep focus shots, creative mise-en-scène, arcs, zooms, pull-outs—a whole host of cinematic effects are utilized to enhance not only the underpinnings of the story, but the inner workings of Zatoichi himself. The candle-slicing scene is a good example of all these creative techniques. Also,

Ichi confesses his sins to Yayoi in New Tale of Zato-ichi

the score is brooding, haunting, a superb effort from Akira Ifukube, composer of music for some 300 films, everything from **Chushingura** to *Godzilla.*

After watching *New Tale of Zatoichi,* we come away with a deeper feel for the central character, a sensitive, conflicted person facing enormous hardships with courage and dignity. Character development is always crucial to any cinematic experience, and it's a tribute to Daiei that they took the time to flesh out Zatoichi this early on. Succeeding films in the series build on this intimate portrayal, and his adventures are that much more compelling for it.

Sleepy Eyes of Death: The Chinese Jade

Nemuri Kyoshiro 1: Sappocho

"Ninja . . . a monk's note . . . and vanishing corpses."
"Oh, how creepy!"

1963, Daiei

DIRECTOR: Tokuzo Tanaka

CAST: Raizo Ichikawa, Tamao Nakamura, Tomisaburo Wakayama, Sonosuke Sawamura, Saburo Date

AVAILABILITY: Tough

COMMENT: VHS from AnimEigo is out of print

She's not kidding, and we're only five minutes into *Sleepy Eyes of Death: The Chinese Jade.*

Nemuri Kyoshiro is the ultimate cynical, suave, super-deadly, totally hip ronin about town. He's filled with existential angst and says things like "I'm just someone who's pissed off at all mankind, even though I'm a man myself. I'm past the point of no return. I know not what my future holds, but in the time that I have left, I shall be the ruin of the evil men that cross my path (laughs)." He has a way with the ladies, and he lets his sword do the talking with those evil men, although he never provokes a duel. "Others always force me to slay," he tells us in this, the first of 12 in the popular Sleepy Eyes of Death series.

Raizo Ichikawa, who plays the title character, was the golden boy at **Daiei** in the late '50s and throughout the '60s. He's been called the James Dean of Japan; more than just a pretty face, he was a charismatic presence, a mesmerizing, compelling force of nature, and always super cool. And like Dean, he died young: struck down by cancer at 37. But he wasted no time—in his brief 14-year career he made upward of 100 films, an outstanding achievement for any actor. In the '60s, his popularity was rivaled only by fellow Daiei superstar **Shintaro Katsu**, their respective films often running as double features to maximize ticket sales.

The Chinese Jade hits the ground running. The first image is that of a shower of flaming shuriken hitting a wooden door. Nemuri Kyoshiro looks up, slightly annoyed. "Ninja, eh?" he says casually. "Don't force me to draw my sword . . . once I draw, you're all dead men." Of course they don't listen and he dispatches six of them in as many seconds. Viewers may notice a ninja in-joke running through the film. Ichikawa had starred the previous year in *Ninja (Shinobi no mono),* the first of a seven-film series wherein he played a variety of famous figures from ninja lore. While those films took being a ninja very seriously, *The Chinese Jade* spoofs the sub-genre by making wave upon wave of ninjas ridiculously easy to kill. In this first encounter, a couple of them even do little back flips before expiring from his slashes. It's hilarious. However, one gets away, a grinning youth whom we'll meet a little later.

We soon learn that the ninjas were sent to "test" Nemuri Kyoshiro by the slimy Lord Nariyasu Maeda (**Sonosuke Sawamura**), daimyo of the million-koku fief of Kaga. Maeda will do anything to get a certain jade statuette back from his foe, the equally reprehensible merchant Gohei Zeniya (**Saburo Date**). Why would a rich man like Maeda be so hung up on a little trifle like the Chinese Jade? Well, like the Maltese Falcon, it's what's inside that counts, but we don't know what it is (yet). In any case, he dispatches his lovely adopted daughter Chisa (Tamao Nakamura) to seduce Nemuri into working for him. Perhaps with Nemuri's help, he can regain the prized possession. Then he'll kill Nemuri.

To get him on the payroll, Chisa offers Nemuri 100 ryo to be her yojimbo. She says she's heard that no swordsman in Edo is a match for him. "You must also have heard that I'm a rogue who slices men like they were radishes," he says snidely, but takes the job. Later he admits, "Without some excitement each and every day I begin to feel like I'm dead, you know, as if all that I can feel is the caress of the wind."

Nemuri Kyoshiro receives an enigmatic note from a monk, who turns out to be Chen Sun (**Tomisaburo Wakayama**), 13th descendant of a Chinese master of Shorinji-style boxing. He's sporting a shaved head and does a lot of fighting in the picture, all with his bare hands. Wakayama's performance is a treat for **Lone Wolf and Cub** fans, as it's the complete opposite of Ogami Itto, who's routinely tricked out with all sorts of weapons. Here we see Wakayama going up against gangs of ninja and samurai with nothing but his fists (there is an instant when he grabs a guy's sword and stabs him with it, but that's all the weapon-wielding you'll see from this bald madman). Chen Sun is in with Zeniya, and he too wants to hire Nemuri Kyoshiro.

Nemuri Kyoshiro meets with Chen Sun, but the two men are interrupted by ninja. Chen Sun leaves a poem for Nemuri hanging from a plum tree: "Crashing waves reflect a full moon upon Tsukuda Island." The full moon refers to Nemuri Kyoshiro's sword technique, the enigmatic Full-Moon Cut: he draws a circle slowly in the air, his opponents become hypnotized by it and rush in, only to be cut down in an instant. The

Full-Moon Cut is his trademark, and we see it in every picture. Therefore the poem is summoning Nemuri to Tsukuda Island. There he finally meets Zeniya, who also tries to hire him. The scene takes place in an underwater room, and as the two men talk, they are bathed in a trippy, proto-psychedelic blue light effect. Here Nemuri learns the secret of the Chinese Jade.

The rest I leave to you, but in closing I leave you with a few more choice bon mots from the mouth of Nemuri Kyoshiro:

"For me the dark world of humanity . . . not the pure and just world of nature . . . is where I belong. To that world, where every man is a ronin, I must return."

"I'm kind of a cynic, you see."

"You will die by the time my sword completes the circle."

"If you were in my arms, would your heart burn for me? I think not."

"Want to taste steel?"

"Don't get too close to me. I've come from killing many men. You'll reek of blood too."

7

The Mid '60s

Adventures of Zatoichi

Zatoichi sekisho yaburi

Daiei, 1964

DIRECTOR: Kimiyoshi Yasuda

CAST: Shintaro Katsu, Miwa Takada, Eiko Taki, Kichijiro Ueda, Mikijiro Hira

AVAILABILITY: Easy

COMMENT: DVD from Home Vision Entertainment

Double your pleasure! Two mystery ronin, two damsels in distress, and two lovable tykes plus the usual assortment of corrupt officials, low-down yakuza, and noble peasants. Add to this an old town drunk who might just be Zatoichi's long lost father, and you're all set for one of the more engrossing, character-driven installments in the blind swordsman franchise.

A kite lands on masseur Ichi's head as he sits gorging himself on rice balls. Soon thereafter, a shady character hits up our hero to deliver a note to a woman named Sen (Eiko Taki) who works at the Musashi Inn in Kasama. Ichi (**Shintaro Katsu**) is a pushover for this sort of thing, and agrees. He delivers the note to Sen and decides to stay at the inn. He shares a room with Miss Saki (**Miwa Takada**), a lady on a mission to find her missing father. It is a couple of days before the New Year festival and Kasama is filled with traveling merchants and performers. One of the merchants gives Zatoichi a Daruma doll that features prominently throughout the picture.

The performers and merchants are informed that Boss Jinbei (**Kichijiro Ueda**) is expecting 40% of their take, effectivly ruining their business. But what can they do? A corpulent, slobby ronin offers his services to Jinbei's men—is he deadly

天然色

1965 Daiei

Adventures of
Zatoichi: *Sen and
Zatoichi have sport-
ive fun*

or just bluffing? We learn that Sen's brother, the man who gave Zatoichi the note, is an escaped fugitive, out for revenge on Boss Jinbei who hired him for a hit and then turned him in.

An old drunk brings Ichi in to Jinbei's gambling house. Zatoichi winds up doing a little topknot-slicing when he realizes that the dice game is crooked. He becomes friendly with the old man, and the more they talk, the more he comes to believe the old codger is his father, estranged when Ichi was five. Although he can't confirm his suspicion, his feelings are stirred and he winds up placing an ill-advised trust in the old reprobate. Soon Miss Saki is imperiled by Jinbei's gang, and Zatoichi asks the old man to escort her out of town. Bad move. Two boy acrobats become Zatoichi's eyes on the street and help him rescue Miss Saki. But a blind swordsman's work is never done. . . .

The plot and characters in *Adventures of Zatoichi* become more and more intertwined. The character development is slow and deliberate, pulling you in deeper and deeper. Character development is really the key to an absorbing film, and here such care is taken that by the end of the film the audience is wholly subsumed in the action. Even ancillary characters are well rounded and compelling, such as the traveling comic duo played by real-life brother act Daimaru and Racquet Nakada, whose antics were popular on Japanese TV in the early '60s.

Other guest stars include Kichijiro Ueda, familiar from such samurai classics as **Rashomon** and the **Samurai Trilogy**. By this time he too had transitioned into TV comedy, although his bearing is certainly gruff and threatening enough to make him a good heavy as Boss Jinbei. Certain Japanese actors of this period had a tendency to age badly, and it's amazing to think that Ueda, here a fat old man with a voice like gravel and a generally unhealthy aspect, was just a dozen years earlier the lively, cynical commoner who berates the priest and the woodcutter in *Rashomon*. For other examples of thespian decline, take a look at Shintaro Katsu in **Roningai** and **Tomisaburo Wakayama** in Ridley Scott's *Black Rain* (Wakayama delivers the devastating "black rain" speech to Michael Douglas at the end of the picture).

Hideo Gosha fans will recognize **Mikijiro Hira** from such films as ***Three Outlaw Samurai*** and *Sword of the Beast*. He also appeared in Hiroshi Teshigahara's bizarre face-transplant film, *The Face of Another.* Here he plays Gounosuke, the other mystery ronin, a truly dangerous fellow working for Boss Jinbei who at one point tells Zatoichi, "All I really care about anymore is finding someone who can out-duel me." Gounosuke belongs to that morose group of ronin who, having fallen through the ever-widening cracks of the **Tokugawa period**, has nothing left to live for except, ironically, a noble death. His character here is similar to that in *Three Outlaw Samurai*, except this time out he doesn't find redemption in friendship.

While not as action-packed as other installments, *Adventures of Zatoichi* still has its moments. At one point Ichi slices a spinning top neatly in half . . . while it's still spinning (after awhile it realizes it's been halved and splits in two). This film is best suited to those who have seen a couple of Zatoichi films and desire total immersion in Ichi's world. The escapist potential is unlimited: you can't get much farther away than feudal Japan. So sit down, pop on *Adventures of Zatoichi* and lose yourself. Shintaro Katsu's sword, Miwa Takada's beauty, and an eyeless Daruma doll await.

Ask Takuan, the Know-It-All Priest

Q: That red Daruma doll is an odd-looking thing. What's the cultural background on it?

A: At last! A proper question for a Buddhist priest. Daruma is the Japanese name for Bodhidharma (470–543), 28th Patriarch of Buddhism and founder of Zen. He is a legendary figure in Japan and of course a venerable personage for us priests. In paintings he is always portrayed with fierce, bulging eyes protruding from a hairy countenance. It is told that he was something of an irascible character, flying into fits of rage at the idiocy of those who sought his council. The Emperor once asked him, "Is there any merit in good conduct?" "No merit at all," was his curt reply. The Emperor pressed, "What then is the whole truth, the first principle?" "The first principle transcends all. There is nothing holy."

Daruma is reverenced in the playful way unique to Asian cultures. He is said to have meditated for nine years in a cave, losing his arms and legs; thus the rounded shape of the Daruma doll. The eyeless Daruma doll was a favorite at New Year's, when children traditionally painted in one eye to make a wish and painted the other if the wish came true.

Kwaidan

Kwaidan

1964, Toho

DIRECTOR: Masaki Kobayashi

CAST: Rentaro Mikuni, Michiyo Aratama, Tatsuya Nakadai, Katsuo Nakamura, Kanemon Nakamura

AVAILABILITY: Easy

COMMENT: DVD from Criterion Collection

Most of the films in this book concern themselves with the lives and deaths of samurai. But what of the afterlife? What becomes of these stern warriors once they've stepped into the netherworld? Do they fight on? Does their proud heritage prepare them for the lonely, lost existence of a ghost?

Kwaidan is made up of four vignettes, magnificently creepy and surreal, disorienting, vivid, sometimes terrifying. Much of the unreality comes from a soundstage-bound, ultra-formalist production: brightly colored, expressionistic sets combined with post-synched sound that often ignores atmospheric noises (such as someone pounding their fists on a wall—they pound in silence). In addition, the soundtrack utilizes strange, threatening, unidentified noises to further confuse and freak out the audience.

Only three of the stories concern samurai, but the remaining one features **Tatsuya Nakadai**, so you can't really go wrong. Each is set in a different historical period, and all concern ghosts. The stories were written by Lafcadio Hearn, an Irishman of Greek extraction afforded the rare privilege of becoming a Japanese citizen in 1895. His tales are based on ancient Japanese ghost stories, and such was his writing skill that you'd never know they were written by a gaijin. In the hands of Masaki Kobayashi, these stories become moody, methodically paced masterpieces with a distinctly Kubrickian flavor.

The Black Hair

In old Kyoto there was a young samurai who had been reduced to poverty by the ruin of his lord. He decided to leave his home and take service with the governor of a distant province.

The samurai (**Rentaro Mikuni**) also leaves his lovely and devoted wife (**Michiyo Aratama**). "I can't live here with you. I have a future," he declares and tosses her aside like a used Q-tip.

He remarries a rich young woman, haughty and homely, with whom he is totally miserable, and soon longs to return to his first wife. When he at last does so, the old place is completely overgrown, and although he finds his wife, who has waited patiently all this time, things have changed. . . .

This first piece is the only one with any location shots, some gorgeous footage of mountain forests and river gorges. There are also scenes of Mikuni on horseback, shooting targets with a bow and arrow. These were most likely added to ease the audience into the extreme formalism to come. The soundtrack makes use of clicks, snaps, deep crunching, wood splintering, scraping, all with a slight echo. These sounds have nothing to do with the action on screen, and against total silence they have a striking psychological effect. Are they bones? Are they the sounds of some giant demon devouring the tenement? We are never told. Doesn't matter, the damage to our quivering psyches is done.

The Woman of the Snow

He's Tatsuya Nakadai. She's a snow ghost. Can they make it work?

Both *The Black Hair* and *The Woman of the Snow* share story elements with Kenji Mizoguchi's *Ugetsu,* a highly recommended film for those interested in the jidai-geki/ghost story. When watching films like these, it's important to bear in mind what's different about Japanese ghosts, compared with the European or American variety: they are completely real. Unlike the floating, see-through phantoms we're all familiar with in the West, Japanese ghosts have physicality. You can live with one, have sex, have kids; a ghost can mutilate, even murder you. This makes them much more freaky and dangerous. Some of these things happen in this vignette. I'll leave it to you to find out which.

Hochi, the Earless

Here is the centerpiece of the film, which begins with a reenactment of the sea battle of Dan-no-ura in 1186 between two powerful clans, the Genji (in black) and the Heike (in red). Things go badly for the Heike clan, and they all perish in the sea. The battle, filmed in a giant pool on a **Toho** soundstage, is intercut with close-ups of different details of a mural depicting the same battle. This cross-cutting makes the painting come alive in a similar staid, mannerist way. A biwa (lute) plays furiously during the fighting accompanied by a slow, chanted ballad describing the action known as the *Heike monogatari* (Tale of the Heike).

Cut to Amidaji temple at Akamagahara, where we meet Hoichi (**Katsuo Nakamura**), a blind biwa player. We realize that he was the one performing the *Heike monogatari,* conjuring the vivid images of Dan-no-ura. Unfortunately for Hoichi, the ghosts of the Heike, whose bodies are buried nearby, are also fans of this young biwa hoshi (storyteller with biwa). They send a warrior (**Tetsuro Tamba**) to fetch him for a command performance. Hoichi is a sweet little guy, and obliges. Soon he's going every night. He doesn't know they're ghosts, and they've sworn him to secrecy. But all this contact with the dead is taking its toll on him, and he's looking more and more like a terminal case. He's worrying the priest (**Takashi Shimura**), who eventually sends two lay brothers to follow him on his nocturnal mission.

The two men find Hoichi playing and singing in the graveyard. "Don't interrupt me before this distinguished assembly!" he screams. "You've been passing your nights among tombstones," they tell him. Back at the temple, the priest warns Hoichi, "You have put yourself in their power. If you obey them again, they'll tear you in pieces."

You can already tell from the title of the story what pieces get torn off Hoichi. But just how it comes about is a fascinating detail I leave to you to discover.

In a Cup of Tea

It is 1680: a procession of samurai stops at a temple in Hongo. One of them, Kannai (**Kanemon Nakamura**), goes to the well for a drink, and notices a strange man's face reflected in the surface of the water in his cup. Thus begins the most curious of the four tales. We learn that the reflection is that of a mysterious samurai who appears to Kannai later that night when the man is on guard duty. Being a guard, Kannai attacks the "intruder" who in turn promptly disappears. Kannai is made to look foolish for causing a stir.

The following night, he's paid a visit by three of the ghost samurai's ghost retainers, who demand satisfaction. The ending is missing, and the frame story, within which this story is contained, provides the shock ending. It's a Twilight Zone moment.

Masaki Kobayashi made *Kwaidan* in 1964, two years after **Harakiri** and three years before **Samurai Rebellion**. Yet it seems to stand alone, wholly apart from the style and content of those two films, a haunting and haunted work of pure cinematic formalism. Nevertheless, you know it's Kobayashi by his hallmark traits of rigorous pacing, painstaking craftsmanship, and the underlying theme of hypocrisy, cruelty, and folly in the ruling samurai class.

Kwaidan won the Special Jury Prize at the 1965 Cannes Film Festival.

Three Outlaw Samurai

Sanbiki no samurai

1964, Shochiku

DIRECTOR: Hideo Gosha

CAST: Tetsuro Tamba, Isamu Nagato, Mikijiro Hira, Kamatari Fujiwara, Miyuki Kuwano

AVAILABILITY: Easy

COMMENT: DVD format from Hong Kong distributor Platinum Classics. Titles from Platinum are hit or miss at best. Do *not* buy their *Hunter in the Dark* DVD unless you're desperate—the transfer is terrible. However *Three Outlaw Samurai* is fine, perhaps because it is black and white.

Three Outlaw Samurai was **Hideo Gosha**'s first feature film, and it's fresh and brilliant right out of the box. Gosha was unique among film directors of his day: he started out in TV in 1953, working as a reporter, then as producer and director. *Three Outlaw Samurai* is based on a TV series he'd developed, and the characters and settings have a cool, stylized, lived-in quality that stems from their previous life on the small screen; there's an easy familiarity, you feel like you know these guys. Add to this the fact that several character traits and plot points have been lifted wholesale from **Yojimbo**, **Sanjuro**, and **Seven Samurai**, and no wonder this movie feels so right. If you're going to steal, steal from the best. However, Gosha's directorial style is so modern and kinetic, the Kurosawa components play more as homage than heist. If you weren't looking for them, you might not notice.

The story concerns the eponymous ronin, Shiba (**Tetsuro Tamba**), Sakura (Shintaro Katsu look-alike Isamu Nagato), and Kikyo (**Mikijiro Hira**). Shiba is all cool, exuding a calm self-confidence and take-charge attitude as only Tamba can.

Sakura is the portly Porthos of the piece whose weapon is the spear. He provides the comic relief but is as deadly as his compatriots. Kikyo is an ultra-cynical, sophisticated samurai working for the dishonorable chamberlain of the local clan, but eventually he comes around and joins the other two.

Shiba happens upon three farmers holding a young woman of high rank hostage in an old ramshackle mill. She turns out to be Aya (Miyuki Kuwano), the daughter of the chamberlain. The farmers, led by Jinbei (**Kamatari Fujiwara**), are starving and desperate to have their petition of grievances heard; however, the chamberlain will have none of it, hence the standoff. Shiba's just looking for a place to sleep for the night and figures the hostage drama will make for some free entertainment. But soon enough he's embroiled in the conflict.

Sakura, sitting in a cell for vagrancy, is offered his freedom and some money if he'll help eradicate the kidnappers. He likes to fight, so off he goes. On his way, he's attacked by another desperate farmer while urinating by the roadside. So keen are Sakura's reflexes that he has slain the man before he knows it, and with a childlike petulance, asks, "What made him do that? Reckless fellow!" When he learns that the men he's been sent to kill are poor farmers fighting for justice, Sakura declares, "I quit. I'm originally from a farm myself. From this moment, I'm on the side of the farmers." Shiba asks Kikyo, also present, whether he'd like to join them for some millet porridge. "No thanks," Kikyo sneers, "I prefer good food, wine, plenty of it." He saunters off, but he'll be back. Circumstances change, characters and groups turn on another constantly, plots shift, there is many an exciting sword battle, an appearance by the "Gods of Death," and before it's over, Kikyo is fighting side by side with Shiba and Sakura, bodies strewn about them like autumn leaves.

Regarding the Kurosawa elements, it's like this: the lead ronin, Shiba, is strongly evocative of **Toshiro Mifune**'s character in *Yojimbo*. Under the opening credits, we follow him as he walks along the lonely road, his back to the camera. A stray dog trots by (albeit without the severed hand). Later we see him deciding which way to go by throwing a lady's hairpin in the air (in *Yojimbo* it was a stick) and following the direction it points. There's also Shiba's brutal beaten-to-a-pulp scene, followed by a crawling escape beneath decking (just like Toshiro Mifune and Clint Eastwood to boot!) as his pursuers chase about right above his head. The theme of ronin helping poor farmers, while not the property of Kurosawa, nevertheless shows the influence of *Seven Samurai,* and one of the three ronin being an ex-farmer certainly sounds like Mifune's Kikuchiyo. Then there's the issue of a savvy ronin helping a bunch of amateurs match the political machinations of a wicked and entrenched authority (see *Sanjuro*). Again, these touches are more circumstantial than outright plagiaristic. I'm merely pointing out how a talented filmmaker can learn his craft by sitting at the feet of the master (and maybe snagging a couple of things on his way out).

Gosha and director of photography Tadashi Sakai have also learned a thing or two about deep-focus framing and mise-en-scène from **Kazuo Miyagawa**'s work in *Yojimbo.* Notice how people are nicely broken off into frames within frames by window slats, prison bars, all manner of architectural latticing. This is not so much stylistically derivative, however, as it is simply good form. In addition, there are plenty of nice touches, such as: light glinting dramatically off sword and spear blades; spookily lit dungeon scenes; a general foreboding darkness throughout (fully half the film takes place at night); and to mark the onset of the grand finale sword battle, a sudden manual tilt of the camera into an extreme dutch angle, communicating the skewing of everything that has gone before.

As for story direction and pacing, Gosha's style crackles with electricity, it pulses, running through the movie like a current. Perhaps it's due to his early training in television that his films are infused with the immediacy that television demands—fast-paced plot and explosive action sequences—yet tempered by the cerebral and contemplative dimensions of film. It's slick, yet deep. It's deceptively simple, yet extremely sophisticated. What results is something wholly complete, finished in a way that films are rarely finished, every element in balance with the rest, providing the audience a sense of satisfaction akin to fine dining or good sex.

As a first effort, *Three Outlaw Samurai* is sublime. When

you consider that each successive film saw Gosha's powers growing, you realize, as you pursue Gosha, that you're in for some of the most formidable and unforgettable of samurai film experiences.

Sleepy Eyes of Death: Sword of Seduction

Nemuri Kyoshiro 4: Joyoken

1964, Daiei

DIRECTOR: Kazuo Ikehiro

CAST: Raizo Ichikawa, Yoshio Inaba, Shiho Fujimura, Tomisaburo Wakayama, Naoko Kubo

AVAILABILITY: Tough

COMMENT: VHS from AnimEigo is out of print

Looking for a film that features a psychopathic princess, a doctor feelgood, a poisoning prostitute, crucified Christians, a suicidal heroine, sleazy drug dealers, a horny, hallucinating priest, a half-breed ronin, a fortune teller, a stray dog, a Japanese madonna, and a Chinese martial artist with an Elvis hairdo? C'mon, you know you want it.

Of the handful of Sleepy Eyes of Death films on video (now criminally out of print), *Sword of Seduction* is far and away the finest, craziest, most twisted, over the top, and insanely great of them all. The fourth film in the series, starring **Raizo Ichikawa** as the super-cool, wickedly snide ronin Nemuri Kyoshiro, was handed to **Kazuo Ikehiro**, one of the more "arty" of **Daiei**'s stable of house directors. Ikehiro uses extreme camera angles, moody chiaroscuro lighting effects, split-screen, psychedelic special effects, anything he can think of to infuse the film with a dreamy, narcotic feeling that mirrors one of the film's primary themes, opium addiction. He deliberately abandons the realistic for the fantastic, conjuring a surreal world wherein the shocking, continually shifting sequence of events flows swiftly and effortlessly onward, sweeping us up along the way. By the end of the film's 87 minutes, we're amazed at how much has happened—it's as if two or three movies have been rolled into one.

As mentioned above, opium figures largely in this film. We see people addicted to it, crawling across the floor in the throes of junk-sickness; we see a villainous rice merchant, Bizenya (**Yoshio Inaba**, one of the *Seven Samurai*), who's smuggling the stuff to sell to the courtesans of the Inner Court (a kind of harem for the shogun); and then of course there is the mysterious and wicked Princess Kiku, forever in shadow, who's not only an addict, but a sadistic, murdering harridan to boot! Oh, and she harbors a horrible secret . . . let's just say if she were to "lose face," it might not be so bad. . . .

Here for another round is Chen Sun (**Tomisaburo Wakayama**) who you'll remember from the first Nemuri Kyoshiro film, *Sleepy Eyes of Death: The Chinese Jade.* This time out, for some inexplicable reason, he's sporting a big Elvis-style pompadour; perhaps he hated his bald look in the first movie and insisted on lots of piled-up hair for his return. In any case, he's now working for Bizenya, whose partner is Dr. Moroya Jundo, official physician of the Inner Court. It is Dr. Jundo who got Princess Kiku and numerous concubines hooked on opium. He is untroubled by guilt, declaring them "nothing but pathetic pigs! Filthy and wicked!"

The other big theme in *Sword of Seduction* is Christianity and the persecution of Christians during the **Tokugawa period**. Early on, Nemuri Kyoshiro meets Torizo, a Christian on the run from the law for, well, being a Christian. He tells Nemuri of a saint, the Virgin Shima (**Naoko Kubo**, who starred the same year in *Zatoichi's Flashing Sword* and *Sleepy Eyes of Death: Sword of Adventure*). Shima is also on the run, and Torizo begs Nemuri to save her. "I flatly refuse to help such a person," says Nemuri. But apparently Shima knows the cir-

Ask Takuan, the Know-It-All Priest

Q: I didn't know Christians were persecuted in Japan. What's the story?

A: In 1549 Spanish Missionary Francis Xavier established the first Christian mission in Kagoshima. Subsequent decades saw a steady increase in converts. This creeping foreign influence alarmed Hideyoshi Toyotomi, first unifier of Japan. In 1587, Toyotomi issued an official edict banning missionaries from Japan. He went on to confiscate Spanish ships and order the crucifixion of Christians.

Toyotomi's successor, Ieyasu Tokugawa, was initially more liberal-minded, but by 1614 had established his own ban on Christianity. Crucifixions resumed, along with burnings at the stake. Things came to a head in the Shimabara Revolt of 1637 with the death of some 37,000 Christians and rebel farmers; over 10,000 were beheaded, while others were burned or boiled alive.

Persecutions continued for the remainder of the Tokugawa period as a matter of official policy, only ending with the Meiji Restoration in 1868.

Nemuri Kyoshiro: When he says, "Go to hell!" you're going to hell!

A young Tomisaburo Wakayama before his pompadour phase

cumstances of Nemuri's birth, something that gets his attention. Later, Torizo is apprehended right in front of Nemuri and pleads for help. "Fool! It's all because of your silly belief in Christianity," Nemuri replies coldly.

Torizo's sister, Kosuzu (**Shiho Fujimura**), tries to secure her brother's release by agreeing to sleep with an old Spanish missionary whom the officials are trying to convert to Buddhism. If she can use her beautiful body to persuade the priest to sign a letter of conversion, Torizo will be freed. "I'll make you want to make love with me," she says as she strips. "Come now . . . please hold me in your arms! Renounce your Christian faith. Abandon your god and take me now!" The old bugger can't refuse, and jumps her bones. In the shadows, Nemuri watches. Next morning when the old priest is released, he hardly takes two steps from the prison door when out of nowhere Nemuri charges up on a horse, draws his sword and, with a hardy "Go to hell!" beheads the old man. What's going on? We get the feeling that our hero has some issues with this foreign faith.

So much more happens in this film that it defies description—you just have to see it. Each seduction, each treachery, every lethal altercation gets more surreal and bizarre. Eventually, Nemuri Kyoshiro learns the truth about himself from the Virgin Shima: he was the fruit of forbidden passion between his Japanese mother and a Portuguese missionary who defiled her during a black mass. This explains his reddish hair and his tortured love/hate relationship with Christians and the Christian faith. The circumstance of his conception also becomes a centerpiece in the series, with the reenactment of the evil ceremony preceding the opening credits in later installments.

If you only see one Sleepy Eyes of Death film, make it *Sword of Seduction.* Way ahead of its time in 1964, it lays the foundation for other outrageous film series like **The Razor, Lady Snowblood,** and **Lone Wolf and Cub.** Where else will you find dialog like this?

"You've been killing helpless souls as if they were merely bugs. I came to tell you to stop doing so."

"What if I say 'I refuse'?"

"I'll kill you!"

Samurai Assassin

Samurai

1965, Toho

DIRECTOR: Kihachi
Okamoto

CAST: Toshiro Mifune,
Keiju Kobayashi,
Michiyo Aratama,
Yunosuke Ito, Eijiro
Tono, Yoshio Inaba,
Takashi Shimura,
Koshiro Matsumoto

AVAILABILITY: Easy

COMMENT: VHS from
AnimEigo

By 1860, things were starting to look pretty black for the **Tokugawa Shogunate**. The symbolism of the moment couldn't have been any more potent than the appearance of four huge, black U.S. battleships commanded by Commodore Perry who, in 1853, showed up and "requested" access to Japanese ports and a general reversal of the shogunate's centuries-old isolationist policies. Perry returned a year later with twice as many ships, and the shogunate caved, opening ports in Hokkaido and Shizuoka. This break in one of the central policies of the Tokugawa government, isolation from the West, led to a splintering of the entire power structure. The samurai class broke off into factions, each with its own radical agenda for the future of Japan. However, they all had one thing in common: plots and plans for killing off the other factions. In other words, assassinations were BIG in mid-nineteenth-century Japan.

If this seems a little overwrought for the beginning of a film review, there's a reason: *Samurai Assassin,* based on real people and events, is one of the most narratively dense, historically detailed films of the samurai genre. Make no mistake, it's a great film, but it's not one you can just waltz into. **Shinobu Hashimoto**, samurai scenarist supreme, was steeped in the history of his nation, and reading his screenplays can sometimes feel like taking a survey course on the subject. Fortunately, he always worked with excellent directors who knew how to stage his material in engaging, stimulating productions. In this film, Hashimoto's depth of detail is balanced by the incendiary action sequences that made director **Kihachi Okamoto** famous in the '60s as one of the new breed of super-violent samurai auteurs.

Samurai Assassin features a veritable who's who of **Toho** stars, including many members of the **Kurosawa-gumi**. In addition to **Toshiro Mifune**, familiar faces include **Eijiro Tono** (*Yojimbo*), **Yoshio Inaba** (*Seven Samurai*), **Takashi Shimura** (*Seven Samurai* and just about every other **Kurosawa** film), **Koshiro Matsumoto** (*Chushingura*) and **Michiyo Aratama** (*Kwaidan*) to name a few. Part of the joy of samurai films is getting familiar with a whole host of great actors you never knew existed and then identifying them with each new film, a pastime I call "samurai spotting." There's certainly much samurai spotting fun to be had in *Samurai Assassin.*

In order to keep up with the complexities of *Samurai Assassin*—the historical facts come fast and furious—you'll need a little more background. So here's the thing: In 1858 the 14th shogun died, and a succession struggle ensued. The power behind the throne, Naosuke Ii (Koshiro Matsumoto), saw to it that the younger of the two candidates, Iemochi (a raw youth he could control), was named the new shogun. Ii was also ready to play ball with the West, which put him at odds with the isolationist supporters of the other shogunal candidate, Hitotsubashi. Ii initiated a campaign of demotion, exile, and execution against those who opposed him, later known as the Ansei Purge of 1859 and earning him the nickname of "Red Devil." The plot to assassinate Red Devil Ii is the central thrust of the film.

However, the plotters, the **Tengu** faction of Mito (yes, there are many, many names to keep track of in this film), are a paranoid lot, and think there is an informer amongst them. Their suspicion falls on Tsuruchiyo Niiro (**Toshiro Mifune**), whom we first encounter picking his nose and rubbing it into his kimono under the opening credits. He's the cynical, shaggy ronin figure, tough, ambitious, and looking out for number one. But he's no spy—he's determined to take Ii's head himself. Confirming his loyalty becomes a convenient MacGuffin for the plotters' neurotic leader, Kenmotsu Hoshino (**Yunosuke Ito**), providing lots of character-developing flashbacks that show the kind of man Niiro really is. From here the film becomes Niiro's story, filled with melodramatic twists and revelations, while the inevitable assassination attempt looms throughout.

There is a pessimistic fatalism that runs through *Samurai Assassin.* The thesis is stated by at least three different characters at various points: "Nothing ever goes as one would hope," notes the plotters' scribe early on; "Nothing ever goes as planned," laments old Kisoya (Eijiro Tono); "This world never works the way you want it to," Niiro declares. And, by picture's end, we see this sentiment played out to its most ironic extreme.

Samurai Assassin is a challenging yet rewarding film, rich and rare and highly recommended. Filled to overflowing with screen talent, both in front of and behind the lens, it's the kind of picture that bears, nay demands, repeat viewings. First rate.

The Secret of the Urn

Tange Sazen: Hien iai giri

Toei, 1966

DIRECTOR: Hideo Gosha

CAST: Kinnosuke Nakamura, Seizaburo Kawazu, Keiko Awaji, Tetsuro Tamba, Wakaba Irie, Isao Kimura

AVAILABILITY: Tricky

COMMENT: Available as an import or through third-party collectors and independent distributors

He wears a white kimono. He has one eye. He has one arm. He is a ronin. He is a monster.

The phrase "monster" occurs again and again in *The Secret of the Urn* to describe its central figure, Tange Sazen (**Kinnosuke Nakamura**). According to his circumstances, his fate, and everything within his historical and cultural context, Tange Sazen is a monster. Yet the monster in film is often simply a symbol for the outsider, and here the metaphor works brilliantly. Being a lone ronin, he is already out of the loop; being severely mutilated increases his isolation and alienation tenfold. Needless to say, he's got something of a bad attitude. . . .

At the outset, *The Secret of the Urn* allows us to see the "before" version of our antihero. In this former life, he is Tange Samanosuke, a member of the Patrol Group for his clan. With shaved pate, fixed topknot, and a solemn look, he's instructed to assassinate a friend who his superior has learned is a spy.

Tange Samanosuke rides out with the man he's been told to kill, and informs him in a straightforward manner of his intentions. But the rogue tricks him: claiming the right of seppuku, he requests Samanosuke be his kaishakunin. They set about the ritual but, at the last moment, up comes the villain's wakizashi, out goes Samanosuke's eye, and a group of clansmen suddenly appear over the horizon. It's all been a setup! The samurai fall on the stricken Samanosuke, the attack culminating in a chilling, slow-motion image of his severed arm flying high into the sky, still clutching his sword. Birds scatter. Fade to black.

One year later: the shogun is considering which clan to assign the Nikko Toshogu shrine's 20th anniversary celebrations, a prestigious yet expensive honor (300,000 ryo). His devious chief advisor Guraku Nomura (**Seizaburo Kawazu**) suggests the **Yagyu clan**, knowing they don't have the dough. Nomura plans to ruin the Yagyu with the honor. Their only hope lies in the Kokezaru Urn, a family heirloom that contains the secret to a million ryo treasure. Clan leader Tsushima Yagyu (**Tetsuro Tamba**) sends his brother Genzaburo (*Seven Samurai* member **Isao Kimura**) to fetch it. Returning with the urn by boat, Genzaburo and his men are attacked by Nomura's forces at the riverside (Nomura wants the urn as well).

There is also a lovely lady thief, Ofuji (Keiko Awaji), who, along with her brother, is also after the urn. They too are at the river when Genzaburo docks, looking to scoop up the priceless object in the melee. This scene is a cracking action sequence; so much is going on at once, and director **Hideo Gosha** finds a way to keep up with it all through the use of tracking shots. The camera follows the urn as it passes from hand to hand, each holder being slashed by the next. One lateral tracking shot along the river lasts for a full 30 seconds of solid slicing and chaotic handoffs, like some relay race of death! A dying Yagyu clansman finally hands the bloody urn to a small boy in a boat, telling him if he takes it to the Yagyu residence in Edo, he'll get a reward. The boy agrees but soon finds himself pursued by more samurai, plus Ofuji and her brother.

The boy hides in a straw hut. A moment later Tange Sazen emerges, his foot on the urn. The transformation is striking; he is barely recognizable from the loyal retainer of the film's opening. A scar runs down his closed right eye, and his left eye rolls around in demented fashion as he surveys the surrounding samurai. Genzaburo approaches and explains that the Yagyu need the urn or there'll be trouble. "Will you give me the urn?" he asks Tange Sazen. "I'm a little bit weird, you know, and I don't like what you said," Sazen replies menacingly. "People seem to have died for this useless urn. I'll keep it so there won't be any more trouble."

And off we go. Tange Sazen has the most antic disposition of any ronin in chambara, a gut-laughing lunatic with a lightning sword and nothing to lose. Later, when ninjas attack, Sazen quips, "I'm beginning to like this urn. Whoever wants this urn more than his own life, come on out!" He's perverse, but with that kick-ass, fuck-it attitude we all admire. He's a stray dog with a bone who won't give it up on general principles. Ofuji becomes his girlfriend in order to get her hands on the urn, but winds up taking a shine to him and before long isn't sure which she wants more, the urn or Tange Sazen.

Things take a heartbreaking turn with the arrival of Hagino (Wakaba Irie), the woman Sazen loved in his past life as Samanosuke. She's fallen on hard times, and is brought to the ruined temple that Sazen, Ofuji, and a gang of thieves have made their hideout. She recognizes Sazen instantly, but he denies her tearful entreaties. Here Kinnosuke Nakamura gives a moving performance, communicating the anguish and conflict within Tange Sazen. The pure love he once felt for Hagino (and obviously still does) cannot live within this monster's heart, and we watch as it tears him up inside. He humiliates her until she runs away, and later, drowning his sorrows in sake, he tells the kid, "Listen, a samurai isn't as strong as you think. He just has a sword. He isn't strong at all. You're living alone without a father and mother. You are stronger than any samurai I know!"

The character of Tange Sazen first appeared in 1927–1928 in *Ooka Seidan—Suzukawa Genjuro,* a serialized tale written by Fubo Hayashi (real name Umitaro Hasegawa, 1900–1935). An ingenious writer of the early Showa period, Umitaro Hasegawa used three different nom de plumes to write fiction, nonfiction, adaptations, and translations. Tange Sazen was initially a supporting character in *Ooka Seidan—Suzukawa Genjuro,* but because of his popularity, *Tange Sazen* was later written (1933–1934) making him a beloved hero figure of the day. His legacy lived on for decades afterward, in scores of film adaptations. Cartoonist Osamu Tezuka even created a manga version of Tange Sazen.

The Secret of the Urn is a must-see Hideo Gosha picture, a must-see Kinnosuke Nakamura picture, and one hell of a ride. Comedic, dramatic, and filled with dialogue like this: "Are you sure you want to commit harakiri? Is this all the **Bushido** Code can offer? (Laughs) Until I became a monster, I didn't realize how foolish the samurai are. Anyway, I'm not going to stop you."

Daimajin

Daimajin

Daiei, 1966

DIRECTOR: Kimiyoshi Yasuda

CAST: Miwa Takada, Jun Fujimaki, Yoshihiko Aoyama, Ryutaro Gomi, Tatsuo Endo, RikiHashimoto, Saburo Date, Otome Tsukimiya

AVAILABILITY: Easy

COMMENT: DVD from Rubbersuit, a division of ADV films; trilogy comes complete in 3-disk box

So you say you're in the mood for a samurai flick but you're kinda tired of **Toshiro Mifune**? Seen one too many **Zatoichi**s lately? Looking for something different tonight? How about a thirty-foot stone god in samurai armor stalking the land, wreaking havoc on an evil lord and his minions? It's chambara/kaiju-eiga and it rocks!

"Kaiju" means "giant monster" (à la Godzilla, Ghidorah, Rodan, Mothra, Gamera) and "eiga" means movie. **Daiei** had a winner on its hands with 1965's *Gamera*, its first entry in the kaiju-eiga arena, and it also had a nice little line in chambara (Zatoichi, **Sleepy Eyes of Death**, etc.). So they decided to blend the two genres. The result is the Daimajin trilogy (all released in 1966). You don't have to be a giant monster fan or a samurai freak to get into this unique genre hybrid.

Seems there's a mountain village full of people terrified by rumblings they attribute to the "Majin's footsteps" ("majin" translates as devil or evil spirit). Their faith rests in their god, upon whom they rely to protect them from the Majin. The villagers perform elaborate, costumed tribal dances (not unlike the one the natives do in *King Kong*) to appease their god, to ask his protection against the Majin and . . . but what's this? A coup has occurred up at Castle Yamanaka! Kindly Lord Hanabusa has been overthrown by the wicked chamberlain Samanosuke Odate (**Ryutaro Gomi**) and his savage henchman Gunjuro (**Tatsuo Endo**), and Odate's men are breaking up the villager's ritual. Now the Majin will not be contained! (You see where this is going. . . .)

Lots of swordfighting ensues at the castle, as clan retainers Chuma (**Saburo Date**) and Kogenta (**Jun Fujimaki**) do what they can to rescue the children of the slain lord (his last words: "This is bitter.") Kogenta gets the kids safely away, and upon the advice of his aunt Shinobu (Otome Tsukimiya), the local Shinto priestess, takes them up to "Majin's Mountain." There they find the giant stone statue that keeps the Majin at bay.

Flash forward 10 years: The young lord Tadafumi (Yoshihiko Aoyama) and his sister Kozasa (**Miwa Takada**) have grown into nice, attractive young people. They've been living in the mountains with Kogenta all this time. Meanwhile, the cruel Lord Odate has enslaved the villagers, making them build a huge fort; they are whipped and abused, toting giant stones ancient-Egypt-style. Something must be done! Kogenta's not the man to do it though; he is captured by Gunjuro and subsequently tortured, confined, and used as bait to catch young lord Tadafumi. Tatsuo Endo's enthusiastic performance as the sadistic Gunjuro is one of the high points in the picture; his wild facial tics and general nastiness during the torture scene rival his stuttering yakuza boss Yasugoro in *Zatoichi's Flashing Sword*.

Ryutaro Gomi as Lord Odate is no slouch either. He often played heavies in Daiei pictures, and here he's so mean, he winds up cutting down old aunt Shinobu when she comes to plead with him not to destroy the stone god. "Destroy the god who protects us and the terrible evil spirit Arakatsuma will come forth," she gasps. He finishes her with one final, slow-motion slice, but she still manages to get out, "Samanosuke! You will know the wrath of our god!" Odate sends Gunjuro and some men to destroy the statue, but they only manage to drive a spike into its forehead before things start shaking, and half the men, Gunjuro included, get swallowed up by a crack in the earth. The spike stays where it is until it is eventually used for some creative retribution. . . .

Young lord Tadafumi tries to rescue Kogenta, gets caught, and it's up to the tears of his sister to move the giant stone god. Here things get a little confusing, as the villagers' god and the Majin get all mixed up together. Kozasa prays to the stone statue, which is supposed to symbolize the god, but when it comes alive, it's clearly the Majin. What gives? Who cares! The last 15 minutes of the film are pure monster mayhem, shot brilliantly with incredible colors and special effects that create more verisimilitude than you're likely to see in any of the other rubber suit affairs. Unless you're actively focusing on the fact that it's really Riki Hashimoto (formerly of the Mainichi Orions baseball team) in a big costume with a green Kirk Douglas grimace mask, you'd swear there really was a giant stone samurai walking around crushing, smashing, impaling, and generally bringing down Tenchu on the heinous exploiters of the good village folk. His menace is put over the top by a typically terrifying score by Akira Ifukube (yes, he did *Godzilla* too).

If you like Zatoichi, you'll be right at home in the world of Daimajin, as the three films of the trilogy (*Daimajin, Wrath of Daimajin,* and *Return of Daimajin*) all feature the same sets, costumes, and Daiei contract players familiar from the blind swordsman series. As with **Yokai Monsters**, it's as if they took a Zatoichi film, removed Zatoichi, and put in a monster instead. But Daiei always did quality work, and you'll be pleasantly surprised by just how good a kaiju-eiga can be when done right. No cheesy monster mash this; rather a giant samurai monster saga fit for a god!

Sword of Doom

Daibosatsu toge

1966, Toho

DIRECTOR: Kihachi Okamoto

CAST: Tatsuya Nakadai, Yuzo Kayama, Michiyo Aratama, Ko Nishimura, Toshiro Mifune

AVAILABILITY: Easy

COMMENT: VHS from Home Vision Entertainment; DVD from Criterion Collection

The sword is the soul. Study the soul to study the sword. An evil mind, an evil sword.

Thus speaks sword school instructor Toranosuke Shimada (**Toshiro Mifune**), having just cut down a dozen attackers in the snow. His words sum up the theme of *Sword of Doom,* a film written by **Shinobu Hashimoto** and directed by **Kihachi Okamoto**. Released one year after their first collaboration, *Samurai Assassin,* Okamoto's powers have grown considerably. *Sword of Doom* is Okamoto's masterpiece. Hashimoto delivered a script that was more suited to Okamoto's directing style; the political intrigue takes a back seat to the human drama.

Sword of Doom and *Samurai Assassin* bear many similarities: once again, the action is set during the last dying gasps of the **Tokugawa period** known as the **Bakumatsu period**, in which the very fabric of the society is disintegrating and factional infighting is boiling over into bloody assassinations. Once again the story centers on a cynical, super-bad, dirt-poor ronin, but here the similarities end. Where *Samurai Assassin* featured Toshiro Mifune as an ambitious-but-basically-alright guy, *Sword of Doom* posits **Tatsuya Nakadai**'s masterless samurai, Ryunosuke Tsukue, as a swordsman of pure evil. To reinforce this evil, the word "cruel" is uttered half a dozen times at the outset of the film in regards to him. But Nakadai really doesn't need this expository aid; his face and body language say it all. This performance, unique in his catalog, is chilling and awesome to behold. He is an enigma, a cypher—there's no one there, just an essence of sociopathic wrongness. Rarely does anything approaching joy flicker in his cold, dead eyes, and these fleeting moments come only when he has killed. He lives to kill—it is the only thing that sustains him in his otherwise empty life.

There are multiple, intertwining plots and subplots that can be divided into political drama and human melodrama. Politically, the Shinchogumi is staging assassinations, and one of their main guys, former **Mito Tengu** member **Kamo Serizawa** (Kei Sato), observes Ryunosuke in a sword competition. Wielding a bokuto (wooden sword), Ryunosuke brains his opponent with ease, and is hired by an impressed Serizawa to do some killing for the Shincho group. Meanwhile, on the melodramatic side of things, Ryunosuke has already slept with his dead opponent's wife, Hama (**Michiyo Aratama**), in an old water mill, the pounding of the grain pestles mirroring the sexual activity. After the match Hama warns him that he's about to be ambushed by her dead husband's friends, and by the way, would he mind having her as his wife? He takes out all attackers in a brilliant sequence, and takes her too.

Then there's the young ingenue, Omatsu (Yoko Naito), whose grandfather (**Kurosawa-gumi** stalwart **Kamatari Fujiwara**) Ryunosuke cut down at the opening of the film for no apparent reason (except to show his casual cruelty). She is imperiled by her flower arrangement instructor who tries (unsuccessfully) to pimp her out to a local debauched lord before eventually selling her to a brothel. Omatsu's protector is her uncle, sneak thief Shichibei (**Ko Nishimura**). Omatsu has fallen in love at first sight with handsome young Hyoma Utsuki (**Yuzo Kayama**) who is, you guessed it, the brother of the man Ryunosuke felled in the tournament. Utsuki's sword instructor is none other than Toranosuke Shimada, the fellow quoted at the beginning of this review, played by Toshiro Mifune. And that's only half of what happens. There are additional characters, and before it's over, they are all revealed to be interconnected in one way or another. Two words of advice: multiple viewings.

Toward the end of *Sword of Doom,* Ryunosuke's evil doings catch up with him—he completely loses his mind. In an eerie, expressionistic sequence, he hallucinates wildly, seeing the shadows of those he's killed appear on the walls around him in finest *Richard III* fashion. He slashes away at the phantoms again and again to no avail. Suddenly, the shadowy apparitions switch to real attackers. It is the Shinchogumi who have, by now, turned on him, and what follows is a magnificent sword battle that seems to go on and on forever. Although mortally wounded time and again, Ryunosuke refuses to go down, symbolizing the immortal tenacity of evil.

While I make a point never to reveal endings in these reviews, for *Sword of Doom* there is no fear, as the movie doesn't have one. It's a post-modernist wet dream. The various plotlines lead inexorably toward two showdowns, Ryunosuke/Shimada and Ryunosuke/Utsuki, which never occur. Instead, the filmmaker simply ends the movie during the final sword battle on a freeze-frame of Ryunosuke in mid-slash. The nihilism of the ending, callously tossing aside the baroque storylines, serves to underline the nihilism of the central character. In fact, the serialized novel upon which the film is based, *Daibosatsu Toge (Great Boddhisattva Pass),* was itself never completed; the author strung it out from 1913 to 1941 but died before finishing it. While *Sword of Doom* only covers the first part of the novel, a full cinematic adaptation had been made several years earlier by **Kenji Misumi** as the Satan's Sword trilogy (1959–1961) starring **Raizo Ichikawa**.

The all-star cast elevates the melodrama of *Sword of*

Doom to an artistic level that complements the action and stylistic flair of the film, but it must be said that the film is confusing, particularly at the outset. Characters are thrown at the audience in rapid succession, requiring some note-taking to keep them straight. As in *Samurai Assassin,* there is a rushed feeling to the exposition. It is unclear whether this is the fault of the writer or the director, but looking at how Hashimoto's scripts play with other directors, one can't help feeling Okamoto is to blame. That said, there are some brilliant action sequences, and the character development, while scant, is enough to serve its purpose. Suffice to say that after a couple of viewings, all the tangled lines of *Sword of Doom* straighten out and you are left with an exciting and intriguing piece of chambara that can be savored indefinitely.

8

The Late '60s

Samurai Rebellion

Joi-uchi

1967, Toho

DIRECTOR: Masaki Kobayashi

CAST: Toshiro Mifune, Tatsuya Nakadai, Go Kato, Yoko Tsukasa, Shigeru Koyama, Michiko Otsuka

AVAILABILITY: Easy

COMMENT: VHS from Home Vision Entertainment

To be a samurai is to submit to the absolute authority of one's lord. But what if there were a samurai who, pushed to the breaking point by cruel and egregious demands, refused to submit and rebelled against his lord? This is the story of *Samurai Rebellion.*

Set in 1725, the height of the **Tokugawa period** (before the onset of its decline in the 1780s), the events of *Samurai Rebellion* take place within the vacuum of peace that marked the period. The first images we see are that of a man, a sword, and another man, the latter made of straw. The sword is being tested on the straw man, a symbol not only of the peacetime in which only straw soldiers need fear a sword, but of the once proud samurai warrior, now something of a straw man himself.

One such samurai is Isaburo Sasahara (**Toshiro Mifune**). He is the man testing the sword, an easy-going, hen-pecked retainer in the cavalry escort of the Aizu clan. He is also an expert swordsman whose approach to martial arts is summed up by his close friend and colleague, Tatewaki Asano (**Tatsuya Nakadai**): "Push and you step back. Push, you step back farther. But at the last moment, you change from a defense to offense." This is essentially the plot of the film.

東宝

脚本 橋本忍
監督 小林正樹
製作 小林正樹

藩の無理非道、もう我慢がならぬ！ 話題騒然！ 巨匠と名優が時代劇の頂点へ斬り込む！

上意討ち

拝領妻始末

三船敏郎
司葉子
加藤剛
仲代達矢

Samurai Rebellion

The first such "push" comes in the person of the daimyo's sinister steward, Geki Takahashi (Shigeru Koyama) who arrives with the directive that Sasahara's eldest son Yogoro (**Go Kato**) marry the lord's cast-off concubine, Lady Ichi (Yoko Tsukasa). This is clearly not what the family would have chosen, particularly Sasahara's harridan of a wife Suga (Michiko Otsuka); she relays the story of why Lady Ichi was dismissed. It seems Ichi had flown into a rage and started beating another of the lord's concubines, as well as the lord himself. Such a firebrand couldn't possibly make Yogoro happy, thinks Suga and the rest of the family. But although Sasahara tries to turn down the "offer," Yogoro relents and agrees to the marriage.

As it turns out, Ichi is a sweetheart and she and Yogoro find love and happiness together. Soon they have a baby girl, whom grandpa Isaburo dotes on. Happy ending, right? Noooo. We learn that Ichi had borne a son to the lord prior to marrying Yogoro, and that the current heir has just died, placing her son next in the line of succession. This is the kind of opportunity that some ex-concubines dream of, but Ichi has found love and a new life with Yogoro. She and her son are called back to the castle, but she refuses to go, wishing to stay with her husband and daughter. Unfortunately, foul treachery is afoot, and before long she is lured there and held against her will. Further outrages lie ahead, ratcheting up the tension until Isaburo and Yogoro can no longer tolerate the injustice, and take matters (and swords) into their own hands.

The oppressive weight of the lord's dominance is felt throughout; everyone is struggling to balance their obligations to the clan with their own feelings and sense of right and wrong. This is known as the **giri/ninjo conflict**, and it is a traditional theme in Japanese theater and literature, particularly samurai dramas. Imagine having to, say, kill your wife to prove your loyalty to your lord. This was not uncommon and obviously makes for intense melodrama. It is this time-honored dramatic convention that Kobayashi draws on, albeit for his own political aims.

Masaki Kobayashi, more than any of his contemporaries, was committed to pointing out the hypocrisies and abuses of power inherent in the Japanese feudal code, and by extension, in the conventions and soul-destroying conformity of the modern Japan of his day. His most potent film to this end is **Harakiri**, but *Samurai Rebellion* is usually mentioned in the same breath. At the heart of both films is a family destroyed by the system; in *Harakiri,* they are destitute ronin, in *Samurai Rebellion,* established samurai retainers. Both films feature a mature protagonist, desperate to preserve the life of his grandchild. And both films were written by **Shinobu Hashimoto**, based upon novels by Yasuhiko Takiguchi. *Samurai Rebellion* is not as narratively dense as *Harakiri,* and so would be a better choice for someone new to the genre.

Filming in deep-focus, Kobayashi utilizes the natural aesthetics of Japanese architecture to create symmetrical, ordered spaces in *Samurai Rebellion.* These balanced, weighted environments highlight the sterility and confinement within which Sasahara and his family must dispassionately accept the offenses heaped upon them. Kobayashi first discovered this dramatic potential while making *Harakiri.* "I was keenly attracted to the stylized beauty of our traditional forms," he said. "At the same time, since I felt I had come to the end of pursuing realism in film, this new mode of expression delighted me" (Linda Hoaglund, "A Conversation with Kobayashi Masaki," *Positions 2-2*, 1994, p. 382). It is a delight for us as well.

Samurai Rebellion won the Fédération Internationale de la Presse Cinématographique Award at the 1967 Venice Film Festival.

Zatoichi Challenged

Zatoichi chikemuri kaido

1967, Daiei

DIRECTOR: Kenji Misumi

CAST: Shintaro Katsu, Jushiro Konoe, Miwa Takada, Yukiji Asaoka, Mie Nakao, Takao Ito, Asao Koike, Kenzo Tabu, Shinya Saito

AVAILABILITY: Easy

COMMENT: DVD from Home Vision Entertainment

The Japanese title translates as "Zatoichi Blood Spurt Highway," which doesn't really tell you much, but it sounds cool. Actually, the story revolves around the blind swordsman's mission to deliver a little boy to his father while facing numerous obstacles along the way (wicked yakuza, corrupt officials, and mysterious ronin). It's a cracking good film, one of the more popular in the series, filled with magnificent sword work and featuring the series' by now standard "special guests."

The plot hinges on the common chambara device of an obligation taken on by the protagonist at the outset of the film. In *Zatoichi Challenged,* this involves a dying mother who pleads with our hero to deliver her son Ryota (Shinya Saito) safely to his father, Shokichi (Takao Ito), who resides in the town of Maebara. After gasping out her plea, Mom promptly dies, leaving Zatoichi (**Shintaro Katsu**) with a five-year-old brat on his hands. The child actor cast as Ryota most likely got the job because of his infant-like facial features, but there's something unpleasant about him, making him seem more like a demon baby. For my money he's not nearly as cute or endearing as he should be, but it doesn't matter; he's just a MacGuffin. The primary interest lies in the rest of the engaging and varied cast of characters.

On the road, Ichi and Ryota hook up with a traveling Kabuki troupe under the leadership of Miss Tomoe (**Yukiji Asaoka**, with whom the camera gets up close and personal in *The Razor: Sword of Justice*). Among the Kabuki performers is the lovely and talented Miyuki (singer Mie Nakao) who enlivens things with an impromptu pop number complete with electric shamisen. This performance, coupled with Shintaro Katsu's melodramatic delivery of the theme song under the opening credits, threatens to turn the whole proceeding into a

"Welcome to my world, kid"—Zatoichi Challenged

"Nobody makes fun of my hat!" —Zatoichi Challenged

rather cheesy chambara musical. Nevermind, it's enjoyable in a harmless, inane way, and passes quickly.

The troupe is accosted by yakuza; they've been sent to escort the entertainers to their boss, Gonzou (**Asao Koike**), even though the performers are en route to play for a rival boss. Things get ugly, but for some reason Zatoichi lays low. A mysterious ronin, Tajuro Akazuka (Jushiro Konoe), steps in and gives the thugs what for.

As it happens, Shokichi (Ryota's father) is an artist, held against his will by Boss Gonzou and forced to paint "forbidden picture plates," platters depicting pornographic scenes. Boss Gonzou, along with the intendant and local businessmen, is making a killing in the forbidden picture plate market, but this means nothing to Zatoichi—our hero has to free Shokichi in order to fulfill his obligation. This is more difficult than it seems, and every time he questions a key player in the dirty plate conspiracy, that person is suddenly struck down by mystery ronin Akazuka. Although Akazuka and Zatoichi are on friendly terms, they seem to be on a collision course. . . .

The mystery ronin is another standard trope in chambara: the hero encounters the mystery ronin early in the film, and they tend to maintain a cordial acquaintance, based on mutual respect. But somewhere along the way, we learn the ronin's true nature, either nice or nasty. One way or the other, the mystery ronin usually ends up on the business end of the hero's sword, uttering "Superb!" or "Magnificent!" before expiring (although that's not necessarily what happens in this picture).

The mystery ronin in *Zatoichi Challenged* is portrayed by chambara veteran Jushiro Konoe, a ferociously virile figure in his early 50s. His presence and sword ability are on a par with the likes of **Tomisaburo Wakayama**, and though rarely seen in the samurai films washing up on Western shores, in Japan he is a chambara legend. His career began in the 1930s but halted during World War II. Starting from scratch after the war, he was soon back in the saddle, a bona fide samurai film star. In 1965 he got the TV show *Suronin Tsukikage Hyogo* (*Samurai Vagabond*), a success that ran for 10 years. It is due to the popularity of this show, as well as his stature in the industry, that he was cast in *Zatoichi Challenged* as a "guest star" in the series.

Also present in *Zatoichi Challenged* is the beautiful **Miwa Takada**, playing Shokichi's love interest, Mitsu. Takada is a familiar face in **Daiei** pictures, appearing in such series as **Sleepy Eyes of Death**, **Daimajin**, **Yokai Monsters**, as well as several Zatoichis. She's a soulful and compelling actress and always easy on the eyes.

Shintaro Katsu, for his part, looks a little puffy here, continuing the trend of a creeping corpulence that increases from film to film. Katsu-shin loved to party, and here, by the 17th film, it's quite in evidence. He's also got an ill-advised goatee going—well hey, it's 1967, gotta get a little freaky. Nevertheless, his sword moves are as swift as ever. Like an old, fat cat that can still execute a magnificent leap, Katsu's weight never seems to really hinder his iaido prowess when the chips are down.

Zatoichi Challenged is one of those films that stands out, a prestige project helmed by legendary sword film director **Kenji Misumi**. It's Zatoichi magic, and continues to deliver the samurai goods after all these years.

Yokai Monsters: 100 Monsters

Yokai hyaku monogatari

Daiei, 1968

DIRECTOR: Kimiyoshi Yasuda

CAST: Miwa Takada, Jun Fujimaki, Ryutaro Gomi, Takashi Kanda, Saburo Date, Ikuko Mori, Ichiro Yamamoto, Shinichi Rookie

AVAILABILITY: Easy

If there's one thing to rival the Japanese love of samurai, it's ghosts. Ghost stories play a large part in traditional Japanese culture, resulting in hundreds of ghost films and more than a few samurai/ghost hybrids (see **Kwaidan** and **Samurai Reincarnation**). "Yokai" more often means ghost than monster—the literal translation of the film's title is "100 Ghost Stories"—making this less a samurai/monster movie than the title would suggest (for samurai/monster, see **Daimajin**). *100 Monsters* is the first of a trilogy of Yokai Monsters films, all featuring the same assortment of traditional Japanese ghosts and all released in 1968 by **Daiei Studios**.

Standard samurai film elements are in place here: There

COMMENT: DVD from
Rubbersuit, a division
of ADV Films

is a corrupt magistrate, a yakuza boss, helpless poor people, and a ronin protector. This is basically a **Zatoichi** film with ghosts filling in for **Shintaro Katsu**. All the other elements are the same: director **Kimiyoshi Yasuda** directed half a dozen Zatoichis (and a few **Nemuri Kyoshiro**s as well); half the cast have appeared in Zatoichi films (remember beautiful **Miwa Takada** from *Adventures of Zatoichi?*) as well as the sets, costumes, writer, all the same deal. So basically, if you like Zatoichi movies and you're intrigued by the prospect of some freaky Japanese ghosts (and they are freaky), this movie trilogy is for you.

The plot concerns an Edo tenement building, its inhabitants, and a nearby shrine, all of which are threatened by yakuza boss Tajimaya (Takashi Kanda), who's got the support of Shrine Magistrate Uzen (**Ryutaro Gomi**). He wants to tear the whole area down and put up a brothel. The kindly landlord of the tenement has a lovely daughter, Okiku (Miwa Takada), whom the wicked Uzen has his eye on. Also living in the tenement is a mysterious ronin, Yasutaro (**Jun Fujimaki**), who behaves in an enigmatic manner, refusing to help the tenement dwellers one minute, then popping up from nowhere to save them the next.

The film opens with the old shrine caretaker relating how he was attacked one dark night in the forest by a Tsuchikorobi ("Earth Roller," a gigantic, furry Cyclops that traditionally moves about in the form of a huge ball of soil). The tenement community regularly participate in a 100 Ghost Story social gathering in which they take turns telling ghost stories. Legend has it, after the last story is told, a curse-eliminating ritual must be performed, or else an apparition will appear.

Boss Tajimaya decides to hire a 100 Ghost Story–telling specialist for a sake and bribery party he's throwing for Uzen and a number of other government officials. But at the end of the evening, the fool stops the old tale-spinner from doing the protective ritual, thus opening the door to apparition city. During the old man's recital we only get to see one of his tales enacted, but it's a doozy. . . .

Two ronin go fishing in a lake with a sign posted in the water reading "Suicide Prohibited." They are warned by a spooky old monk that this is a lake of death and no place to do their fishing; if they catch a fish, he warns, they'll be cursed, "and you fellows don't know the horrors of being cursed." Of course not, which is precisely why they ignore his warning and the skinny ronin (Ichiro Yamamoto) catches a big koi. The other, bigger ronin (**Saburo Date**) takes his pal home for some sashimi and sake, ordering his wife (Ikuko Mori) to prepare the koi as they enter. This being Japan, this just means a little slicing, so it's done in a jiff. Problem is, his wife can't wash the fish's blood off her hands, and the next thing we know, her head is rising off her shoulders on a snaking, ever-elongating neck. She has become a Rokurokubi (literally "potter's wheel neck," from the image of elongating clay on a potter's wheel). The two ronin now know the horrors of being cursed, but not for long, as they end up dead. Was it the Rokurokubi that killed them?

The central drama of the boss, the magistrate, the ronin, and the tenement dwellers progresses. The poor folks endure numerous, escalating harassments and, finally, murder at the hands of Tajimaya's thugs, but things start changing up on the villians when the yokai community gets involved. Soon Tajimaya's henchmen are either turning into Nopperabo ("no-face goblin") or being tormented by an Okubi ("big head"), a vast, hideous face in the sky. Uzen even mixes it up with an Oni ("ogre") and a Hifukibaba ("fire-breathing granny"). And let's not forget lovable Karakasa ("bamboo and paper umbrella"), the popular one-eyed, one-legged, long-tongued umbrella-ghost. Karakasa has become friends with Tajimaya's addle-headed, childlike son Shinkichi (Shinichi Rookie).

Anyone interested in Japanese folklore will get a real kick out of *Yokai Monsters: 100 Monsters* and the other two films of the trilogy (*Spook Warfare* and *Along with Ghosts*), as the ghosts are all genuine, centuries-old cultural artifacts full of history and tradition (you can use this line on your wife or girlfriend when she gives you that look—you know the one I mean). Kids will certainly enjoy it, although it's a bit rougher stuff than what's on offer from Disney and Dreamworks; there are plenty of people being run through with swords here, but hey, life is cruel, might as well get them used to it now. In fact, even if you don't know a thing about Japan and you've never seen a samurai film, you will dig these films. Samurai, ghosts, and Miwa Takada? What's not to like?

Samurai Banners

Furin kazan

1969, Toho

DIRECTOR: Hiroshi Inagaki

CAST: Toshiro Mifune, Kinnosuke Nakamura, Yoshiko Sakuma, Kanemon Nakamura, Katsuo Nakamura, Akihiko Hirata

AVAILABILITY: Easy

COMMENT: VHS from AnimEigo

This is the story of a man blinded by ambition. No, really— he's literally blinded: in a stunning close-up, an arrow shoots right into his eye. Such a man is he, he pulls it out and continues on about his business, surveying the battlefield where his dreams are wrought in the fires of war.

This man is Kansuke Yamamoto (**Toshiro Mifune**), general and chief strategist to the great **Sengoku-period** warlord **Shingen Takeda** (**Kinnosuke Nakamura**). *Samurai Banners* focuses on the battles waged by Takeda, and features, among other things, the brilliant red flags and samurai armor that were Takeda's trademark. Directed by **Hiroshi Inagaki**, this is a large-scale, full-blown war epic, highlighting magnificent scenic vistas, stirring battle sequences, and penetrated through and through with equal parts **Bushido** and vile treachery.

Little is known of the shadowy yet legendary Yamamoto. Crippled and battle-scarred, he walked with a cane—understandable for a man who fought his way through the **Warring States** period to the age of 69. He seems to occupy the role of a Sengoku Machiavelli, renowned for his morally reprehensible yet nevertheless realistic and effective approach to power politics. For example, early in the film, Yamamoto advises Takeda against a full-scale invasion of the neighboring Suwa han, opting instead for negotiations that lead to such a cozy relationship that Lord Suwa (**Akihiko Hirata**) comes to Takeda's mansion for frequent visits. On his third such visit, Yamamoto suggests that he be slain. During a Noh performance, Yamamoto's lieutenant suddenly approaches Lord Suwa, and with an abrupt "I've been ordered to take your life," does so.

The story of how Yamamoto gets the job working for Takeda is illustrative: he hears from a down-at-heel ronin that one of Takeda's chief vassals, Nobukato Itagaki (**Kanemon Naka-**

mura), will be passing through town. He convinces the ronin to attack Itagaki, but not to kill him, just display some fancy swordwork. He will defend the retainer and they'll both get work, having shown their prowess as fighters. Of course when the time comes, he chops the wretched ronin's arm off and fatally slashes his back. Itagaki, impressed, instantly hires Yamamoto. From there, his rise is inevitable. Soon even Takeda himself is gleefully remarking what a "terrifying man" Yamamoto is, coming to rely wholly on his plots and stratagems.

Following the assassination of Lord Suwa, Yamamoto and Itagaki talk, their exchange providing timeless gems of realpolitik. Itagaki asks Yamamoto whether he fears retaliation from other regional daimyo. Yamamoto is unconcerned: "Lending strength to the strong, and thus profiting from it is common sense." Itagaki reflects, "In this age of war, survival requires complex conspiracies, secret dealings, and assassinations. They're inevitable." Itagaki asks Yamamoto what he really desires in his heart. "To seize castles and land. Then seize more castles and land. At this moment, sir, this is all that Yamamoto Kansuke desires."

Soon afterward, Takeda's army attacks Suwa, and in the castle they find numerous soldiers who have committed harakiri. But the princess Yu (Yoshiko Sakuma) has no such intention. She wants to live, even though her ladies-in-waiting, and Yamamoto himself, urge her to die honorably upon her own blade. Yamamoto, clearly smitten, nevertheless lectures her on convention and protocol, how her unwillingness to die

Ask Takuan, the Know-It-All Priest

Q: What's the big deal about Takeda's banners?

A: Shingen Takeda was a proud warlord and larger-than-life figure. Not for him some mere banner displaying his clan crest. He had these to be sure, but for the lead banner, he had a complete slogan, 14 kanji in all: "Fast like the wind, calm like the forest, conquering like the fire, invincible like the mountain." In addition, there were four battle divisions which bore the kanji for wind (fu), forest (rin), fire (ka), and mountain (zan). Takeda himself wore the mountain kanji on his helmet and was known as "The Mountain," so solid and unmovable was he. But the mountain finally crumbled in 1573 when the great Takeda died. All things dissolve and fade away into the void, my son. Better to sit and contemplate the sutras of the blessed Buddha.

1969/Toho

Samurai Banners

Kinnosuke Naka-mura as Shingen Takeda in Samurai Banners

will bring shame upon the family name. "You're ruthless," she screams. "You're a beast who knows no remorse! So how dare you talk to me about shame or my behavior, as if you were a normal human being?!" Now he *really* digs her. Unfortunately, Takeda wants her for his concubine and gives Yamamoto the unsavory task of talking her into it. Professional that he is, he does so (amid falling cherry blossoms—*symbolic*), and the unlikely love triangle that develops provides a subplot for the remainder of the picture.

But what of the battles? Can we expect a cast of thousands, samurai warriors in close combat, knights on horse, and all those banners? You get all you can handle and more in this 166-minute marathon. Plus there's the dazzling red armor, used to such striking effect in **Kagemusha** and **Heaven and Earth**; however, here it's limited to Itagaki's division. Itagaki's son Nobusato (**Katsuo Nakamura**) comes up with the idea, and in a pivotal battle sequence late in the film the "Men in red" come swooping down to save a foundering Takeda force. Because director Hiroshi Inagaki saved it up, their arrival packs an extra emotional punch.

There are other superb touches during battle: at one point we see a 10-foot-long battle sword being wielded by several soldiers; they run across the battlefield holding the hilt horizontally, literally mowing down enemy soldiers in bunches. Elsewhere we see the fighting with multi-colored flowers blooming poetically in the foreground (much is made of nature imagery to contrast the carnage). The battle strategies are explained with extensive use of animated maps and title cards (albeit in kanji), and even though what's happening during the fighting is at any given moment almost completely incomprehensible, it's nevertheless thrilling. And let's not forget those costumes. Mifune wears the most gigantic horned helmet you've ever seen, enough to shame the mightiest Viking. Takeda and the other generals are similarly decked out to the nines.

And through it all there is Yamamoto, a ruthless, mass-murdering bastard whom Mifune manages to transform into an alright sort of guy once you get to know him. Mifune's natural good nature and decency as a man usually had this effect when playing homicidal sociopaths (see his Isami Kondo in **Band of Assassins**). That's what makes samurai films so fascinating: the conflicts, the contradictions, both within the characters and the audience. But somehow it all manages to work, and we emerge refreshed and elated, completely satisfied, even though we rarely if ever get a happy ending. Take that, Hollywood!

Red Lion

Akage

Toho, 1969

DIRECTOR: Kihachi Okamoto

CAST: Toshiro Mifune, Etsushi Takahashi, Shigeru Koyama, Minori Terada, Shima Iwashita, Yunosuke Ito, Tokue Hanazawa, Shin Kishida, Bokuzen Hidari, Hideo Sunazuka, Hideyo Amamoto

AVAILABILITY: Easy

COMMENT: VHS from AnimEigo

Disclaimer: There is no actual lion in this film. There is, however, **Toshiro Mifune** roaring and blustering in a bright red Kabuki wig, dispensing his full range of broad mannerisms and rubber-faced mugging in this striking blend of slapstick comedy and tear-jerking tragedy.

The year is 1869. We're a year into the **Meiji Restoration**, yet the transition of power is not yet complete. The Imperial Restoration Force, some 50,000 Satsuma, Choshu, and Tosa clansmen, are advancing the Imperial flag from town to town toward Edo. In order to secure the support of the common people, an advance troop of some 130 peasants is sent ahead as a vanguard, promising the poverty-stricken, overburdened people tax reform and forgiven debts. Led by Commander Sozo Sagara (Takahiro Tamura), they are known as the Sekiho Troop, and among their numbers is one Gonzo (Toshiro Mifune). And gonzo he is. A lively, effusive, stuttering hothead, he begs Commander Sagara to let him ride ahead to the next town, Sawando, to notify the villagers of the approaching Imperial Force. This is Gonzo's hometown, and he hasn't been back in 10 years. Wishing to return a bigshot, he borrows Sagara's official akage (red hair) wig-hat signifying troop leader status, and he's off on a horse, whooping and hollering all the way.

From this point on, the story revolves around Gonzo's attempts to clean up Sawando which has become a model of **Tokugawa-period** corruption. The town is filled with colorful characters, drawn in broad strokes, whom we come to know

Red Lion

1972 Toho and Mifune Productions

and love (or hate), and whose personalities and antics make the film come alive. They include:

KOMATORA (Tokue Hanazawa): Sleazeball yakuza boss. Ten years earlier he had Gonzo beaten, bound, and thrown in the river to drown. He runs the local brothel full of indentured village women.

SANJI (Minori Terada): An eccentric pickpocket from Edo, "Sanji the Wallet Collector" becomes Gonzo's loyal lieutenant, helping him in pivotal situations, such as when something has to be read (Gonzo, illiterate, always has something in his eye. . . .)

OYO (Jitsuko Yoshimura): Beautiful and mysterious daughter of the stable-keeper. She's friendly to Gonzo, but asks a lot of questions and seems to have a secret agenda.

KAMIO (**Yunosuke Ito**): Corrupt intendant. In the new political climate, he's unsure of his standing, and vacillates between brutally oppressing the people and trying to curry favor with Gonzo. Standout comedic performance from the always excellent Ito.

THE "WICKED MANAGER" (**Shin Kishida**): This scheming wretch works for Kisoya, the local Mr. Potteresque merchant and moneylender, but is really running the show. Like Oyo, he too has a secret purpose.

HANZO (**Etsushi Takahashi**): Cynical ronin. He's a sword-for-hire, and Komatora has hired him to kill Gonzo. He spends his time drinking sake from a wooden box and musing on the meaningless of existence.

TOMI (Shima Iwashita): Gonzo's long lost love, now one of Komatora's prostitutes. She's fragile and traumatized and makes some bad choices, but she loves Gonzo with all her heart of gold.

Also on tap are Amagaeru (Hideo Sunazuka) the "reporter"/spy, Gensai (Hideyo Amamoto) the old sensei who incites the young men of the village to riot, and lovable grandad Gohei (legendary rubber-faced old fart **Bokuzen Hidari**), who's trying to hang himself because his granddaughter's been taken by Komatora. Add to this the aforementioned legion of young rebels, the horde of prostitutes freed by Gonzo, and a clandestine group of shogunate operatives known as "Mobile Unit

One." And let's not forget the approaching Imperial Force. This volatile combination of elements can only result in one thing: a violent, devastating explosion.

The atmosphere of *Red Lion* pulses with the uncertainty and menace of changing times, the so-called "World Renewal" of the Meiji Restoration. The chant of "Eijanaika," variously translated as "ain't it grand," "who cares," and "nevermind" is heard across the land as peasants realize that the era of the Tokugawa Shogunate is over. "The world has been turned upside down," Gonzo tells Komatora. Later, in one of many abortive confrontations with cynical ronin Hanzo, Gonzo declares, "The world is changing!" Hanzo replies, "How so? The only thing that will change is the flower on the official crest." He's right. Hanzo represents worldly wisdom in the midst of chaotic agenda clashes and power shifts and gets all the best lines. Late in the film, Hanzo is approached by members of Mobile Unit One. They want his help in their pro-shogunate suicide mission, claiming that it's the only way to die with grace as a samurai. "Is there any grace or ugliness in death?" he asks incredulously. "Everything goes into the void. It all becomes nothing. That is all there is to it." No **giri/ninjo conflict** for Hanzo!

Anyone who enjoyed Toshiro Mifune's unhinged over-the-top antics in **Rashomon** and **Seven Samurai** will enjoy

Character Actor Hall of Fame

Yunosuke Ito (1919–1980)

One of the more versatile and prolific character actors of the '50s and '60s, Yunosuke Ito could convey menace, compassion, incompetance, charisma, idiocy, sagacity, or inscrutability, all with a gravitas that made his performances, even in small roles, more memorable than most. He also had a face like a horse. Homely yet striking, there's no mistaking his long face, protruding jaw and low-lidded eyes. Ito often worked with Akira Kurosawa (his first screen appearance was in Kurosawa's 1949 crime drama *Stray Dog*), but also worked with great directors like Kon Ichikawa (*The Burmese Harp*), and Masaki Kobayashi (*I'll Buy You*). His range of characterizations includes: the bohemian novelist who shows a terminally-ill man a good time in the pleasure districts of Tokyo in *Ikiru;* the cynical, lecherous photographer in Yasuzo Masumura's brilliant advertising industry satire, *Giants and Toys;* the duplicitous, disguise-donning leader of two competing ninja clans in the grandaddy of all ninja films, *Shinobi no Mono.* And of course he was always great in the samurai genre, appearing in *Lone Wolf and Cub: Sword of Vengeance, Red Lion, Samurai Assassin,* and *Sanjuro* among others.

his Gonzo as a refreshing return to form. Although approaching 50, Mifune has lost none of his charm and zaniness as he portrays this exuberant country bumpkin who, as everyone continually reminds him, once fell out of a persimmon tree and landed on his head. His performance stands in stark contrast to that of Kondo in **Band of Assassins** the following year. Watch these back to back for an increased awareness of the range of this magnificent actor. Mifune's energy and invention are at the heart of *Red Lion,* and along with strong, delirious performances from the rest of the cast, it's sure to make you smile and weep and watch again.

Tenchu!

Hitokiri

1969, Shochiku

DIRECTOR: Hideo Gosha

CAST: Shintaro Katsu, Tatsuya Nakadai, Yukio Mishima, Yujiro Ishihara, Mitsuko Baisho

AVAILABILITY: Tricky

COMMENT: Available as an import or through third-party collectors and independent distributors

Tenchu! has long been considered the holy grail of samurai pictures. Why? For one thing, it's so hard to find! It was made by **Hideo Gosha**, one of the finest directors in the history of Japanese cinema, and yet a director criminally unknown in the U.S., hence the paucity and relative obscurity of his titles here. Made for **Shochiku Studios** in 1969, *Tenchu!* fuses the political cynicism of '60s samurai films with the ultraviolence of early '70s chambara; it has both elements in spades. Starring **Shintaro Katsu** of **Zatoichi** fame and the legendary **Tatsuya Nakadai** at his silky, sinister best, the film also features novelist and ultra-right nationalist Yukio Mishima; his unsuccessful real-life takeover of the Japanese Self Defense Forces' Ichigaya Headquarters in 1970 ended in his committing seppuku. Guess how he dies in the film? Getting interested?

Tenchu!, based on a true story, was a joint venture between Shochiku and Katsu Productions, Shintaro Katsu's production company (the latter would go on to produce the **Lone Wolf and Cub** series). By 1969, Katsu had made 19 Zatoichi films, as well as a host of other features and film series, and it shows: he's portly and somewhat the worse for wear. A notorious partier, he ate, drank, smoked, and caroused himself to ill health. But in *Tenchu!,* Gosha has tapped something in Katsu that positively burns up the screen. All the natural magnetism and energy Katsu was known for intensifies exponentially; it is the role of his life.

The year is 1862, the beginning of the end for the **Tokugawa** Shogunate, and the air positively pulsates with plots and power politics. Katsu plays rumpled roughneck Izo Okada, a member of the **Tosa** clan, a "loyalist" faction dedicated to the restoration of the Emperor. The Tosa restoration effort seems to require lots and lots of bloodletting, and Hanpeita Takechi (Nakadai) is behind it all. When Okada comes to him for work, he's told, "Your swordsmanship is in need of discipline. You fight like a wild animal." But Takechi knows raw talent when he sees it. He's decided to groom Okada, and make him the assassin extraordinaire.

When we first meet Okada he has never killed anyone. This is unique: rather than entering as the scraggly stray dog, killer of countless assailants (think **Toshiro Mifune** in *Yojimbo* or Nakadai in *Harakiri*), we actually get to watch his transformation. At the beginning of the film he's instructed by Takechi to go along with an assassination party, but only to hide and watch. As he witnesses the brutal assassination he says to himself, "Damn, I could do better than that. I could kill . . . I'll kill!" His eyes bulge with horror, then narrow with determination, rain pouring over his hairy visage. It's an incredible moment, and cuts right to the big red kanji of the title card, "Hitokiri" (Assassination). (The alternate title, *Tenchu!,* is the cry of the Tosa clan assassins, and literally means "Heaven's punishment.")

What follows is the rise of Izo Okada. Rising too are the heaps of corpses, as Hideo Gosha works his chambara magic. Never will you see such gruesomely realized sword fights as you find in a Gosha film. He strives for the realism, the physicality, the sheer strenuousness of men (and women) fighting with swords and knives. When the blade goes in, you see it, and you *hear* it, with gushing, ripping, tearing sound effects that are harrowing, yet always balanced, never camp. And there is much blood. Gone are the squeaky-clean sword fights of the '50s. This is no **Hiroshi Inagaki** watercolor. This is visceral. This is the real deal.

Also in the mix is Ryoma Sakamoto (Yujiro Ishihara),

real-life renaissance samurai and architect of the **Meiji Restoration**, who pops in and out of the plot like the Conscience of the Nation. Then there's Okada's girlfriend, the prostitute Omino (Mitsuko Baisho), doomed to a lifetime of "service" because of a 30-ryo debt she can never repay. And let's not forget Shinbei Tanaka (Yukio Mishima), the other top swordsman in Kyoto with whom Okada shares a friendly rivalry until things go horribly wrong. . . .

If there is a weakness in the film, it is the over-reliance on the audience's foreknowledge of the historical setting and its component players, something with which every Japanese school kid would have been familiar. This can happen with a **Shinobu Hashimoto** script. Hashimoto wrote in a variety of styles for all the major filmmakers of the day (his first screenplay was *Rashomon* for **Akira Kurosawa**). But whenever the subject turned to the **Bakumatsu period**, his scripts had a tendency to become quite dense (see *Samurai Assassin*). His knowledge of the period is fathoms deep, and at times the pressure just becomes too great. Fortunately it's nothing a few repeat viewings and this book can't handle!

Tenchu! is a must-see for the serious samurai afficionado, and worth seeking out. Like a samurai sword, it is forged from the finest materials by a master craftsman, creating something at once new and timeless.

9

The '70s

Zatoichi—The Festival of Fire

Zatoichi abare-himatsuri

1970, Daiei

DIRECTOR: Kenji Misumi

CAST: Shintaro Katsu, Tatsuya Nakadai, Reiko Ohara, Masayuki Mori, Peter, Ko Nishimura

AVAILABILITY: Easy

COMMENT: DVD/VHS from AnimEigo

An excellent cast, stunning cinematography, and a star turn from chambara auteur **Kenji Misumi** combine to make *The Festival of Fire* one of the more remarkable pictures in the Zatoichi series. In 1970, after nearly a decade of success, the Zatoichi franchise had become respectable enough to attract truly world-class talent, and the '70s-era installments boasted a roster of the greatest names in samurai film. *The Festival of Fire* is no exception. The great **Tatsuya Nakadai** gives an incendiary performance as the most ferocious, psychotic mystery ronin our blind masseur has ever faced (the previous year Nakadai had co-starred with **Shintaro Katsu** in **Hideo Gosha**'s **Tenchu!**). Also present are revered stage actor **Masayuki Mori** (who played the murdered samurai in *Rashomon*), appearing here as the blind and sinister "Dark Imperial Lord" of the yakuza, as well as **Ko Nishimura** as his diminutive sycophant and heir to his throne. (In 1970 Katsu-shin also went up against uber-star **Toshiro Mifune** in *Zatoichi Meets Yojimbo*. Later co-stars would include the likes of **Rentaro Mikuni** in *Zatoichi at Large* and **Takashi Shimura** in *Zatoichi's Conspiracy*.)

The year 1970 marked a pivotal shift in the production

of the Zatoichi series: all films would henceforth be made by Shintaro Katsu's own production company, the innovatively named Katsu Productions (Katsu-shin had taken a tentative step in this direction with 1967's *Zatoichi the Outlaw*). Unleashed as they were from the Daiei (and later Toho) studio system, the '70s Zatoichis have a broader range both emotionally and visually. In *The Festival of Fire* there's more room to breathe, to move, to experiment; the set-ups are more fanciful and composed (a misty forest, a lively mistress auction, a haunting dream), the comic set-pieces more playful, even silly. The film opens with Ichi being chased by a stray dog; in another sequence he walks on stilts to soothe a crying child, passes scenes of a serene watermill, children catching dragonflies, a horse pissing (spraying the masseur), and baby birds being fed. There is also an outrageous slapstick act performed by a bickering couple and a bizarre Go game between Ichi and the blind boss.

And of course the swordplay is bloodier. An ambush in a bathhouse finds our hero fending off a horde of naked yakuza in a frenzied blur of bare asses and colorful tattoos. Unarmed, he fights his attackers with buckets until he can secure a sword, thereafter changing the bathwaters from crystal clear to billowing crimson. Blood red is a dominant hue in director Kenji Misumi's palette. Compare Misumi's work as a Daiei contract director with films like *The Festival of Fire* (and later **Lone Wolf and Cub**) and witness a genre veteran's powers expanding in scope and depth, an artist truly coming into his own.

Storywise, there isn't much we haven't seen before. The joy of *The Festival of Fire* is more in the telling than the tale. On the road, Zatoichi, disguised as a ghost, rescues a beautiful woman from the clutches of a disgusting oyaji who has just purchased her at auction, unaware that she is the wife of the aforementioned psycho ronin played by Tatsuya Nakadai. The latter appears seconds later and cuts down the oyaji and his party with a splendid flourish, then proceeds to pull the most amazing, tortured, eyeball-rolling grimace you've ever seen. Meanwhile, hiding out in a nearby farmhouse, the wife takes Ichi's money pouch and steals off into the night only to be slashed by her husband. Now he thinks Ichi's had her and pursues the masseur throughout the remainder of the film.

Following the carnage at the bathhouse, Nakadai strolls past Ichi, casually whispering, "Your death is reserved to my sword." Later they face each other in a stunning long shot on a wind-buffeted bridge. They fight, then Nakadai abruptly quits and turns to go.

"Am I pardoned because I'm innocent?" asks Ichi.

"Heh, heh, you're my only reason for living. If I killed you now . . ."

"You'd have nothing to live for."

"I will kill you. Eventually."

Zatoichi is also on a collision course with Yamibuko, the blind "Shogun of the Underworld" (Masayuki Mori). This boss of bosses makes speeches about the loneliness of the blind and seems magnanimous enough, but in reality he's a nasty piece of work and means Ichi no good. And of course there is a love interest, Okiyo (**Reiko Ohara**), the young daughter of Migi (Ko Nishimura), the blind boss's creepy favorite. Okiyo is spying on Ichi for the boss but winds up falling for the charming masseur. Also in the mix is the girlish Ume (played by an actor named simply Peter), a pimp looking for a position with the local yakuza gang and willing to do anything to get it. . . .

The Festival of Fire will reward Zatoichi fans both old and new. See it for the stunning set pieces, see it for the numerous exercises in superior cinematic composition, see it for the gags, see it for Tatsuya Nakadai. But don't miss this magnificent example of what I would call arthouse chambara.

Wicked Priest 5: Cast a Net of Drunken Anger

Gokuaku Bozu: Nomu utsu kau

1970, Toei

DIRECTOR: Takeshi Saito

Will you listen to my story? I drink, gamble, and buy prostitutes. I am a wicked priest. I don't understand why I behave like this since I do God's work. But I can't forgive people who say good things while actu-

CAST: Tomisaburo
Wakayama, Bunta
Sugawara, Takashi
Shimura, Tatsuo Endo

AVAILABILITY: Tricky

COMMENT: Available as
an import or through
third-party collectors
and independent
distributors

ally doing the opposite of what they say. . . . Drinking,
gambling, and women are honest images of real life,
wouldn't you agree?

These are the words of Shinkai, the eponymous Gokuaku
Bozu or "Wicked Priest." Alternate titles include *Evil Priest,
Scoundrel Priest, Killer Priest,* and *Priest Killer*—"Wicked
Priest" seems to be the predominate default title. While he
may be relatively obscure in the West, make no mistake:
Shinkai stands shoulder to shoulder with **Zatoichi**, Nemuri
Kyoshiro, and Ogami Itto in the samurai film pantheon.

The series stars **Tomisaburo Wakayama**, and it is a revelation for anyone who has only seen him as the stern, frowning assassin or over-the-top heavy. Here we find him laughing,
mugging, falling for girls, drinking, screwing, and generally
displaying all manner of exaggerated, comedic reactions to a
host of predicaments, both ludicrous and lethal. Truth is, he's
not really wicked at all, quite the opposite: he's a sweetheart.
Just don't get him mad. He has an explosive temper and when
pushed too far is liable to unleash some cold steel or, just as
fatal, a rain of devastating blows with his fists. Either way,
blood will gush, bodies will fly, and fortunately for the dead,
he's available for prayer services afterward.

The setting is the turn of the twentieth century, the middle
of the **Meiji period**, and Shinkai is in a Tokyo brothel, devouring prostitutes like rice balls and shouting, "This woman isn't
good enough! Get me another one!" The proprietors note that
he's gone through five already, when in walks the Busogumi,
a bad-news yakuza group. They interrupt Shinkai *in flagrante
delicto* (not advisable) and, wearing nothing but a loincloth,
he procedes to pummel them to a collective bloody pulp. All
this mayhem is happening under the opening credits, as the
air is filled with the sonorous voice of Wakayama himself,
crooning the series' theme song, "Gokuaku Bozu."

Shinkai is exiting the establishment just as the police
arrive and runs off in the cold winter night with only said
loincloth and no place to stay. He's befriended by a local con
man who brings him to the dilapidated "Dunghill Mansion,"
a den of thieves, hookers, and general riff raff of the day. He

falls for Ogin, the beautiful croupier at the house crap game. She tries to scam him using a midget under the floor to flip the dice in the cup. Shinkai's infatuation is mixed with savvy, however; he knows what's going on. He unsheathes his sword (concealed in his priest's staff) and plunges it into the floor to make a point. Lucky Shinkai: the bet was for Ogin's body, just the thing he was craving. He spends a glorious evening with her—she for her part, like the female interrogatees of **The Razor**, is equally enraptured—but in the morning she's gone, along with all his money.

The next day, Shinkai gets duped again by these con artists, and thrashes them accordingly. Eventually they develop a mutual respect and he becomes their champion. This is fortunate for them, as the boss of the Busogumi has construction plans that involve the demolition of Dunghill Mansion. Kindly Boss Wajima (**Takashi Shimura**) of the Jinsokugumi (a rival gang) holds a crucial license the evil Busogumi boss is after. Wajima is also on the Dunghill denizens' side, and befriends Shinkai. Unfortunately the Chief of Police, Tomita (**Tatsuo Endo**) is not only working with the Busogumi, he's also keeping Ogin as his mistress. Things soon lead to an all-out gang war with hordes of strange assassins pursuing Shinkai. Pandemonium!

Above and beyond all these subplots stands the ongoing rivalry between Shinkai and the blind priest Ryotatsu, aka The Whipmaster (yakuza film star Bunta Sugawara). In the first installment of *Wicked Priest,* Shinkai and Ryotatsu had a showdown resulting in Ryotatsu's blinding and Shinkai's banishment from the priesthood. They renew their struggle in every episode, facing off twice in *Wicked Priest 5: Cast a Net of Drunken Anger,* once early on and then again at the end of the film. The latter confrontation is a great hand-to-hand fight on desolate sand dunes. The actors do all their own stunts— no phony stunt doubles. In fact, this is usually the case in samurai films. The stars are always trained martial artists who know how to throw, take, and fake a blow.

Bunta Sugawara's Ryotatsu is somewhat terrifying. His screen presence is amazing, bubbling over with barely contained rage. Yakuza film fans know and love Bunta from his many appearances in early '70s jitsuroku-eiga including **Kinji Fukasaku**'s seminal Modern Yakuza (*Gendai yakuza*) and Battle Without Honor and Humanity (*Jingi naki tatakai*) series. He has some great lines here. Upon their first encounter, he snarls, "Shinkai, no matter where you are, my deep-seated hatred brings you to me." Later he intones, "There's always the smell of blood wherever you are. And this smell of blood is what always calls me." Well, which is it Bunta, your deep-seated hatred or his bloody reek? Whatever it is, you can't keep these two apart. That is until Wakayama gets the **Lone Wolf and Cub** gig. . . .

Band of Assassins

Shinsengumi

1970, Toho

DIRECTOR: Tadashi Sawashima

CAST: Toshiro Mifune, Rentaro Mikuni, Kinya Kitaoji, Keiju Kobayashi

AVAILABILITY: Tricky

COMMENT: Available as an import or through third-party collectors and independent distributors

A splash of blood. Then, narration:

> We will expel the barbarians. It's the only thing to do. We can't let foreign barbarians disgrace Japan! Our government was forced to conclude an open port treaty with foreign trade ships which has angered the Emperor! The Tobaku clan took advantage of the Emperor's anger, and radical Tosa and Choshu samurai claim that it is Tenchu for them to assassinate the shogun along with many other government officials. Those who oppose the Emperor and the shogun have united in Kyoto where they are trying to topple the shogunate.

This big-budget **Bakumatsu** blow-out comes to us courtesy of **Toshiro Mifune**'s production company, Mifune Productions, and features the superstar looking every one of his 50 years (and a few more to boot). He also sweats a lot in this picture, probably to make him seem rugged and earthy, but all that sweat on his face catches the light, showing every greasy wrinkle (yikes!). In fact, one of the earliest scenes finds Mifune's character showing how strong he is by standing very close to a big bonfire, sweat pouring down him—not a good look. Sweaty guys in their 50s are kinda creepy and usually up to no good.

But I kid Mifune. This is among his finest performances, certainly one of his grimmest. He is **Isami Kondo**, leader of the Shinsengumi, a paramilitary group of pro-shogunate ronin formed in Kyoto in 1863, during the period when everything was starting to unravel. The story of the Shinsengumi, like that of the **Loyal 47 Ronin**, is a perennial favorite in Japan; their exploits have been dramatized on film since the silent era. One reason for the popularity of the Shinsengumi, one that they share with the Loyal 47, is their tenacity and adherence to **Bushido** in the face of certain doom. We know they're going to lose, they know they're going to lose, but it never dampens their ardor nor diminishes their fighting spirit. That makes them makoto no bushi—true samurai!

At the outset of the film there are two pivotal figures, **Kamo Serizawa** (**Rentaro Mikuni**) and Isami Kondo (Mifune). You may remember Serizawa and Kondo from *Sword of Doom;* they had hired **Tatsuya Nakadai**'s psychotic ronin to help them with their assassinations. Here they meet for the first time (onscreen) by the aforementioned bonfire which Serizawa has built in protest after not getting a room at the local inn. Kondo shows up and they get into a staring contest by the fire until Serizawa can't take the heat anymore (symbolic foreshadowing for events to come). At this point, Serizawa is still a member of the **Mito Tengu**, but he and Kondo soon join forces to head up the Shinsengumi (literally "newly appointed group") with Serizawa as Bureau Chief. Ironically, the aims of the Shinsengumi, protection of the shogun and support for his rule, are the opposite of the anti-shogunate Mito Tengu, making Serizawa look somewhat disingenuous.

The Shinsengumi take as their flag the kanji for "makoto" (truth) and set up a rigid code of conduct:

1. Do not act against the samurai code
2. Nobody is allowed to resign from the group
3. Money cannot be raised without permission
4. No fighting among the members
5. High moral standards must be observed

1970 Toho and Mifune Productions

Band of Assassins

The penalty for breaking the rules is seppuku. However, this doesn't stop Serizawa from drinking and murdering and extorting everything in sight (here, Rentaro Mikuni is at his bestial best). He's a drunken thug totally out of control, which doesn't make the Shinsengumi, the body of which he is the head, look very good. Kondo, the more balanced personality, knows he has to do something. At a social gathering of group members, Serizawa gets drunk, insults the head geisha, and starts some shit with one of the senior ronin. Right as swords are about to be drawn, Kondo knows there's only one thing to do: Gotta dance! He springs into a little Kabuki number, diffusing the situation (nice singing voice, Tosh!). Later he stabs Serizawa repeatedly in his bed and, the following day, announces that he's the Shinsengumi's new Bureau Chief.

From there, *Band of Assassins* follows the exploits of the Shinsengumi, featuring some spectacular sword battles. The Ikedaya incident in particular is fantastic, with lots of moving camera work that puts you right in the action. In a later scene, a swordsman attacks Kondo and his lunging movement is translated into a string of jump cuts. The technique sustains the moment, creating a kind of static movement effect. Many innovative techniques are utilized by the filmmaker to enhance the action in what is essentially a high-profile, showcase film. Much is made of natural scenery and its attendant symbolism as well: shots of rivers (transience of existence), cherry blossoms falling (death), snow storms (turmoil), wind (violence)—all have their place. There is even a stone demon that seems to represent Serizawa's mental instability and alcoholism.

Although the Shinsengumi is essentially a band of brutal killers doing the shogunate's dirty work (and various atrocities of their own), the tone of the film is supportive, at times providing corny musical cues that sound like they were lifted from an old western. The film is saying that sure, they're vicious, sure they slaughter people for a living, but they're really good guys. While it may be hard for a non-Japanese audience to reconcile these factors, it's only because of the relative honesty of the violence. Blood sprays everywhere, and there are the usual massacre scenes, much more extreme than what you'd see in a Hollywood film. So maybe that's why U.S. audiences could accept a Dirty Harry or Terminator but might choke on the gore in films like this.

It should be noted that the names and historical facts come flying so fast that to watch *Band of Assassins* without your finger glued to the pause button is not recommended. The filmmaker rushes through the background information faster than **Kihachi Okamoto** on his fifth cup of coffee. Perhaps it's simply that Japanese audiences are so familiar with the material; only a word is needed, and casually in passing. It's a little tougher for us Western audiences, but in the end well worth the effort.

Lone Wolf and Cub: Sword of Vengeance

Kozure Okami: Kowokashi udekashi tsukamatsuru

1972, Toho and Katsu Productions

DIRECTOR: Kenji Misumi

CAST: Tomisaburo Wakayama, Akihiro Tomikawa, Yunosuke Ito, Saburo Date, Ryutaro Gomi

AVAILABILITY: Easy

COMMENT: DVD/VHS from AnimEigo

A mysterious ronin pushes a wooden baby cart through a pastoral Japanese landscape. In the cart is his cherubic two-year-old son, a lively tyke for whom the man cares deeply. They go everywhere together. Sometimes they camp out under the stars, other times they stay in a picturesque inn or rural Buddhist temple. So it is, this heart-warming pair travel from town to town, cutting people to pieces in a series of gruesome assassinations for money, utilizing a vast array of lethal weapons. In the world of the samurai film, *Lone Wolf and Cub* stands out as the most notorious, outrageous, over-the-top, ultra-violent chambara action series of them all.

The Lone Wolf and Cub saga, six films in all (1972–1974), was adapted from the popular manga of the same name (available in English translation in some 28 paperback volumes from Dark Horse Comics). If you've never seen one of these films, I highly recommend reading the first two or three volumes of the manga beforehand. Seeing the manga come alive on the screen is a real kick; you'll be struck by how much care and attention to detail went into the dramatic realizations and spurting gore.

The film opens with the beheading of a child. It's not graphic (as are later decapitations), but it sets a tone and may

1972 Toho and Katsu Productions

Lone Wolf and Cub: Sword of Vengeance

be the signal to some audience members that this type of fare is not for them. The scene is the first of three flashbacks that provide exposition throughout the film. The child is the young lord of a clan that has just been dissolved by the shogun. The little daimyo is required to commit seppuku; he kneels dutifully, holding a folded fan in place of the ceremonial dagger, amidst a crowd of weeping retainers. An imposing figure enters the frame. Now we get our first look at Ogami Itto (**Tomisaburo Wakayama**), the Kogi Kaishakunin (shogun's official executioner). He stands behind the tyke, focused, dispassionate; the camera zooms in on his face, he swings, fade to red.

But Ogami Itto is not to hold his prestigious post for long, as treachery is afoot. Yes, the evil **Yagyu clan** wants his job (and his head). They murder his wife and frame him for treason. Before long two officials (**Saburo Date** and **Ryutaro Gomi**) come a-calling with a seppuku order for both Ogami and his infant son, Daigoro (**Akihiro Tomikawa**). Ogami knows he's being set up and refuses to cooperate; he's seen this type of thing before, and is not about to go quietly. He hacks his way through a throng of swordsmen and runs out the gate, only to be confronted by Retsudo Yagyu (**Yunosuke Ito**), the old bearded Yagyu patriarch and mastermind behind it all. Ogami Itto brazenly displays the shogunate crest on his kimono, a symbol for which he no longer has any respect but which spooks Retsudo—like a talisman, the crest keeps him at bay, afraid to strike at it. Finally Retsudo proposes a duel between Ogami and the top Yagyu swordsman, Kurato Yagyu. If Ogami Itto wins, the Yagyu will let him go. You already know who wins. But the slow-motion image of blood spurting out of the neck of the still-standing Kurato's headless corpse will stay with you forever!

Ogami Itto resolves to get revenge on the Yagyu. He will become a demon assassin, walking the paths of Meifumado (Buddhist Hell), killing for 500 ryo per job. He offers his son the choice of a sword or a colored ball: choosing the sword means Daigoro will live in Meifumado with dad, accompanying him and occasionally helping out with the killings; choosing the ball means Daigoro will "join his mother"—we know what that means. Psychotic? Yes, but within the conceptual framework of the manga/movie, it works. We're on Ogami It-to's side, we identify with his skewed perceptions, his warped bloodlust, his twisted **Bushido** rationalizations. This is because he is the heroic figure in the oldest of dramatic forms, the revenge tragedy.

The remainder of *Lone Wolf and Cub: Sword of Vengeance* is a frame-by-frame dramatization of the manga series' eighth vignette, "Wings to the Bird, Fangs to the Beast." Ogami Itto and Daigoro find themselves in a mountain village held by egregious outlaws and are soon taken prisoner as well. One particularly unpleasant knife-throwing bandit (**Daigo Kusano**) forces Ogami Itto to perform sex with a prostitute while he and his friends watch. The brigands will not hold the town for long, however, and their comeuppance is swift and excruciating.

As great as all this sounds, the film is not without its flaws. Despite the action sequences, *Lone Wolf and Cub: Sword of Vengeance* still feels somber and morose. There is a lugubrious quality to the whole affair. This is due in part to the subject matter, but more to the disruptive nature of the flashbacks, which take too long and break up the action of the present. You get the feeling that the filmmakers were still coming to grips with how to adapt the material to film; manga is a series of static shots, and the static quality shouldn't come into the film, as it frequently does here. The manga was written

Shogun Assassin

Back in 1980, long after the Lone Wolf and Cub series had ended, two guys from Los Angeles named Robert Houston and David Weisman decided it would be a good idea to chop up the first two installments, rearrange the pieces, rewrite the script, redo the score, and dub the whole thing into English. It wasn't. Imagine the effect of slicing up Da Vinci's *The Last Supper* and rearranging who sits where; what's the point? While you can still admire the artistry, there's no denying that the original version was vastly superior and didn't need to be cut up like this. And it certainly didn't deserve the bad dubbing—when I see lady ninja Sayaka from *Baby Cart at the River Styx* and hear Sandra Bernhard's voice coming out of her mouth, that's just wrong. Along the way Retsudo Yagyu somehow becomes the shogun, the original storylines get dumbed way down, and Daigoro winds up narrating the film (with the help of interminable voiceovers by a kid who sounds borderline mentally retarded). *Shogun Assassin* did good business upon its release, due in part to timing: its opening coincided with the original broadcast of popular TV series *Shogun* (starring Richard Chamberlian and Toshiro Mifune). However, it should have come with a disclaimer: "The film you are about to see does not reflect the quality and artistic vision of the fine films from which it was cut."

by **Kazuo Koike** and illustrated by **Goseki Kojima**, and Koike also wrote the screenplay for the movie, his first. Fortunately he learned from mistakes made here, and the second film is much better, considered by some the best in the series.

Then of course there is the matter of Tomisaburo Wakayama's appearance. He looks nothing like the buffed, strapping Ogami Itto of the manga. It's not detrimental; you can get used to a portly, craggy oyaji in the role, but only because it's Wakayama, an outstanding martial artist and chambara star since the mid '50s. He's still in fine form, hasn't lost his chops over the years, and when he lashes out with his dotanuki (jumbo samurai sword), or slashes masterfully with his naginata (curved sword on spear), or goes flying through the air, or chops an adversary off at the knees (literally!) you really do believe it. It is a testament to his greatness. For his part, Akihiro Tomikawa is every bit as cute as his manga counterpart.

I encourage everyone to read the manga in tandem with watching the films. It's a rare pleasure, a multi-media samurai hybrid of death and dismemberment with family values built right in. Magnificent!

Lone Wolf and Cub: Baby Cart at the River Styx

Kozure Okami: Sanzu no kawa no ubaguruma

1972, Toho

DIRECTOR: Kenji Misumi

CAST: Tomisaburo Wakayama, Akihiro Tomikawa, Kayo Matsuo, Akiji Kobayashi, Minoru Oki, Shin Kishida, Izumi Ayukawa

AVAILABILITY: Easy

What can you say about a film where the dismemberment count includes three legs, three fingers, one nose, three arms, and an ear? Plus one completely split head, two partially split heads, numerous impalings, iron claws in heads, bleeding walls, bleeding sands, underwater knife fights, arson, massacred labor agitators, and lady assassins hurling daikons of death? That's entertainment!

Baby Cart at the River Styx is by far the best of the six-part film series concerning former Kogi Kaishakunin and all 'round badass Ogami Itto (**Tomisaburo Wakayama**) and his cherubic son Daigoro (**Akihiro Tomikawa**). Creator and scenarist **Kazuo Koike** learned quickly from mistakes made in the first film (his

COMMENT: DVD/VHS
from AnimEigo

debut sceenwriting effort) and tightened the screws on this one so much you can hardly get a breath. Also, since all the exposition is out of the way, this film literally hits the ground running with an opening shot of a basket-headed **Yagyu** assassin running right at you. It's a POV shot through Ogami Itto's eyes, and in a flash his dotanuki is embedded in the ill-fated samurai's forehead. Just then, an unexpected second Yagyu jumps on the stricken samurai's shoulders—it was all planned! No good, though; our demon assassin has his spear through the assailant faster than you can say "shish kabob."

And we're off. The evil Lord Retsudo, hoary head of the Shadow Yagyu, doesn't make an appearance in this film, but his presence is felt nevertheless. He's sent Ozunu (Akiji Kobayashi), head of the Kuroguwa ninja, with a message to Sayaka (**Kayo Matsuo**), leader of the Akashi Yagyu clanswomen, an elite squad of female assassins. The message is simply, "Kill Ogami Itto." Sayaka is one intense lady, played to the hilt by the truly frightening Kayo Matsuo (look for her doing a similar yet even more freaky character in *Hunter in the Dark*). Matsuo's over-the-top performance is one of the things that makes this movie truly great. Her diabolical laughter, her sadistic demonstration of what her girls can do (using Ozunu's best ninja as a handily dismembered test case), the way she escapes from a tight spot by jumping straight up out of her kimono and running away backward—these are the standards against which all lady villains should be measured.

Then of course there are the three Hidari brothers, the so-called "Lords of Death" (a popular moniker in samurai films—see *Three Outlaw Samurai*). They're official escorts of the shogunate, heading to Takamatsu by boat to pick up a prisoner, the headman of the indigo farmers of the Awa clan. This headman has trade secrets the shogun wants. Needless to say the Awa clan wants to keep their indigo monopoly and have hired Ogami Itto to take the headman out. This puts Itto on the boat too, as well as on a collision course with the Lords of Death.

Each of the three Hidari brothers has a special weapon that he wields with expertise: Big bro Benma (Akiji Kobayashi) uses a wicked armor claw; Tenma (Minoru Oki) prefers a flying club (an iron club that doesn't really fly, except into your head); and Kuruma (**Shin Kishida**) is most comfortable goring faces with his mailed fist, a kind of spiky leather glove. They get a chance to show off a little when they're confronted on deck by a band of pathetic Awa hirelings. Particularly nasty are those iron claws, 12-inch talons that tear right through their fleshy adversaries.

Ogami Itto first encounters the Hidari brothers below deck, after the melee. Chancing upon one another, the brothers give Itto the old "even though I admire you, I'm going to have to kill you"–type warning. We'll see. In the meantime, they've all got trouble on their hands, as an Awa-hired arsonist has just set the ship on fire! Fortunately the baby cart floats, and Ogami Itto uses his long spear to pole-vault off the flaming vessel.

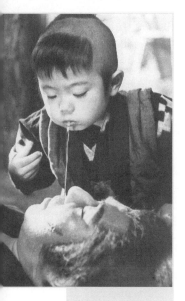

Lone Wolf and Cub: Sword of Vengeance: *Daigoro gives dad a drink*

Lone Wolf and Cub: Baby Cart at the River Styx also features Daigoro getting into the act, helping daddy kill. During a clash with some of Sayaka's killer clanswomen, he sits in his baby cart, calmly hits a button, and a hidden spike shoots out, skewering one of the attackers. Later, as dad sends him careening down a hill in the perambulator toward a band of ninja, Daigoro operates another secret switch, and blades extend from the wheels, sheering off shinobi shins. He's also captured and dangled down a "bottomless" well for awhile.

Fans of the Lone Wolf and Cub manga, and Daigoro in particular, will be excited to learn that as of this writing, Kazuo Koike, still alive and kicking at 67, is hard at work on a new chapter in the saga. "People who read *Lone Wolf and Cub* are very interested in the fate of Daigoro," Koike told *Giant Robot Magazine* (Issue 30, Winter 2003). "I am coming out with a sequel to *Lone Wolf and Cub* called *Lone Wolf*. It's what happens when Daigoro grows up." Two words: serial killer.

While I've focused on the outrageous exploitation aspects of *Lone Wolf and Cub: Baby Cart at the River Styx,* it should be noted that it's also a really fine piece of filmmaking. **Kenji Misumi** was a **Daiei** veteran and bona fide chambara auteur by the time he came to make these films (he did parts 1, 2, 3, and 5) and his craftsmanship and cinematic flair really show on the screen. Atmospheric lighting, hyperkinetic editing, and masterful use of scenic locations all contribute to and enhance the action and gore, resulting in a quality picture that you'll find enjoyable again and again. That's why it's remained a favorite of samurai film fans for over thirty years.

Lone Wolf and Cub: Baby Cart to Hades

Kozure Okami:
Shinikazeni mukau
ubaguruma

Toho, 1972

DIRECTOR: Kenji Misumi

CAST: Tomisaburo
Wakayama, Go Kato,
Isao Yamagata,
Akihiro Tomikawa,
Yuko Hama, Saburo
Date, Daigo Kusano

AVAILABILITY: Easy

COMMENT: VHS from
AnimEigo

What will you get from this, the third Baby Cart movie? A powerful meditation on the True Way of the Warrior; a surreal soundtrack that moves from symphonic swells to weird, low synth belches to jazzy improv flute solos; more stunning location scenes highlighting the natural beauty of the Japanese countryside; a point-of-view shot from the eyes of a rolling, severed head cutting to a shot of the head smiling as it dies. All this and so much more await you in *Lone Wolf and Cub: Baby Cart to Hades*.

While the first film was a little slow and the second was totally OTT, this third entry finds the series hitting its stride. It is more balanced in its pacing, more sober, lyrical, and evokes the feeling one gets when reading the manga. It also features samurai stars **Isao Yamagata (*Gate of Hell*)** and **Go (aka Tsuyoshi) Kato (*Samurai Rebellion*)**. The range of styles (and at times bizarre application) of the film's score creates a surreal quality, again reinforcing the manga feel: this is not the real world—this is a heightened, graphic novel world where even the most mundane aspect is infused with an element of the fantastic.

Kanbei Magomura (Go Kato) is "makoto no bushi," a true samurai, but he's working as a watari-kashi, a kind of temp samurai, usually hired as a yojimbo to accompany daimyo on their biannual treks back and forth to Edo. Watari-kashi were essentially road scum, drifters one step above ronin, and the group Kanbei's fallen in with are a bunch of real low-lifes. They rape a traveling mother and daughter, but before they know it Kanbei has appeared out of nowhere, slain the two women, and forced the men to draw lots to see which one dies for the crime. Does he kill the women to spare them a life of shame, or is he protecting his current lord? Probably both, but Ogami Itto (**Tomisaburo Wakayama**) has witnessed the scene, and Kanbei approaches him. They've both heard of each other, and Ogami Itto asks him what a samurai of his caliber is doing working as a watari-kashi. "We need not concern ourselves with that," Kanbei replies. "For now, I'd like to request a duel." They begin, but to avoid wasting such a fine samurai, Ogami Itto declares the duel a draw and moves on. Kanbei laments, "Once again I have lost a chance to die."

Ogami Itto and Daigoro (**Akihiro Tomikawa**) encounter a young girl recently sold into sexual slavery, and defend her against a group of Bohachimono (flesh peddlers) led by beautiful, gun-totin' babe Torizo (Yuko Hama) and her henchman (**Saburo Date**). Torizo explains that, as Bohachimono (a branch of the yakuza) she and her men have lost all trace of the Eight Things: piety, respect, honesty, trust, justice, courtesy, uprightness, and shame. In addition, they have no intention of relinquishing their claim on the girl, who has killed her buyer by biting off his tongue. (Biting one's own tongue off is a standard method of suicide among women in samurai films; death presumably results from either drowning in the blood or blood loss. Perhaps the girl was considering this option when the nasty fellow stuck his own tongue in her mouth.)

In order to vouchsafe the poor farm girl's release, Ogami Itto endures the torture of buri-buri (you'll see) on her behalf. Afterward, he is hired by Torizo and her father (whom the former Kogi kaishakunin had inadvertently dismembered during a difficult beheading). They want to put a hit on Genba Sawatari (**Isao Yamagata**), a local corrupt deputy. Genba gets wind of this and sends his yojimbo to kill Ogami Itto. In the first of several spaghetti western–influenced scenes, his sharp-shooter yojimbo (the ever-moustachioed **Daigo Kusano**) demonstrates his prowess on a series of targets with a flourish to put Clint Eastwood to shame. Daigoro watches and claps excitedly, charming the gunman. The boy then lures the man to his death.

After losing his bodyguards one by one, Genba marshalls all the men he can get, including those of neighboring clans and the **Yagyu** as well. This action culminates in one of the great set pieces in samurai film history: in a dusty desert valley (à la Sergio Leone) Ogami Itto takes on something like 200 samurai (archers, gunners, swordsmen) with the help of a gattling gun concealed in the baby cart and his trusty naginata. He does so much slicing, it becomes a regular naginatathon, and when it's over, the arid plain is littered with corpses as far as the eye can see.

Along the way to the desert valley of death, Ogami Itto slays various ninja, goes fishing, has a playful splash fight with Daigoro, and performs a neatly executed leap over an adversary while driving his sword straight down into the man's skull. Oh, and he eventually has that duel with Kanbei. Kanbei asks him what the true way of the warrior is, and is told simply, "to live to die."

Some people complain about the pace of this film, but pay no attention. Such dissenters probably never read the manga, and so have no frame of reference. In any case, it's a fine film, a mature effort from the great **Kenji Misumi**, a chambara director par excellence. This was Misumi's third Baby Cart film, and he would return again for #5, *Baby Cart in the Land of Demons*. In Misumi's capable hands, Tomisaburo Wakayama (along with **Raizo Ichikawa** and **Shintaro Katsu**) did some of his finest work. *Lone Wolf and Cub: Baby Cart to Hades* is one of those films.

Character Actor Hall of Fame

Saburo Date (1924–)

If you've seen a Zatoichi film, chances are you've seen Saburo Date. With his imposing frame, protruding brow, and pushed-in nose, he looks more like a professional boxer than the standard yakuza thug he invariably portrays. As a contract player for Daiei, Date was cast in scores of films, but often criminally underutilized. A towering, macho presence, he appeared in prestige pictures during the 1950s like *Ugetsu* and *Sansho the Bailiff* (directed by Kenji Mizoguchi) and *Gate of Hell*. During the '60s he was a frequent face in the Zatoichi, Sleepy Eyes of Death, Yokai Monsters and Shinobi No Mono (Ninja) film series. In the '70s he appeared in a number of Lone Wolf and Cub and Zatoichi films. So if you've always wondered what that prize fighter-looking guy's name was, it's Saburo Date. And if you're already a Saburo Date fan like me, it's worth seeking out a copy of *Sleepy Eyes of Death: The Chinese Jade* to see him actually get a full-on villain role. Also recommended is his turn as the unwitting husband of a Rokurokubi (long-neck ghost) in *Yokai Monsters: 100 Monsters*.

The Razor: Sword of Justice

Goyokiba

1972, Toho

DIRECTOR: Kenji Misumi

CAST: Shintaro Katsu, Ko Nishimura, Yukiji Asaoka, Daigo Kusano, Keizo Kanie

AVAILABILITY: Easy

COMMENT: DVD from Home Vision Entertainment

1972 Toho

The Razor: Sword of Justice

After a decade as **Zatoichi**, **Shintaro Katsu** decided to start a new franchise, one based on a character as diametrically opposed to the blind swordsman as possible. He found what he was looking for in the character of Itami "The Razor" Hanzo, an Edo-period constable from the brilliantly twisted manga of **Kazuo Koike**. Where Zatoichi was blind, Hanzo had fierce, armor-piercing eyeballs. Where Zatoichi was a criminal, Hanzo was a cop. Where Zatoichi was humble and didn't get much action, Hanzo was loud and overbearing and not only got a lot of sex, but possessed an enormous member that he used to interrogate shady ladies. Oh, and Hanzo would be super kinky, too, for good measure. As things turned out, the appeal of this new character was limited; only three Razor films were made. But what incredible films they are! If you haven't seen one, brace yourself. I guarantee you've never seen anything like it.

The Razor: Sword of Justice opens with a multi-split-screen, '70s cop show montage-style credit sequence complete with funky bass, guitar, and trumpet, sounding somewhere between Starsky & Hutch and a blaxploitation soundtrack. The images of **Edo-period** Japan and Katsu strutting his tough mofo stuff against the music is a glorious cultural train wreck.

In the opening scene, Hanzo speechifies about the corrupt state of Edo politics and unfair police restrictions, and the next thing we know we find him torturing himself with "crushing stones" placed on his legs by his henchmen, Onibi (**Daigo Kusano**) and Mamushi (**Keizo Kanie**). "The torturer ought to know what it feels like to be tortured," he gasps through gnashing teeth. "It's said that, somewhere beyond the limits of endurance, one can reach a point where pain becomes pleasure. Knowing that point would make it possible to devise the most effective torture." This all sounds very logical, but afterward, when he stands up, he's got an unmistakably tumescent member. All business indeed, Mr. Hanzo!

Then there's Hanzo's daily schlong-strengthening ritual. It involves (1) cleansing his huge phallus with hot water, (2) beating it with a stick on a customized, grooved wooden board, and finally (3) jamming it repeatedly into a bag of rice.

This last bit is accompanied by a sequence shot with what can only be described as a "cock cam," a point-of-view shot, moving into and out of the grains of rice. Just imagine putting a camera on the end of your pecker and you get the idea. What a movie!

Hanzo works for the Kitamachi Constabulary under a corrupt chief, Magobei Onishi (**Ko Nishimura**), whom the cops on the force call "Magobei the Snake." Hanzo is constantly enraged by the corruption he sees all around him, and is determined to do something about it. That's right, he's an honest cop. But when he learns that Onishi's current flame is also the ex-girlfriend of an escaped convict, he begins to suspect something and takes matters into his own hands.

Knowing he'll get nothing but bullshit from Onishi, he apprehends the woman, Omino (**Yukiji Asaoka**), and interrogates her in his own unique way. This involves using his massive tool on her and then stopping suddenly. "No, don't stop," she cries, and the deal is she has to provide information about her old boyfriend. She resists, but he stops again, and it's too much. She tells all. This softcore porno scene is made artistic by the use of superimposed close-ups of her mouth, his eye, his bobbing forehead, as well as the aforementioned cock cam: the camera moves in and out of a deep red, impressionistic, soft-focus image of Omino's . . . interior . . . providing a penis-eye view of the sexual action. It's quaint and smutty at the same time, but completely original.

Later, as they relax in a hot tub over sake, Hanzo demonstrates his tricked-out pad. With the push of a button or pull of a lever, swords shoot out of the walls, spears jut down from the ceiling, and concealed panels in the walls reveal a wide range of weapons. His house is a nineteenth-century high-tech fortress worthy of James Bond. "Anyone stupid enough to barge in here will leave in pieces," he tells Omino.

Hanzo follows the trail of clues, each one leading to a bigger revelation, until he realizes that it's all heading straight into the shogun's Inner Castle. Along the way, he fights hordes of assailants using his customized jitte (it has a weighted chain inside the handle for strangling, wrapping around swords—he even swings from it!), a set of spiky iron knuckles, and the variety of lethal devices in his house. Much blood gushes everywhere. He also interrogates another woman using a variation of his standard technique, this time hoisting her from the ceiling in a net and having Onibi and Mamushi raise and lower her while he lies beneath. Then he takes her for a spin. Use your imagination.

So there you have it. Male fantasy? You bet. Prurient nonsense? Of course! But in the hands of director **Kenji Misumi**, an old pro and long-time Katsu collaborator, it somehow works. But don't take my word for it. There's no way to adequately describe the Razor films. They have to be seen to be believed.

The Razor: The Snare

Goyokiba: Kamisori Hanzo jigoku zeme

1973, Toho

DIRECTOR: Yasuzo Masumura

CAST: Shintaro Katsu, Toshio Kurosawa, Ko Nishimura, Daigo Kusano, Keizo Kanie

AVAILABILITY: Easy

COMMENT: DVD from Home Vision Entertainment

The Japanese title translates as "Hanzo the Razor's Torture from Hell," which is apt, as this is the kinkiest entry in the highly kinkoid Razor trilogy. It's also the best. While the first one drags a little and the third is a straight-up comedy, the second is balanced, thematically integrated, and extremely well written. The latter is due to the writing/directing efforts of Yasuzo Masumura, renowned director of pictures such as *Blind Beast* and *Giants and Toys* (recommended). The original source material is yet another manga written by the brilliant and prolific **Kazuo Koike** (**Lone Wolf and Cub**, **Lady Snowblood**). Contrary to some sources, the picture was not directed by Masumura, but by perennial chambara favorite and Katsu cohort, **Kenji Misumi**.

The themes this time out are, once again, government corruption, the decadence of the upper classes, and torture; but this time each has been expanded and pushed to the limit. Torture, for example, is no longer just **Edo-period** cop Itami Hanzo's personal hobby; there are other S&M weirdos running around, and they aren't troubled by victimizing innocents to get their jollies, something Hanzo can't allow. The government corruption is more cruel and premeditated this time around, and the decadent rich are the same sadistic freaks just mentioned. But these deviants don't know who they're messing with—Hanzo is the King of Kink, and these bad boys are going get an ass whooping (literally)!

The film opens in mid-chase, with Hanzo (**Shintaro Katsu**) and his comical henchmen, Onibi (**Daigo Kusano**) and Mamushi (**Keizo Kanie**), in pursuit of two crooked-looking peasants. The two guys make a run for a bridge where a procession of samurai with a palanquin are passing, something you just don't do if you're in the lower classes (you're supposed to kneel and wait). The samurai attack the hapless fellows, and are in turn rebuffed by Hanzo: "You're interfering with an officer of the law! Move it, you stupid retainers!" He winds up in a duel with one of the samurai, an imposing swordsman named Junai Mikoshiba (**Toshio Kurosawa**, with an even bigger '70s hairdo than the one he sports in *Lady Snowblood: Blizzard from the Netherworld*).

The duel is halted by the nobleman in the palanquin who happens to be the Treasury Commissioner. He lectures Hanzo: "When you break one of the customs of the samurai, you are not only dishonoring the Way of the Warrior but also tarnishing the image of the shogunate." He reminds Hanzo of his rank. Hanzo roars back, "Rank my ass! Ranks are like any useless ornaments! Got it?! All this honoring and ancient custom crap . . . I'll destroy it all before I die!" That's our Razor. As the procession leaves, Hanzo is advised to wash his neck and prepare for death. "No need for that," Junai counters in passing, "I'll be the one to slay you."

Unruffled, Hanzo turns his attention back to the men he's caught. They're holding stolen clothing they got off a dead girl they found in a nearby water mill. They swear they didn't kill her. Upon investigating the body, Hanzo and his men learn she died of a botched abortion and she smells of monastery incense. The "nunsploitation" theme begins here. He sets off to investigate the shrine where she got the abortion, as well as the temple Kaizanji where she got pregnant servicing the depraved sexual demands of rich merchants. Both places are distinctly creepy, almost satanic.

In the shrine, Hanzo witnesses a freaky priestess doing a spooky "purge the unborn" dance, chanting the operative phrase, then taking one of the women arrayed before her and

1973 Toho

The Razor: The Snare

undressing her. The priestess undresses as well, and things look like they're going in the direction of a lesbian encounter when she suddenly reaches for a long, thin knife. . . . Hanzo busts in at the last moment and breaks it up.

Later, at Kaizanji temple, Hanzo gets past the guards by having himself buried alive in place of the dead girl from the mill. After the funeral party has departed, he pops out of the ground forcefully, manfully, . . . and in full drag! It's a hilarious scene, but things soon take the darkest of turns as he manages to get inside the temple and see what's doing. He witnesses a sadistic merchant named Tanbaya beating a young, naked woman bloody with a bamboo stick, and it's a hard scene to watch. Hanzo finally stops Tanbaya and gives him a healthy dose of his own medicine.

Things get more complex as we learn that the Treasury Commissioner is debasing the coinage, and another subplot involving a master criminal (also a pervert) comes into play. Along the way we get to see the old "net trick" (see **The Razor: Sword of Justice**), Hanzo uses the lethal devices of his James Bond–style bachelor pad (as well as the secret weapon in his loincloth), and he once again rebukes and humiliates his corrupt boss, Onishi the Snake (**Ko Nishimura**).

The Razor: The Snare has a great look. The cinematography was done by **Kazuo Miyagawa**, the genius behind *Rashomon* and *Yojimbo*. The score is unique too, a synthesizer-driven funk-prog extravaganza by Isao Tomita. The synth, which is present throughout, is at times just Jan Hammeresque noodling, elsewhere working up into a frenzy for the freaky scenes, and even imitating a bamboo flute during more contemplative moments. And of course there is always the '70s waka-jawaka guitar funk whenever Hanzo is strutting around Edo. The music really makes these Razor movies, adding a vital component. They just wouldn't be the same without it.

Only one question (and installment) remains: *Who's Got the Gold?*

Lady Snowblood: Blizzard from the Netherworld

Shurayuki-hime

1973, Toho

DIRECTOR: Toshiya Fujita

CAST: Meiko Kaji, Ko Nishimura, Toshio Kurosawa

AVAILABILITY: Easy.

OMMENTS: DVD from AnimEigo

So you say you're tired of all these *guys* doing the slashing? Ready to see a beautiful woman in some sword-wielding action for a change? You came to the right place. *Lady Snowblood: Blizzard from the Netherworld* is a dark and lurid bloodbath reminiscent of blaxploitation movies like *Coffey* and *Foxy Brown,* with one bad-ass mama out for revenge. It is a tribute to the porous nature of the samurai genre that it can absorb the ethos of early '70s American exploitation cinema and blend it with the distinct essence of chambara. What results is a hybrid of wicked intensity.

The film opens and closes with the anguished cry of one Yuki (**Meiko Kaji**). At the start of the film, it is the cry of a newborn baby girl in a women's prison. Snow swirls outside the barred windows as Yuki's mother Sayo declares, "Yuki, you were born for vengeance." She's not kidding. Yuki was literally conceived to this end; her mother, in prison for murder, slept with every guard, priest, and lawyer she could get her hands on, just so she could have a child to wreak her bloody vengeance (she was hoping for a boy, but there you go). Cut to the window: the snow turns bright red. Title card.

Actually, the original title of the film, *Shurayukihime,* translates as "netherworld snow lady"—no mention of blood. No worries though, you don't have to wait long to see it, gallons of it, spurting, spraying, gushing everywhere. Five minutes into the movie someone's arm is off, severed at the shoulder by our ravishing heroine. The early '70s was a time when samurai films were really pushing the gore factor to the limit, making Sam Peckinpah look like Vincente Minnelli, and this film is a fine example. It's probably one of the bloodiest, right up there with **Lone Wolf and Cub**. This comes as no surprise, since both films are adaptations of manga created by **Kazuo Koike**, a writer whose specialty was ultra-violence presented in meticulously researched historical settings. Indeed, panels from the Lady Snowblood manga are used during the movie at several points to provide historical background and exposition under the voice-over narration.

Flash forward: it's 20 years later and our little creature of vengeance has grown up. The year is 1894 and Yuki is hot on the trail of the four low-life criminal types who murdered her would-be father and raped her mother. Through flashbacks we get the whole sordid story, how the villains had come to the town of Koichi to sell phony letters of exemption to a recently passed national conscription law. As it happens, back when this law was passed in 1873, it was extremely unpopular with the general population. Bizarre rumors began to spread about the so-called "men in white," government agents up to all sorts of weird rackets such as selling the blood of new recruits. (You can rest assured that all this really happened; Koike's specialty is digging up particularly heinous moments in history and exploiting them to their full potential.)

So guess who has the unfortunate fashion sense to wear a white suit to his new job as the schoolteacher in Koichi? Sayo's husband, the man who would have been Yuki's father had not fate shown up in the person of three guys and a gal of undeniably bad character (I'll refrain from listing their incredibly long names here). The four fiends fall on Sayo's husband like a pack of wolves, hacking him to pieces. The white suit highlights the bright red blood to great effect here, and there's even a close-up of a trickle pouring out of the body and forming a little stream (a representation in miniature of **Akira Kurosawa**'s standard "rivers of blood" line spoken in so many of his samurai efforts). Sayo is taken to a nearby water mill, where she is raped repeatedly. The scene contains only the sounds of the mill, the creaking of the wheel, and the pounding sound of the grain pestles (see *Sword of Doom*).

So the upshot is that Yuki pursues the four with her lethal lady-sword concealed in her purple umbrella. This is historically accurate as well; in those days, a woman was forbidden by law to openly carry a sword. We see more flashbacks, this time of her martial arts training as a child. She is schooled by a rigorous and demanding priest, Dokai (**Ko Nishimura**), who puts the seven-year-old through all sorts of ordeals, getting her ready for her mission of destruction. He rolls her down a hill in a barrel; he deals out punishing bokuto training; during a katana drill, he slices her kimono off and gets a weird look on his face. At one point he tells her: "You are a child of the netherworld. You are not a being of this earthly realm. You are a devil that abides by netherworldly principles . . . a beast, a devil . . . one whose disguise is human . . . one so evil that even Buddha cannot save you now." It's a reworking of the **Lone Wolf and Cub** "We live in Meifumado" thing, and doesn't quite come off here, as the little girl looks so gentle and sweet.

Yuki meets novelist and muckraker Ryurei Ashio (**Toshio Kurosawa**), who decides to publish her tale. We think he's just capitalizing on her sad story, but later learn it was all priest Dokai's idea, a way to bring one of the foul four out of hiding. Ashio happens to be a hunky sort, and provides a love interest for Yuki. He has a secret as well. Before long there's a false ending, and you really think it's all over (unless you're hip enough to remember the clues); and then the bloodletting and body-segmenting continues.

Starring in the title role is Meiko Kaji, no stranger to Japanese exploitation cinema. During 1972–1974, while filming *Lady Snowblood: Blizzard from the Netherworld* and **Lady Snowblood: Love Song of Vengeance** for Katsu Productions, she was also starring in the Female Convict Scorpion *(Sasori)* series for Toei. The Sasori pictures comprise a brutal female prison saga in which Kaji is betrayed by her detective boyfriend, set up on a drug bust, and incarcerated (with all the attendant horrors). She continually escapes and is continually dragged back to the living hell of the prison system to endure further torture and humiliation. Watching a Sasori film is similar to encountering a bloody pile-up on the freeway: ghastly, yet you can't look away.

The same goes for *Lady Snowblood: Blizzard from the Netherworld*—samurai pulp, but well made. It's a gem, a dark little blood ruby of a film in which the chambara corollary to Pam Grier kicks righteous ass in the name of sisterhood and revenge. No wonder then that it's one of Quentin Tarantino's favorites; the influence on *Kill Bill Vol. 1* is hard to miss.

Lady Snowblood: Love Song of Vengeance

Shurayuki-hime:
Urami renga

Daiei, 1974

DIRECTOR: Toshiya Fujita

CAST: Meiko Kaji,
Yoshio Harada, Juzo
Itami, Shin Kishida,
Kazuko Yoshiyuki

AVAILABILITY: Easy

COMMENT: DVD from
AnimEigo

Lady Snowblood, beautiful, and cold as befits your name. . . . What's left for you in this life then? Without blood you would be merely snow that melts into the dirt. Snowblood! Your life as a fugitive drained you and made you forsake fighting. But there can be no such thing as peace for you. You're forever bound to live a life of inhuman carnage!

Thus speaks Seishiro Kikui (**Shin Kishida**), head of the Japanese government's secret police, circa 1905. His operatives (wearing Otafuku masks) have rescued Yuki Kashima (**Meiko Kaji**), our eponymous heroine, en route to her execution for 37 counts of murder. It seems Kikui has other uses for Ms. Snowblood, specifically the assassination of one Ransui Tokunaga (Juzo Itami). "He is an advocate of anarchism, an absurd yet devastating idealism," he tells Yuki. Tokunaga has a document that Kikui wants badly (we'll find out why later). Yuki's mission: get close to Tokunaga, get the document, then kill Tokunaga. This sets up the plot for the picture and away we go.

Keep in mind this meeting with Kikui comes after several nicely staged and artistically filmed swordfight sequences, Yuki making neat work of numerous attackers with her umbrella-concealed tanto sword. She's chased by unnamed assassins as well as the police (the latter led by a chief in a deerstalker-and-tweed ensemble right out of Sherlock Holmes). The most striking scene takes place in the calm waves of a beach in early morning. Following a night spent (platonically) with a mysterious stranger who has treated a wound Yuki received stepping in a rabbit trap, she finds herself moved by the man's kindness. In the bright morning sunlight, as she cuts down cop after cop, the waves lapping at the bodies strewn about her, she gets a glimpse of the stranger and something in her gives up. She's had enough. She surrenders.

But remember she's "forever bound to live a life of inhuman carnage," and next thing we know she's got a gig working for Ransui Tokunaga as his maid. She unexpectedly comes to like this romantic, intellectual radical who turns out to be quite a cool guy. Living in the same house, observing him reciting Russian poetry, getting into kinky foot fun with wife Aya (Kazuko Yoshiyuki), getting drunk, reading, writing, living the life of the bohemian anarchist about town, she starts having second thoughts about her mission. Not only that, but Tokunaga is on to her. He takes her to a cemetery where his murdered anarchist colleagues are buried and gives her the lowdown: the document he holds contains damning evidence of conspiracy and murder that will bring down not only Kikui, but also his superiors and perhaps the whole government! The two of them head home, but are arrested by the police. Yuki escapes but Tokunaga isn't so lucky.

Up to this point, the story has a sophisticated feel, a mature, complex political thriller uncommon in this type of film fare. There's a picture of Bakunin on Tokunaga's wall, he's quoting Kropotkin, it's *heady*. Where's the exploitation? It kicks in right after Tokunaga is arrested. He's beaten to a bloody pulp by the cops who also pour boiling water on him while Aya looks on in horror. They finally shoot him up with bubonic plague and dump him by the side of the road. Aya seeks revenge on the police chief by feigning drunken amorousness and then (in a dazzlingly graphic close-up) jamming her hair pin right into his eye. (Yuki will get the other eye later, leaving the gory blind man to fire his shotgun randomly about the room, nailing his own men!) There are assorted amputations, impalements, and other such blood-spurting butchery in store for the bad guys as well. There's also the burning of several slums by the secret police, crisping the inhabitants. Not to mention what happens to Tokunaga; we get to see every stage of the black death as it slowly consumes him.

Putting in a fine performance is **Yoshio Harada** who plays Tokunaga's poverty-stricken brother, Shusuke. Shusuke was the mysterious stranger who helped Yuki in the beginning of the film. He's a doctor, as well as one third of a love triangle that is revealed midway through the picture. He nurses his brother, but he's bitter and conflicted and hates living in a slum. Harada's specialty is the tortured loner struggling to keep his dignity, his magnetic presence conveying the indomitable fighting spirit of the makoto no bushi. Watch for him in **Hunter in the Dark**, **Roningai,** and **Shogun's Samurai.**

Also worthy of note is Juzo Itami, who plays Ransui Tokunaga. His name will no doubt ring a bell as the director of such breakthrough Japanese films as *The Funeral* (1984), *Tampopo* (1985), and *A Taxing Woman* (1987). These films were part of the Japanese cultural invasion of the '80s (along with all that sushi) and introduced many a Western filmgoer to contemporary Japanese culture, as well as the exquisite natural talent of their director, who decided to become a filmmaker at age 51. Much of the sensual zest for living that permeates *Tampopo* also comes through in Itami's performance as Tokunaga, making the character's downfall all the more tragic. Tragic as well was Itami's eventual demise: in 1997 he leapt to his death from an eight-story building. In suicide notes, Itami blamed false tabloid reports of infidelity with a 26-year-old woman as the cause of his suicide. He was 64.

As is the rule with second films in a series, *Lady Snowblood: Love Song of Vengeance* is better than the first film. There are no flashbacks to burden the flow of the story, and the story itself is more engaging and not quite as nonstop exploitational as its predecessor (which could be a good thing or a bad thing depending on your disposition). In any case, both are great, gory samurai fun with a feminist twist.

The Razor: Who's Got the Gold?

Goyokiba: Oni no Hanzo yawahada koban

1974, Toho

DIRECTOR: Yoshio Inoue

CAST: Shintaro Katsu, Ko Nishimura, Mako Midori, Etsushi Takahashi, Asao

With *Who's Got the Gold?*, the third and final chapter of the Razor trilogy, we find the franchise starting to run out of steam and realize why it remained a trilogy. While it's the funniest of the three, with over-the-top comedic performances from everyone (particularly **Ko Nishimura** as Onishi the Snake), the plot once again revolves around money, sex, and corruption in much the same way it did before. There's not much variance in the plot structure, and the film underplays the series'

Koike, Mikio Narita, Daigo Kusano, Keizo Kanie, Hiroshi Nawa

AVAILABILITY: Easy

COMMENT: DVD from Home Vision Entertainment

unique features (Hanzo's kinkiness and huge dong), almost as if the filmmakers themselves were tiring of the whole affair. In fact, there's no torture in this one at all! Nevertheless, it is a Razor film, and that alone puts it in a class by itself.

There are a few things we haven't seen before: a ghost, an orgy, lots of hysterical comic blind men, and a homemade, Western-style cannon. The ghost, whom we see first, is haunting the lake next to the Shogunate Treasury where we find Onibi (**Daigo Kusano**) and Mamushi (**Keizo Kanie**), Hanzo's henchmen, indulging in a little late-night fishing and drunken Kyogen improv. Right off the bat we're laughing, until an eerie lady *Ghost of Yotsuya*–type specter comes looming up on them, causing them to cower, whimper, and loose their buzz. When Hanzo (**Shintaro Katsu**) hears of the ghost, he's intrigued, declaring, "I've always wanted to do it with a ghost, at least once."

Hanzo captures the ghost who is, of course, just a woman with gooey make-up on, but in the course of splashing around in the lake trying to apprehend her, he comes across some big bamboo poles full of koban (1-ryo gold coins). Hanzo takes the ghost lady back to his place, and after rigging her up in The Net (See ***The Razor: Sword of Justice***) and giving her his special love torture, she confesses that her husband is a treasury guard. She doesn't get to say much more, however, as she sud-

Character Actor Hall of Fame

Ko Nishimura (1923–1997)

During the '60s, with his rectangular visage and broad nose, Ko Nishimura was a frequent face in samurai films like *Sword of Doom* (as Matsu's kindly yet thieving uncle Shichibei) and *Yojimbo* (as the hapless yakuza Kuma). During the late '60s Nishimura became a favorite of Shintaro Katsu, who cast him in several Zatoichi films including *Zatoichi's Fire Festival*. In the early '70s, Katsu used him again as the unforgettable "Onishi the Snake," Katsu's corrupt cop boss in all three installments of *The Razor*. During this period he also played the somewhat disturbing priest Dokai in *Lady Snowblood: Blizzard from the Netherworld* and Retsudo Yagyu in the Japanese TV adaptation of *Lone Wolf and Cub*. Ko Nishimura was equally compelling in contemporary gendai-geki, giving what is perhaps his finest performance as a salaryman driven insane by Toshiro Mifune's Hamletesque revenger in *The Bad Sleep Well*. Look for Ko Nishimura in Kinji Fukasaku's 1968 cross-dressing kitsch classic, *Black Lizard*, Daiei's 1962 ur-ninja film *Shinobi no Mono*, Akira Kurosawa's terse kidnap thriller *High and Low*, and the fifth Nemuri Kyoshiro installment, *Sleepy Eyes of Death: Sword of Fire*.

The Razor: Who's
Got the Gold?:
*Elder Hotta busted
by Hanzo*

denly dies. "Hey . . . I wonder if she liked it a bit too much?" he asks. No Hanzo, you're not that good, she's got a dagger in her back. Treasury guards storm in, only to get shot with arrows from secret panels in the walls, impaled on spikes under trap doors, and generally hacked to death by Hanzo, who wields a sword for the better part of the film. His action sequences are fairly gonzo this time out, and it's always good to see Katsu with a sword in his hand. After the fight, Hanzo realizes that the gold-filled bamboo must have been lobbed out the window of the Treasury into the lake: an inside job.

The Razor: Who's Got the Gold? also features yet another totally corrupt shogunate official, the elder Hotta (Hiroshi Nawa). Hotta is accosted by a consumptive doctor, Gen'an Sugino (**Etsushi Takahashi**), who begs that he help save Japan by opening up trade. "We must incorporate the ideas of the West at once," he pleads, "and use their steam engines to drive trains and ships, and to weave cloth. We must make the nation prosperous." The elder is unmoved, replying flatly, "Japan shall remain Japan. There's no reason to dishonor our traditions." Hanzo is ordered to arrest the doctor, but is intrigued by Gen'an's talk of new technology, particularly new high-tech weaponry like the cannon (plans for which are in the doctor's possession). Hanzo decides to put the good doctor up in his secret room. There, he instructs the doctor, who only has a month or two to live, to commence construction of the newfangled cannon.

Meanwhile, blind High Priest Ishiyama (**Asao Koike**) is giving koto lessons to all the wives of the elders and high-ranking shogunate officials while setting up secret orgies for them with his monks. He also has a nice little loan-sharking business on the side, and an evil yojimbo with a red scabbard named Bansaku Tonami (**Mikio Narita**). Ishiyama has lent money to a childhood friend of Hanzo's, and when the poor ronin can't pay his debt, the High Priest sends a gang of blind men to harass him by screaming and chanting at his door. The actors portraying the blind men play it to the hilt, making all manner of screwed-up faces, their heads lolling on their necks like rag dolls. It's unexpectedly hilarious, and one can only speculate whether a certain former blind swordsman egged them on during the shooting.

As mentioned earlier, keep an eye on Ko Nishimura, playing Hanzo's sleazy boss Onishi the Snake. His sycophantic histrionics before his superiors and verbal sparring with Katsu are beyond anything in previous films. At one point, upon receiving reward money from the elder, he does a backward, tip-toed knee-walk that's laugh-out-loud funny. John Cleese, look out!

Music-wise, the synthesizer from the second film is back, more frenetic, more febrile than ever, and the funk level seems to have increased in general, with lots of wah-pedal guitar and cool bass lines. There's no soulful Hanzo ballad, as there was at the end of the first film, but you can't have everything. All in all, I'd recommend this movie. If you've seen the others, you kind of have to see this one, and even if you haven't this one is still crazy and action-packed enough to leave you, like Hanzo's female interrogatees, panting for more.

Shogun's Samurai

Yagyu ichizoku no inbo

1978, Toei

DIRECTOR: Kinji Fukasaku

CAST: Kinnosuke Nakamura, Sonny Chiba, Hiroki Matsukata, Tetsuro Tamba, Toshiro Mifune, Reiko Ohara, Yoshio Harada, Isuzu Yamada, Mikio Narita, Etsushi Takahashi

AVAILABILITY: Tricky

COMMENT: Available on DVD from Ventura Distribution, although

Kill your father if he stands in your way. Get rid of Buddha if he interferes. You need determination more than justice. If you're unable to do this, I have nothing more to say. I beg you to execute me immediately.

This is the essence of shogunate statecraft, and it's spoken by a towering figure in the history of the **Tokugawa period**, Tajima no Kami Munenori Yagyu, head of the notorious **Yagyu clan**.

It's 1624 and the second Tokugawa shogun has died under suspicious circumstances. What's more, a succession struggle has developed between his two sons: the stuttering and purple-birthmark-faced Iemitsu (yakuza film star Hiroki Matsukata) and the young and handsome Tadanaga (Teruhiko Saigo). Yagyu, official sword instructor to the shogun, is backing Iemitsu, and, as his words above indicate, he'll stop at nothing to see his man become the next shogun. "Starting today,"

I cannot vouch for the quality; the list price is $10, which doesn't bode well. I would recommend the Region 2 version from Eureka Video (available on Amazon.co.uk).

Iemitsu pledges, "I'm ready to go to hell with you." Together, they don't quite manage to get rid of Buddha, but everyone else is definitely fair game. Tajima Yagyu perpetrates numerous treacheries, resulting in the proverbial rivers of blood and mountains of corpses.

This late-'70s star-studded extravaganza (also known as *Yagyu Clan Conspiracy*) was **Toei Studio**'s first samurai film in 12 years, and they really went all out. The original trailer for *Shogun's Samurai* claims that it's "a big-boned drama played by big-boned actors." I'm thinking that's a good thing.

Tajima Yagyu is played by samurai screen legend Kinnosuke Nakamura (he changed his name to Yorozuya in the early 1970s). It's a crying shame that more of Nakamura's films aren't available in the West. He was a contract player for Toei, a studio with few titles in circulation outside Japan. He portrayed Ogami Itto in the 1973 television version of **Lone Wolf and Cub**; he played Musashi Miyamoto in the five-part Toei saga, *Zen and Sword;* he was Ryoma Sakamoto in *The Ambitious,* Tange Sazen in ***The Secret of the Urn***, Shingen Takeda in ***Samurai Banners,*** and on and on. He appeared in scores of features from the '50s through the '80s, but his most prolific period by far was the 1960s. He died in 1997 of pneumonia at the age of 64.

Also starring among the cast of thousands are **Toshiro Mifune** in a small role, and **Sonny Chiba** in a big one. As Tajima Yagyu's son, Jubei, Chiba enlists the help of the Negoro clan of mountain ninjas, unwittingly drawing them into his father's evil machinations. Members of the ninja clan include members of Sonny Chiba's Japan Action Club, a group of highly skilled martial artists assembled and trained by Chiba as literal swords for hire (to movie studios, of course). Look for young JAC stars **Hiroyuki Sanada** and Etsuko Shihomi as Hayate and Man, the dynamic power couple of the Negoro clan.

Also appearing in *Shogun's Samurai* is **Yoshio Harada**, the one-eyed samurai from ***Hunter in the Dark,*** here playing a love-struck flautist and warrior. He'll have more eye trouble in this picture. He'll also wind up skewering his love Okuni (**Reiko Ohara**) with his sword (it's alright, she asked him to). Also on tap is **Isuzu Yamada**, a Japanese screen legend whom you'll recall as Lady Washizu, the Lady Macbeth–like character in ***Throne of Blood***. Keep an eye out for **Mikio Narita** as the fey yet deadly Imperial courtier. And let us not forget the mighty **Tetsuro Tamba** as Genshinsai Ogasawara, a swordmaster with skills comparable to Tajima Yagyu, who sides with Tadanaga and goes after Yagyu personally. He wears a monk's robes and is very cool and menacing.

Shogun's Samurai was director **Kinji Fukasaku**'s first stab at the samurai genre. Previously, Fukasaku had made movies in a variety of genres, including sci-fi, heist, campy pop-art, and yakuza. His Battle Without Honor and Humanity *(Jingi naki tatakai)* series is legendary for its gritty depictions of the brutal yakuza underworld; his *Black Lizard* set new standards for drag queen noir; and his sub-cheesy *Message from Space* was a cash-in on the *Star Wars* craze. Whatever the genre, Fukasaku's films could always be relied on to put asses in seats, making him among the most successful filmmakers in the history of Japanese cinema. His masterpiece, of course, is *Battle Royale,* the millennial school kid massacre movie starring **Beat Takeshi** and a brilliant ensemble of teenaged actors (like Chiaki Kuriyama aka Go Go Yubari in *Kill Bill Vol. 1*). For more on Fukasaku, see Patrick Macias's excellent reference, *Tokyoscope: The Japanese Cult Film Companion.*

In *Shogun's Samurai,* Fukasaku does not disappoint, although the film has something of a TV movie feel. This is due in part to the music, which sounds very much like what

Ask Takuan, the Know-It-All Priest

Q: It seems the Yagyu Clan appears often in samurai films. Can you tell me more about them?

A: From the dawn of the Tokugawa Shogunate, the Yagyu and Tokugawa clans were allied at the highest levels. The Yagyu provided the ruling clan with fencing prowess, political strategy and espionage services. The most famous member of the Yagyu Clan was Tajima no Kami Munenori Yagyu (1571–1646), official sword instructor to the first three Tokugawa shoguns, Ieyasu, Hidetada, and Iemitsu. His close affiliation with these rulers brought the Yagyu immense wealth and influence, and he eventually received the title of Ometsuke (Inspector General). His father, Muneyoshi Yagyu (1527–1606), had previously developed the Shinkage-ryu sword style practiced by the clan. His son, Jubei Mitsuyoshi Yagyu (1607–1650), was a colorful character and folk icon known for his eye patch and ferocious sword-fighting abilities.

you'd get in a late-'70s American movie-of-the-week-type drama. Camera movement and editing are also more suited to television than cinema, and so it's no surprise that the movie wound up serving as a pilot for what became a Japanese TV show of the same name, with much of the same cast, including Sonny Chiba. Several characters that were killed or took their own lives in the film were resurrected for the television series, which ran for 39 episodes.

It should be mentioned that there are some pretty brutal scenes that might not sit well with more sensitive viewers— massacres, beheadings, dismemberments, that sort of thing. At times, elements of cheese intersect with the violence. For example, a scene with Sonny Chiba pulling a spear out of a dead kid and cradling her in his arms as he cries. Later he gets mad and chops off someone's head (I won't say who) and throws it in his father's lap. Chiba's acting is fine, but that head is the WORST FAKE HEAD EVER. Nevertheless, you're so engrossed in the story at this point, it doesn't really matter. The cheese factor makes the whole affair a little surreal, but never really ruins the film.

I've often said, "Everything you need to know about politics, you can learn from samurai films," and this one is a perfect example. Just change the names and dates, replace Japan with the country of your choice, and voila! You're looking at the story behind the headlines. Except for maybe the severed head. . . . or maybe not.

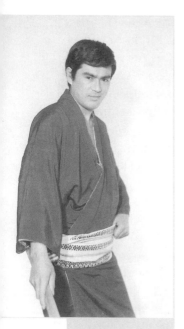

Young Chiba with bokuto

Hunter in the Dark

Yami no karyudo

Shochiku, 1979

DIRECTOR: Hideo Gosha

CAST: Tatsuya Nakadai, Yoshio Harada, Sonny Chiba, Ayumi Ishida, Keiko Kishi, Ai Kanzaki, Kayo Matsuo, Tetsuro

Hunter in the Dark is an absorbing, devastating work of cinema and one of director **Hideo Gosha**'s finest moments. While technically a yakuza film, it is in fact one part puzzle picture, one part Shakespearean tragedy, and two parts film noir, perhaps the most atmospheric film of Gosha's oeuvre. Stalking through the dark Edo underworld like the wolves to which the title refers, the story concerns an evil samurai and a noble underworld boss, a jilted geisha with a vendetta, an amnesiac

Tamba, Mikio Narita

AVAILABILITY: Tough

COMMENT: Out of print VHS from World Artists Home Video features good transfer and vivid colors—worth searching for. **Warning**: Do **not** buy the DVD from Hong Kong distributor Platinum Classics unless you're desperate—the transfer is terrible (dark and muddy)

ronin whose affliction causes him to destroy everything he holds dear, plots, treachery, and knife-throwing lady assassins. All this and **Shinichi "Sonny" Chiba** too!

Set in Edo in 1784, *Hunter in the Dark* unfolds against a political backdrop of total government corruption, during the last high years of the **Tokugawa Shogunate**. Profiteering officials, bribable cops, the yakuza, everyone is making pots of money. However, no one lives happily ever after in this dark fable—in fact, no one lives! I tell a lie, one character survives, but I won't say who. In any case, the plot is so labyrinthine, the characters interwoven to such a Dickensian degree that to try to synopsize the film would take longer than to just watch it, so instead let's meet the main characters:

KIYOEMON GOMYO **(Tatsuya Nakadai)**: Super-cool Yakuza boss. Cat-like, sleek, and smooth, Gomyo's no hothead and nobody's fool, choosing rather to hide and watch, play the angles, and strike only when the moment is right. This cerebral quality leads some to think him weak and vulnerable. They seldom think so for long. . . .

YATARO TANIGAWA **(Yoshio Harada)**: A one-eyed ronin with no memory. He is the lost shell of a "makoto no bushi," a true samurai. Brave, resourceful, yet haunted, he works now as a yojimbo/assassin for Gomyo. Will he recover his memory and learn his true identity? If so, will such knowledge lift his curse, or destroy him?

ORIWA (Ayumi Ishida): Gomyo's girlfriend. The two met after Oriwa, attempting suicide, jumped in the river, only to be saved by the boss (who immediately fell for her). She loves Gomyo and makes snow geese patterns for his revolving lantern shop. As they make love, the birds glide round and round the purple walls of Gomyo's love den.

OMON (Keiko Kishi): The madam of the Kamesen Teahouse and Gomyo's old flame. She still carries a torch for him, but he is obsessed with Oriwa. A scorned woman, she plots with a new lover to see Gomyo dispatched. Their plan involves Tanigawa. They're in for a surprise.

OREN **(Kayo Matsuo)**: Beautiful in a psychotic, terrifying way, she was the knife-wielding yojimbo of Gomyo's rival boss before things got ugly at their sit-down and she found herself

Hunter in the Dark:
*Gomyo & gang
question Omon*

out of a job. She vows revenge on Gomyo and Tanigawa. A dangerous adversary, she'll stop at nothing to get her man.

OSAKI (Ai Kanzaki): Tanigawa's girlfriend. Hired by Gomyo's rival boss, Osaki was supposed to spy on Tanigawa and Gomyo. The only problem is she's fallen in love with Tanigawa and is now on the deadly Oren's radar. . . .

SAMON SHIMOGUNI (**Sonny Chiba**): A nasty piece of work, this former chamberlain of the Kitamae clan betrayed his own clansmen and is out to seize control of Ezo (known today as Hokkaido), the Kitamae fief. Ezo is full of wild horses, fish, and snow geese. . . .

OKITSUGU TANUMA (**Tetsuro Tamba**): The real-life corrupt shogunate prime minister, so rich that comic songs were written about his supremacy over the shogun himself. Shimoguni works for him, the two having colluded to abolish the Kitamae clan. He will reward Shimoguni with the governorship of Ezo, if the latter does his evil bidding.

GOSUN (**Mikio Narita**): One of Gomyo's men, he's tasked

Hunter in the Dark:
*Oriwa, Gomyo &
Tanigawa stress out*

with executing Omon for her treachery. This isn't as easy as he thinks. Down at a local swamp, he plans to drown the Machiavellian madam, but it's Gosun that winds up choking on his assignment.

KASUKE (Makoto Fujita): A bum in a boat, Kasuke observes the deadly doings in the swamp and winds up taking Omon in. He learns of Tanigawa from Omon and remembers witnessing a very similar guy losing an eye during an assassination. He figures this information is worth 100 ryo . . . to Shimoguni!

The plot twists and turns and intertwines around itself, gradually pulling all of the characters together in an ever-tightening spiral of existential dread. Visually, the atmosphere is infused with a noirish chiaroscuro, playing out in saturated colors that create a heightened sense of reality. The sound effects are fairly elaborate, enhancing the many show-stopping duels, knife fights, samurai massacres, and general carnage with an impressive range of ripping, slicing, and crunching

*Gomyo is attacked
by soy beans and
a swordsman in
Hunter in the Dark*

noises. The violence is staged with a realism that is particular
to Gosha: when someone is stabbed, you feel it. And when
they turn the blade (and they do), you feel that too. People
don't just drop when they're sliced or skewered, they scream!
It's a harrowing proposition, and something that makes any
Gosha film a memorable experience.

Adding to the delicious ambience of *Hunter in the Dark*
is the Mancini-esque score by **Akira Kurosawa**'s house composer **Masaru Sato**. Although the film was released in 1979,
the music features a harpsichord and arrangements that sound
like a throwback to the mid-'60s. This is in no way a bad thing;
rather, the halcyon days of the '60s samurai film are constantly evoked by the score, blending with the more modern visual
style to fine effect.

And the performances! Everyone is great in this film. Yoshio Harada is at his tortured, brooding best. He fights like
a demon, receiving near-mortal stab wounds throughout the

picture. At one point, as he fights a dozen attackers in a burning temple with his arm in a sling (stab wound) and with only one good eye, he strongly resembles Tange Sazen (see **The Secret of the Urn**). Tatsuya Nakadai is stately and elegant as always, and while morally ambiguous at best, he nevertheless wins us over from the very start. Special kudos to Kayo Masuo as the freaky, feral knife queen Oren. She chews up the scenery like there's no tomorrow, and even shows her sexy side in a performance to rival that of Sayaka in **Lone Wolf and Cub: Baby Cart at the River Styx**. And as for Sonny Chiba, he turns in one of the finest performances of his career: balanced, focused, and ferocious. Chiba is pure class and pure evil!

Hunter in the Dark has it all. Chambara action, suspense, a film noir–style plot, compelling characters including a host of strong female roles, arthouse sophistication, and lots of blood and flying limbs. It's a little hard to find, but well worth the quest for the discerning samurai aficionado.

10

The '80s and Beyond

Kagemusha

Kagemusha

1980, Toho/20th Century Fox

DIRECTOR: Akira Kurosawa

CAST: Tatsuya Nakadai, Tsutomu Yamazaki, Daisuke Ryu

AVAILABILITY: Easy

COMMENT: VHS from Twentieth Century Fox; DVD from Criterion Collection

When **Akira Kurosawa** was a boy, his father would often take the family to see the silent films of the day. These early experiences shaped young Akira's sensibilities, and the importance of the pure image never left him; it is central to his films, which often feature long passages containing no dialogue. In 1949's *Stray Dog,* he lets an entire reel go by in silence, judging that dialogue would add nothing to the dramatic information. In his later films, while never abandoning dialogue, he turned more and more to a kind of total *pictorialism,* the image taking precedence over other filmic content. *Kagemusha* is one such film.

Based on some 250 paintings and drawings by the director (produced during the late '70s when he couldn't get funding for his movies), the film, a medieval war epic, is a vital, eye-poppingly colorful tableau of pure art. Samurai armies march out of the rising sun, casting long, expressionistic shadows against the dust kicked up by a hundred horses. Color-coordinated banners and heraldry dominate the landscape, encoding it with a thousand fluttering kanji. Dazzling sets, intricate costumes, mounted processions full of grandeur and pageantry, and everywhere such color, at times almost psychedelic in its scope and intensity.

1958 Toho

Akira Kurosawa shares a joke with Kagemusha producers Audie Bock, Francis Ford Coppola, and George Lucas

Kagemusha is an epic. It also has no plot, no cohesion, nor much character development. On first seeing the picture, I felt these were major drawbacks. But upon repeated viewings, I decided, "Who cares?" It's beautiful. It's beautiful in the way that Kubrick's *Barry Lyndon* is beautiful (although *Kagemusha*'s pacing is better). You can just stare at it and get lost in it. That's the best way to experience *Kagemusha*.

The action takes place during 1573 to 1575, toward the end of the **Sengoku period**, a time of nonstop warfare that characterized the whole of the sixteenth century. The country is dominated by three warlords, all vying for the job of ruler of Japan. These are Nobunaga Oda, **Ieyasu Tokugawa**, and **Shingen Takeda**. Takeda (**Tatsuya Nakadai**), like many powerful daimyo of his day, employs a kagemusha (double) to throw off his enemies and give him an added measure of security in dangerous situations. Until now his brother Nobukado (Tsutomu Yamazaki) has had the job, looking much like him. But as the story begins, Nobukado has brought a new kagemusha to Shingen, one whose resemblance to the lord is almost uncanny.

The thief is overwhelmed by it all in Kagemusha

Kagemusha: Horse-mounted Takeda samurai

The double is a petty thief whom Nobukado found in the prison yards awaiting crucifixion, and Shingen takes an immediate liking to this cantankerous character. The double (he has no name) is given a crash course in daimyo impersonation, and kept on tap until needed. This happens sooner rather than later, as Shingen Takeda is hit by a sniper's bullet and mortally wounded. Next thing you know, our cranky crook is doing his show for real, full-time. Can he pull it off? The fate of the Takeda clan depends on it.

The dual role of Shingen Takeda and his kagemusha was originally written for none other than Zatoichi himself, **Shintaro Katsu**. It was hoped that he would bring a comic lightness to the film and, as the double, portray a variant on the mangy ronin character from **Yojimbo**. However, on the first day of shooting, Katsu, a big star with an ego and entourage to match, brought along his own video crew to document his performance. Kurosawa, control freak extraordinaire, had no intention of allowing another film crew on his set and told Katsu to forget it in no uncertain terms. Katsu stormed off the set; he was used to telling the director what to do, not vice versa. He'd never worked for "The Emperor" before. He awaited Kurosawa's apology, but it never came. By day's end, Katsu was fired and Tatsuya Nakadai called in.

As the lord Takeda, Nakadai is stately and imperious, but as the double, he seems a little at a loss. The performance is clumsy and confused, as if he simply doesn't know how to act it. I attribute this to the direction; Nakadai is a film veteran, having appeared in over 100 features, and a magnificent talent at that. If he's lost, it's because Kurosawa was too busy with his moving painting to bother much with the actors in it. Pauline Kael, in reviewing *Kagemusha* for *The New Yorker,* noted that Kurosawa was "in love with the aesthetics of warfare—he's a schoolboy setting up armies of perfect little soldiers and smiling at the patterns he has devised." Perversely, he cast many amateurs in pivotal roles as well. Ieyasu Tokugawa is played by a Tokyo businessman who had never acted before. Here we see the pattern of pictorialism over people.

Nevertheless, *Kagemusha* is a stunning visual experience depicting the glory days of the samurai, a time when the loyal warrior was in his element, in full armor, fighting and dying magnificently for his lord in open combat. Contrast this image with all those downtrodden, debased ronin of the **Tokugawa period**, a time of enforced peace—no wonder Kurosawa preferred the Sengoku period: the horses, the pitched battles, the armor! Where suits of samurai armor are just empty symbols or reminders of former glories in *Harakiri* and *Tenchu!*, here they are worn proudly by endless columns of brave bushi going forth to die glorious deaths and be piled in large, colorful heaps. Perhaps in *Kagemusha* we see the samurai as he saw himself: majestic, powerful, and gloriously elevated from the base realities of blood and battlefield.

Samurai Reincarnation

Makai tensho

1981, Toei

DIRECTOR: Kinji Fukasaku

CAST: Shinichi "Sonny" Chiba, Kenji Sawada, Akiko Kana, Ken Ogata, Hiroyuki Sanada, Ai Kanzaki, Naoko Kubo, Noboru Matsuhashi, Hideo Murota, Mikio Narita, Tetsuro Tamba, Tomisaburo Wakayama

AVAILABILITY: Easy

COMMENT: DVD from Tokyo Shock. **Note:** Check out the in-depth interview with Sonny Chiba included on the disk. Great stuff!

Welcome devils of hell! Come into my body and give me your power! I, Shiro Amakusa, shall burn this country with the fire of anguish and hatred! I shall make this hellish scene appear again on the earth before the shogun who massacred us!

Back in 1637 in Shimabara, Kyushu (southern Japan), teenage Christian prophet Shiro Tokisada Amakusa led his fellow worshipers in revolt against the oppressive Tokugawa **Bakufu**. Unfortunately, it was Amakusa's 37,000 Christians against 120,000 shogunate soldiers. The result was perhaps the most brutal massacre in Japan's history. In addition to burnings, boilings, crucifixions, and the like, roughly one-third of the peasants were beheaded, including Amakusa. The central premise of *Samurai Reincarnation* is what would happen if Amakusa had come back to life, renounced his Christian God, and become a wrathful demon, enlisting the great warriors of the day in his quest for revenge against the shogun. The result? A rip-roaring supernatural romp featuring legendary samurai film stars kicking ass as legendary samurai. In addition to the carnage of the Shimabara Rebellion, we see satanic rituals, cannibalism, sexually depraved ghosts, magic swords, and not one but two duels between the great **Sonny Chiba** and the inimitable **Tomisaburo Wakayama**.

Since *Samurai Reincarnation* is a fairly straightforward revenge story, let's look at a breakdown of the *dramatis personae:*

Shiro Amakusa (Kenji Sawada): We first see Amakusa's severed head on a plank at Shimabara as the soldiers enjoy their triumph with a little **Noh** performance. Suddenly an unnatural lightning strikes, causing Amakusa's head to go flying around the stage. Soon the Noh dancer is possessed by the young man's spirit, and off he sets to assemble his lethal ghost squad.

Lady Gracia Hosokawa (Akiko Kana): In life she had been a devout Christian convert, but she suffered greatly at the hands of her unfaithful husband. Finally, in 1600, finding herself in a burning castle on the wrong side in the Battle of Sekigahara, she was forced to meet an untimely death, leaving her spirit embittered and vengeful. Amakusa raises her spirit and provides a beautiful young girl for it to inhabit. Soon she will become the shogun's new concubine. . . .

Unstoppable action man Sonny Chiba

Musashi Miyamoto (Ken Ogata): "I am 62 years old," the great swordsman tells us. "My life's work completed, now I am going to die." However, there is one niggling desire that he has never fulfilled: a duel with Tajima Yagyu, the shogun's sword instructor. Amakusa appears just in time to convince Musashi that becoming a yokai (ghost) is the best way to achieve his ambition to fight Yagyu. Musashi joins Amakusa's demonic dream team.

Jubei Yagyu (Sonny Chiba): Chiba reprises his roll as the wild, one-eyed, pompom-pony-tailed master swordsman from **Shogun's Samurai** (and its resultant Japanese TV series). Here he becomes an unwitting ghost-buster when he learns that Musashi Miyamoto, whom he'd been seeking out for some sword fighting lessons, has been literally spirited away, as has Jubei's father and one of his best friends. He soon gets hold of a weapon that is as effective on ghosts as it is on humans and sets about dispatching the wicked specters to the fires of hell.

INSHUN HOZOIN (Hideo Murota): Another legend of Japanese martial arts, this monk is a master of the Hozoin lance, a spear with a trident-shaped triple blade on the end that he fantasizes using to skewer passing women. Yes, this monk is tortured by a sadistic sexual desire so strong that when Lady Hosokawa appears, wearing a Hannya mask and taunting him with her bare breasts, he goes berserk and charges her again and again to no avail. Finally he stabs himself to end his torment, but his desire knows no bounds. He is promised all the women he can eat (literally) if he joins Amakusa's crusade. He's in.

KIRIMARU IGA **(Hiroyuki Sanada)**: You'll remember this character (and the handsome young actor who plays him) from *Shogun's Samurai,* although this time out he's got a different name. He's a hotshot mountain ninja whose Iga clan is attacked and massacred by the rival Koga clan. During the fighting, Kirimaru is mortally wounded by Lady Koga (whose breasts later provide a tasty snack for hungry/horny ghost Hozoin). Against his better judgment, he becomes a ghost for Amakusa (who appears to fancy him) in order to get revenge on the Koga clan.

IZUMORI MATSUDAIRA **(Mikio Narita)**: He's the leader of the troops that vanquished the folks at Shimabara. He's not happy about this new girl "Otama" with whom the shogun (Noboru Matsuhashi) has become smitten and taken as his concubine (she's possessed by Lady Hosokawa). He's also at the top of Amakusa's shit list; he's eventually murdered by the latter in an original and rather fitting manner. (Appearing in a brief scene with Narita is **Naoko Kubo**, the beautiful actress who appeared in *Sleepy Eyes of Death: Sword of Seduction* as the Virgin Shima, a faux-Christian saint. Perhaps this had something to do with her casting here.)

TAJIMA YAGYU (Tomisaburo Wakayama): Official sword instructor to the first three Tokugawa shoguns, master strategist, and Jubei's dad, Lord Yagyu has decided that Otama is nothing but trouble and decides to feign madness, kill her, then commit seppuku. Before he can do this, however, he happens upon Hozoin munching on another female victim. They fight, and Yagyu miraculously kills the ghost with a neatly executed vertical head slice. Too bad he receives a fatal blow during the duel. About to die, Yagyu realizes that what he really wants more than anything is to have a sword fight with Jubei. Amakusa, drawn by this desire, makes him a ghost, thus rounding out his ghoulish group.

MURAMASA **(Tetsuro Tamba):** A master swordsmith who makes "wicked swords," such as the one that killed Hozoin. Jubei, realizing that Muramasa is capable of making a sword that can kill a ghost, contracts one for himself. He helps Muramasa forge the mighty blade, and once it's ready, he uses it against the now-demonic Musashi Miyamoto. Muramasa's daughter (Ai Kanzaki) happens to be the niece and spitting image of Otsu, Musashi's one great love, and to add a little extra psychological pressure, Jubei has her play the flute while the two swordsmen duel on the beach (à la *Samurai 3: Duel on Ganryu Island*).

Samurai Reincarnation is great fun, but it's not without its flaws. For one thing, the shogun in the picture is identified as Ietsuna, the fourth Tokugawa shogun. However, this man did not ascend to power until 1651, five years after the death of Tajima Yagyu and over a decade after the Shimabara Rebellion; *Shogun's Samurai,* which this film echoes in several places, is more accurate in its chronology. Also there is a glaring continuity error in Mikio Narita's character, Izumori Matsudaira: at the beginning of the film we see him and his men killed by the otherworldly lightning blast that re-animates Amakusa, but later we find him alive and well. Huh?

These problems aside, *Samurai Reincarnation* is still pure supernatural samurai entertainment from the masterful hand of **Kinji Fukasaku**, a director who knew how to establish compelling characters and keep things exciting. The film was produced by Haruki Kadokawa, heir to the Kadokawa publishing empire who would go on to direct *Heaven and Earth* a decade later. Fans of cult director Takashi Miike might recognize Kenji Sawada here as a young version of the father/innkeeper in Miike's *Happiness of the Katakuris* (the ubiquitous Tetsuro Tamba also appears as the grandpa). And then of course there is a certain 52-year-old man named Tomisaburo Wakayama who hasn't lost his chops; he's thinner here and if anything he's even more dynamic than he was in his **Lone Wolf and Cub** days. He leaps, he spins, he slices and dices, he is a wonder. Together with Sonny Chiba, Wakayama elevates *Samurai Reincarnation* from campy horror kicks to sublime samurai satisfaction.

Heaven and Earth

Ten to chi to

1990, Haruki Kadokawa Films

DIRECTOR: Haruki Kadokawa

CAST: Takaaki Enoki, Masahiko Tsugawa, Tsunehiko Watase, Atsuko Asano

AVAILABILITY: Tricky

COMMENT: VHS from Universal is out of print; however, at the time of this writing half a dozen used copies were available on Amazon.com.

First came **Kagemusha**, then *Heaven and Earth*. You can't really talk about this film without comparing and contrasting it with **Akira Kurosawa**'s 1980 epic, because they're just too similar. One thing's for sure, between the two, there are enough samurai in bright red armor to last a lifetime.

The reason for all the red samurai is that the armies of sixteenth-century warlord **Shingen Takeda** figure prominently in both films, and their armor was, you guessed it, red (at least in these films). While Kurosawa opted for lots of other colors too, creating a kind of rainbow warrior collage, *Heaven and Earth* director Haruki Kadokawa was doing tighter color combos. The two major battles of the film are red vs. black, the latter being the chosen look of warlord Kagetora Nagao, the protagonist of the piece.

Kagetora (later known as Kenshin Uesugi and played by Takaaki Enoki) is introduced as a brilliant yet idealistic young daimyo who prays to the fierce, multi-headed Bishamonten, Japanese God of War, but still can't bring himself to kill helpless women and children—yet. He has, however, battled and killed his brother Harukage for control of his home province of Echigo. Only problem now is, Shingen Takeda (Masahiko Tsugawa) is out to take all of Japan for himself and Echigo is the next han on his list. The film revolves around the struggle between these two historical personalities, giving ample time to huge, epic battles with hundreds of horsemen and thousands of infantry. One sequence features 800 horses, a world record.

Like *Kagemusha,* this is a big, sprawling, breathtaking-in-its-scope film event. Unlike *Kagemusha,* which was filmed

Kagetora and Takeda take it personal and make it personal in Heaven and Earth

in Japan, *Heaven and Earth's* location shoot took the massive cast and crew all the way to Goodstoney Indian Reservation on the Morley Flats of Alberta, Canada. Shooting in Canada allowed the production to purchase some 500 horses locally, a shrewd financial move, as hiring trained horses would have cost much more. The horses were put through a rigorous four-month training period, and the final outcome is nothing less than stunning: wave upon wave of mounted samurai riding in geometric formations, red and black riders flowing into each other, mixing like oil paints running together. While *Heaven and Earth* is no *Kagemusha,* it's as close as anyone is likely to come.

When not staging gargantuan battle sequences, Haruki Kadokawa presents the audience with a pastoral beauty and an awareness of nature and seasonal change that's just as striking. The spiritual resonance of nature, the essence of the Japanese aesthetic, is everywhere here. No scene or sequence is unaccompanied by its attendant nature cues, be it Kagetora

Heaven and Earth

meeting his love interest Nami (Atsuko Asano) amid a flurry of falling cherry blossoms, or the young lord, sick at heart from all the killing, fleeing his han through massive white snowdrifts on a silvery, sylvan footpath. Everywhere there's a layer of natural symbolism underpinning the proceedings.

The Zen serenity, the natural splendor, the poise and grace of these passages are all due in large part to Haruki Kadokawa's background as a Shinto priest. Reverence for the mysticism of nature is central to Shinto, and the director communicates this, albeit with a New Agey score. It's worth noting that Kadokawa has managed to stay in touch with his spiritual side, as he is probably the richest Shinto priest in Japan. His father was the owner of Kadokawa Shoten, one of the largest publishers in Japan. When Haruki inherited the business, he formed Kadokawa Eiga, a division for making films. Following a pot bust, he had to step down as president of Kadokawa Shoten, but he still continues to make movies, and more power to him!

One more aspect of the story should be noted. As hinted earlier, Lord Kagetora eventually grows cruel, a prerequisite for a warlord. We know the metamorphosis has taken place when he grows a mustache, a perennial sign of the bad guy in many Japanese films (spot the mustachioed villain in Akira Kurosawa's *Sanshiro Sugata* and *Men Who Tread on the Tiger's Tail* or **Hideo Gosha**'s *The Wolves,* to name a few). "Sometimes one must be cruel and terrify the people," Kagetora tells a general (does he mean with his bad mustache?). Later he casually shoots Takeda's wife right off her horse. Takeda's response? "Exellent!" As for Kagetora's love life, the most Nami ever does for him is play her flute. It's not her fault, she really digs him, but he's taken a vow of celibacy for Bishamonten. (In **Samurai Banners**, he does it for Buddha.)

Weaknesses of *Heaven and Earth* include: in the U.S. release, a voice-over narration by old-time character actor Stuart Whitman, who sounds like a TV commercial every time he speaks; the aforementioned New Age score, particularly inappropriate during the mounted sword fight between Kagetora and Takeda; and, finally, the general bloodlessness of the battles. *Kagemusha,* itself a war fantasy, was a bit more honest in regards to the carnage of war. Here, it's just tin soldiers, an approach that tends to rob much of the impact from what is essentially a story about war. That said though, it's still a fine work, and a must-see for anyone interested in full-scale recreations of battles of the **Sengoku period**.

Roningai

Roningai

1990, Shochiku

DIRECTOR: Kazuo Kuroki

CAST: Yoshio Harada, Kanako Higuchi, Shintaro Katsu, Renji Ishibashi, Kunie Tanaka

Vermin like you are making the world filthy.

These are the last words heard by a hapless old prostitute as she faces the business end of a samurai sword. Who is murdering all the whores of the village? Will the besotted ronin at the tavern wake up from their apathetic, sake-induced paralysis and do anything about it?

AVAILABILITY: Easy

COMMENT: DVD format from Hong Kong distributor Platinum Classics. **Beware**: Titles from this distributor are hit or miss at best. However, *Roningai* is alright. Subtitles are sub-par.

Roningai is memorable for a number of reasons, one being that it is **Shintaro Katsu**'s last starring role in a Japanese movie (he had a walk-on the same year in the Hong Kong fantasy *Saga of the Phoenix*). He plays Bull, the bouncer of the local tavern/brothel. If you didn't know he was in *Roningai,* it would likely take you a while to realize that this hulking, rotund brute was our own Katsu-shin—Wow! He's huge! Noted for his lusty appetites, Katsu is a one-man cautionary tale on the consequences of excess. On the other hand, he's lost none of his charisma and presence; there's just a whole lot more of him to embody it.

There are a number of oldsters making an appearance, like the ubiquitous character actor **Kunie Tanaka** as Magohachiro, a one-time samurai retainer who's reduced to eking out a meager living selling birds. He wants to get a position with his old clan, but the system being what it is, his only chance is to come up with 100 ryo to buy his way back in. His sister desperately wants to help him, and her attempts to secure the huge sum make up one of the intertwining subplots.

Also starring is **Yoshio Harada**, veteran samurai actor in such films as ***Hunter in the Dark, Lady Snowblood: Love Song of Vengeance***, and ***Shogun's Samurai***. Here he's low-life drunkard Gennai Aramaki, a ronin whose talents have dwindled to drinking and screwing—oh, and doing the odd astrological chart for his girlfriend Oshin (Kanako Higuchi), one of the prostitutes at the tavern. God help her, she loves him, and we in the audience are left continually puzzled as to why she hangs on to this loser. But she's got a strong spirit, and her character is much more developed than most women's roles in the samurai genre.

Then there's the ronin Gonbei Tanomo (Renji Ishibashi), the only one we recognize as coming close to the stoic, cynical loner we've come to expect. He's in love with Oshin, creating the classic love triangle and providing an opposite number for the sleazy Gennai. Yet Gonbei too seems inert, alienated beyond simple contempt of the society; like Bull, Magohachiro, and Gennai, he is lost, stultified, cut off from any fragment of his former active self. What we get from all these men is that they have nothing left to live for. Only Magohachiro is still trying to get back what he once had, but his efforts are futile and he is all the more a pathetic figure for it.

What finally winds up galvanizing these men is the string of murders that takes out several prostitutes, and finally the kindly boss who runs the tavern. The murderers eventually walk into the tavern and reveal themselves as a group of shogunal retainers. This is bad news, as it means they're basically untouchable. "Whores are contaminating the world," says their leader. Another chimes in, "Anyone who tries to seduce a man shall be punished by death." Yikes! Time for a career change. Unfortunately, in **Edo-period** Japan, there's no such thing.

There is a scene in *Roningai* that's worth mentioning, as it shows us something we rarely see in samurai films: the happy ronin. Bull stops at a noodle stand for a bite, and the chatty vendor starts telling him, "I used to be a samurai. But a samurai meant something when there were wars. The time of wars ended long ago." Bull is bored by his chatter until he tastes the noodles. They are superior "Osaka noodles" and they're so good that he's literally brought to tears. The noodle vendor continues, "I quit being a samurai, but I'm still fighting. If you like my noodles, I win. If not, you win." He sees Bull's face, and as the big man attempts to pay him, the vendor refuses his money, saying, "You paid with your tears."

There is a veracity, a realism that runs through *Roningai*. One gets the feeling watching the characters interact and go through their daily existence that this is really how life was in the 1830s when the story is set. The rhythm of speech, body movement, the dingy environments, the fight scenes, all have a fresh, non-stagey feel. This is due in part to the director's background in documentary film. Many of the dialogue scenes feel improvised, something unique in this genre. The film was made in 1990, so many of the old conventions have been tossed. Fortunately the film retains the essential elements, however it might deconstruct them, giving us a unique blend of the modern and the traditional.

Taboo

Gohatto

1999, Shochiku

DIRECTOR: Nagisa
Oshima

CAST: Takeshi Kitano,
Ryuhei Matsuda,
Tadanobu Asano,
Masa Tommies,
Yoichi Sai, Tomorowo
Taguchi

AVAILABILITY: Easy

COMMENT: DVD/VHS
from New Yorker
Video

What if the Shinsengumi, the super-macho paramilitary police force in **Bakumatsu**-period Kyoto, was in fact a hotbed of
homosexuality? That's the premise of *Taboo*, a film by world-
renowned director Nagisa Oshima. Oshima is best known for
his 1976 epic of sexual obsession, *In the Realm of the Senses*,
and 20 years later, he's back at it, applying his deft touch to a
story of what happens when desire clouds the mind and stifles
the spirit, leading to jealousy, revenge, and madness. But just
who is the mad one? The desirous, or the object of desire?

The best way to see *Taboo* is on a double bill with **Band
of Assassins**, a traditional, nostalgic portrayal of the "straight"
story of the Shinsengumi. (Or you could try **Daiei**'s 1963 version, *Shinsengumi Chronicles*, starring macho superstars
Raizo Ichikawa and **Tomisaburo Wakayama**.) The contrast is
stark. *Band of Assassins* features **Rentaro Mikuni** and **Toshiro
Mifune** heading up a group of very butch ronin-turned-shogun-
supporters who keep order in Kyoto. In *Taboo*, the principal
leaders are Isami Kondo (Yoichi Sai) and his second-in-com-
mand Toshizo Hijikata (**"Beat" Takeshi Kitano**), both in their
50s, surrounded by a host of young, thin, delicate-looking fellows in their 20s (with a couple of brutes thrown in for good
measure).

Into their midst steps Sozaburo Kano (Ryuhei Matsuda),
the most strikingly androgynous samurai you're ever likely
to see. With delicate, cat-like features and a long ponytail,
the 18-year-old immediately gets more than a few of his fellow samurai hot, including new recruit Hyozo Tashiro (**Tadanobu Asano**, star of Takashi Miike's notorious *Ichi the Killer*).
Tashiro makes a move on Kano their first night, but the latter
appears to sleep right through the former's advances. Henceforth, and for the remainder of the movie, rumors fly about
these two, and various samurai try to determine whether they
are an item or not. Hijikata is convinced of it. Tashiro continually professes his love to Kano, but Kano is the picture
of inscrutability—no one in the film, no one in the audience
for that matter, can tell what's going on in his head. He is an
ice queen, definitely the femme fatale of the picture, driving

Taboo

men mad with desire as he pursues mysterious motives of his own.

Taboo is a mood piece; it doesn't have a plot so much as a series of events or incidents. Shortly after Kano's dojo competition and subsequent admittance (he is of course an expert swordsman), Bureau Chief Kondo assigns him to kaishaku duty to test his mettle. The Shinsengumi was extremely strict (see the *Band of Assassins* review for a list of their rules), and here one of their members has made the poor choice of taking loans in the name of the group. Kano, the model of cold efficiency, beheads the samurai in a tasteful shot taken from directly behind the doomed man, a gush of blood shooting forth. Just before the sword comes down, we hear the thoughts of Hijikata: "He's killed before." Hijikata is the wisest and most astute of the militia members. But even he can't figure out this enigmatic boy-man. Later, another samurai asks Kano, "Why does a rich man's son join the Shinsengumi?" "To have the right to kill," Kano replies. (Perhaps he has somethng in common with Ryunosuke in **Sword of Doom**?) In any case, whether it's his doing or someone else's, corpses soon start piling up.

One thing we do know about Kano, he's definitely having liaisons with fellow samurai Tojiro Yuzawa (Tomorowo Taguchi), although the reason is a mystery—Yuzawa is not particularly attractive, and Kano doesn't seem particularly attracted to him. Is he trying to make Tashiro jealous? But then, we don't know if they're together either. The emergent theme in the piece is ambiguity. What's up with Kano? And by extension, what's up with the rest of the Shinsengumi? Nagisa Oshima seems to be pointing to a larger ambiguity, sexual and otherwise, in Japanese culture. By doing a gay take on one of the most sacred symbols of Japan's martial tradition, he's also saying, "Where does that leave the rest of us?" One thing's for sure, it leaves Yuzawa in a pool of blood. But who . . . ?

Hijikata is portrayed by Beat Takeshi, an amazing talent and a household name in Japan. Over the last few decades this former strip-joint emcee has made successful careers as a stand-up comic, talk show host, game show host, writer, painter, actor, director, recording artist, and all around self-proclaimed "genius." In 1983 he appeared in Oshima's *Merry*

Christmas, Mr. Lawrence alongside another androgynous icon, David Bowie. During the '90s, he directed and starred in a string of dark, nihilistic, exceptional films that defined him as a cinematic force to be reckoned with, including *Boiling Point (3–4x jugatsu), Sonatine,* and *Fireworks (Hana-bi).* In 2000 he turned in an unforgettable performance in **Kinji Fukasaku**'s blood-drenched magnum opus, *Battle Royale,* as the toughest high school teacher in the world, and in 2003 he attempted to step into the sandals of Shintaro Katsu in his own production of ***Zatoichi***.

Beat Takeshi often takes gay roles in movies, fueling speculation about his sexuality. In *Taboo* however, while there is one mention of his "leaning," Takeshi's Hijikata never acts on any sexual impulse. Most likely this is in order to keep him aloof from the action, allowing him to observe. Nothing escapes him. He is our stand-in—we see Kano, and the increasingly bloody events surrounding him, through Hijikata's eyes. Although he sometimes misinterprets situations (providing us with red herrings), he eventually gets it right in the end, so to speak.

Taboo is a unique film, full of beauty and formalist perfection. The execution of the story is achieved with a light touch; there is no heavy-handed didacticism, no authorial statements about homosexuality one way or the other. Homosexuality is treated merely as a reality in the setting, and in the end it moves the plot just like any other sexuality. In this way, Oshima achieves what might seem, at the outset, to be hopelessly unachievable: a good gay samurai film.

Zatoichi

Zatoichi

2003, Shochiku

DIRECTOR: Beat Takeshi Kitano

CAST: Beat Takeshi Kitano, Tadanobu Asano, Yuko Daike, Daigoro Tachibana

Beat Takeshi does **Zatoichi**. You'll notice I didn't say, "Beat Takeshi *is* Zatoichi." That title belongs to **Shintaro Katsu**, a fact of which Mr. Kitano is all too aware. A writer, director, actor, and true original in his own right, Beat Takeshi is not the kind of man to step willingly into another man's sandals—he makes every effort to re-create Zatoichi (with blond hair, bright red cane sword, and his own bewildering array of facial ticks), as

AVAILABILITY: Easy

COMMENT: DVD from Buena Vista Home Video

well as deconstruct the whole paradigm of the series (rather than being the central focus of the film, he takes a back seat, becoming part of an ensemble cast). Gone is the charm, the gregarious good nature, affable chuckle, and nuanced, multi-layered character made iconic by Katsu-shin. Instead, Beat Takeshi opts for doing the same enigmatic, taciturn figure he portrays in the rest of his films. This picture should really be called *Beatoichi,* so altered is the title role. All of this is not to say that *Zatoichi* isn't a fine film, but one's reaction to it will depend to a certain degree on how much of a Zatoichi fan one is.

Zatoichi combines standard genre conventions (warring yakuza gangs, gambling dens, a mystery ronin, sword fights) with unconventional elements (drag queen geisha, fakey digital effects, tap dancing) to create a playfully lyrical hybrid of old and new. The film is shot through with Kitano's trademark Zen calm punctuated by sudden explosions of violence, a technique that, when combined with the period setting, goes a long way to generating the feeling of the "floating world." There is a buoyancy to the proceedings, a lightness of touch that makes the movie feel more like a dream of **Edo-period** Japan than the real thing. At the same time, there are also moments where a bit of realism is interjected to undermine the genre, such as in the opening scene where a young yakuza draws his sword and accidentally slices the shoulder of one of his fellow thugs. It's funny and shocking and reminds us that while this sort of thing probably happened a lot in real life, the tight fight choreography of traditional samurai/yakuza films would never have allowed it.

A key strength of *Zatoichi* is character development, achieved through the extensive use of flashbacks. In fact, we are barely given a glimpse of each main character before we are thrust into his or her respective flashback, creating some chronological confusion at the outset. The ronin Gennosuke Hattori (**Tadanobu Asano**) is shown walking into town with his wife and a moment later we see him somewhere else killing two men with his sword. Huh? Things clear up with the next pair of characters, two geisha, who are likewise seen passing along the street, then suddenly in a room garroting a man with shamisen strings and subsequently stabbing him with a tanto concealed in the neck of the instrument. As the story progresses, additional flashbacks answer questions raised by initial ones, creating a peeling-an-onion-style backstory. It's all very well done, particularly in the case of the two geisha who turn out to be sister and brother.

It seems that the geisha, Okinu (Yuko Daike) and Osei (Daigoro Tachibana), have been on the path of vengeance for the last ten years, out for the blood of the men who murdered their family and household staff. Most recently they caught up with Heihachi, their father's treacherous accountant, who secretly let the killers into the family compound (he was the garroted guy in the first flashback). Little do they know now how close they are to realizing their dream of revenge. . . .

Then there's the intrigue between rival yakuza gangs which is Byzantine to say the least—you've got the Ginzo gang, Ogi gang, Izutsu gang, Funahachi gang, plus some mysterious old fellow known only as the "Kuchinawa boss." This last character seems to be the puppet-master behind the scenes; the mystery of his identity provides an additional narrative thread and a cracking double denouement at film's end. But in the meantime, the ronin Hattori has hired himself out to Ginzo as a yojimbo, much to the consternation of his consumptive wife (for whose sake the noble man takes such objectionable work). Hattori's character is a trope taken straight out of the genre handbook: the mystery ronin who will, whether friend or foe, eventually duel with Zatoichi at some point in the film. To his credit, Tadanobu Asano handles a sword quite well for a twenty-first-century Japanese actor, and conveys the poise and bearing of a makoto no bushi. His sword skills are also on display in **Taboo,** and when you compare these performances with those in contemporary pictures like *Ichi the Killer* and *Shark Skin Man and Peach Hip Girl,* you realize why he's considered one of the most versatile and talented actors working in Japan today.

Which brings us around to Beat Takeshi. For a guy playing the title role of the film, he's barely in it! So involved are the multiple story lines that long passages go by before we finally see him again, appearing at times as an afterthought. When he *is* on screen, he says little or nothing, creating zero personality. His screen time is largely devoted to slicing and dicing, which he does silently as well. One of the most enjoyable aspects of Shintaro Katsu's performances was what he would say in the midst of sword battle, chiding wicked bosses and warning assailants that they were all about to die. We get none of this with Kitano, just the sword mayhem.

And speaking of mayhem, at one point during a gambling session Kitano commits the ultimate genre transgression: he attacks an unarmed man. It is essential to Zatoichi's character that he only fights defensively, never offensively. Even surrounded by swordsmen with weapons drawn, he waits until attacked before going into action and would certainly never dismember a shady dice-thrower (leaving him literally *unarmed*) as Beatoichi does here. However, as mentioned earlier, Kitano is trying to get as far away from Katsu as possible. He's said as much in interviews, frankly admitting that he initially didn't want to make the picture, that he was talked into it and wooed with complete creative control. But he could have made better choices, like giving more of himself to the role, stretching a little, instead of doing the same laconic loner from films like *Sonatine* and *Fireworks.* And the computer-generated blood, limbs, and swords were also a mistake, so sadly lacking in verisimilitude that they look one step away from cell animation. Traditional blood spurts from concealed bags and hoses would have worked just fine without the cheesy CGI augmentation.

Beyond these shortcomings, it must be said that Kitano's *Zatoichi* is a beautifully made film, more than worthy of the acclaim it received on the international film festival circuit. The costumes look great thanks to costume supervisor Kazuko Kurosawa (daughter of director **Akira Kurosawa**). The minimalist score perfectly punctuates the action, and is itself complemented by rhythmic set pieces such as farmers hoeing their fields in syncopated time to the music and various dance numbers. The big mambo tap-dance extravaganza at the end, if confounding, is nevertheless deliriously enjoyable, infusing the whole proceeding with a colorful, "what the fuck, let's party" vibe.

If you've never seen a Zatoichi movie, you're sure to enjoy

this one. Even if you have but aren't an obsessed fan, you'll still more than likely to have a ball. And my advice for genre purists is simply to sit back, relax, let go of your preconceptions, and enjoy the show. Don't think of it so much as a Zatoichi film as a Beatoichi film.

Twilight Samurai

Tasogare Seibei

2003, Shochiku

DIRECTOR: Yoji Yamada

CAST: Hiroyuki Sanada, Rie Miyazawa, Tetsuro Tamba, Ren Osugi, Miki Ito, Erina Hashiguchi

AVAILABILITY: Tricky

COMMENT: Region 3 DVD from Panorama Entertainment

A serious fight, the killing of a man, requires animal ferocity and calm disregard for one's own life. I have neither of those within me now. Perhaps in a month, alone with the beasts in the hills, I could get them back. But tomorrow, I'm afraid, is completely impossible. I ask that you extend the honor of this commission to another man.

This is not the kind of talk we've come to expect from a samurai. However this is no ordinary samurai. This is Seibei Iguchi (**Hiroyuki Sanada**), aka "Tasogare Seibei" ("Twilight Seibei"). His fellow samurai call him Twilight behind his back because he always heads straight home after work (he's a supply clerk for the Unasaka clan), declining all invitations to go drinking with the boys, and with good reason: he's broke. His wife died recently, and the funeral just about ruined him. He's supporting two daughters and a senile mom and is in debt up to his eyeballs. The poor guy never stops working: tilling the soil, chopping wood, staying up late making little insect baskets for a few extra coins on the side. So preoccupied is Seibei with trying to keep his family afloat, he's become unkempt and grimy; his kimono is dirty and torn, and he smells bad. He's even upbraided by the lord of the clan: "Clan retainers must serve as examples to the common folk. Keep yourself clean." This admonishment brings scorn and derision down on Seibei. The poor guy just can't get a break.

But Seibei isn't as miserable as you might think. His haughty and obnoxious uncle Tozaemon (the immortal **Tetsu-**

ro Tamba) comes by to sell him on the idea of remarrying a homely local woman ("You need a healthy wife with big haunches to bear children"). Seibei politely declines, explaining, "Watching my daughters as they grow day by day is . . . how shall I put it? It's like watching crops ripen or flowers grow in a field. I enjoy it very much. I'm not sure if the lady of whom you speak would understand that." There is someone special, though, Seibei's childhood sweetheart Tomoe (Rie Miyazawa), recently divorced from her alcoholic and abusive husband Toyotaro Kodo (Ren Osugi). Will they get together?

At this point you're probably thinking, "That's all very well and good, but how is this Seibei with a sword?" And while he'd never admit it himself, he's superb. He makes quick work of Toyotaro Kodo with nothing more than a hastily made bokuto and is eventually called upon to dispatch a renegade retainer. Although he protests (the quote at the beginning of this review), he is after all makoto no bushi and eventually accepts the assignment.

But *Twilight Samurai* isn't really about swords. It's about love, family, and the realities of life as a petty samurai in a rural han during the **Bakumatsu period**. The film employs gorgeous vistas, natural lighting, fine performances, and striking cinematography, imparting an earthy authenticity to every frame. Traditional tropes and genre conventions are largely jettisoned in the service of genuineness. As Hiroyuki Sanada told *Giant Robot Magazine* (Issue 33, Fall 2004), "*Twilight Samurai* is special because it changed the history of samurai films. For a long time, Japanese samurai films were so stylized that they were not real. This time, we tried to show more authentic human drama in the samurai period." A great success at home, the film won 12 Japanese Academy Awards.

Twilight Samurai owes much to the subtle, lived-in performance of Hiroyuki Sanada. An actor from the age of 5, Sanada first gained fame in **Sonny Chiba**'s Japan Action Club as a martial arts superstar, appearing in ninja/samurai films like ***Shogun's Samurai*** and ***Samurai Reincarnation*** during the '70s and '80s. Dissatisfied with running, jumping, and fighting, however, Sanada turned his back on action films at the age of 25 to seek a serious acting career. In addition to his prolific film work, the intervening years saw him taking on live theater, appearing in a Royal Shakespeare Theater production of *King Lear* (as Lear's fool), as well as a stint in the musical comedy *Little Shop of Horrors.* More recently he's gained fame for star turns in the horror megahit *Ringu* (1998) and the surprisingly good Tom Cruise vehicle *The Last Samurai* (2003).

Also on tap is lovely Rie Miyazawa as Seibei's love interest Tomoe. Born in 1973 to a Japanese mother and Dutch father, Miyazawa started appearing in commercials in grade school. She developed a career as model and "campaign girl," her perky charm used to promote all manner of products from candy bars to phone cards. In 1991 Miyazawa ascended to national prominence with the publication of *Santa Fe,* a book featuring nude photos of the 18-year-old, transforming her literally overnight from pretty teen spokesmodel to notorious sex kitten. She went on to a film career and troubled personal life (anorexia, suicide attempts, failed public relationships), but proved a survivor and compelling national figure. Her award-winning performance in *Twilight Samurai* is proof that Rie Miyazawa is much more than just a pretty face.

Ren Osugi appears in a small role as the drunken lout/abusive husband Toyotaro Kodo. Fans of directors Takashi Miike and Beat Takeshi will recognize Osugi, a frequent face in the pictures of these fine filmmakers, as well as in J-horror classics like *Don't Look Up* (1996), *Cure* (1997), and *Uzumaki* (2000). At the age of 52, Osugi shows no signs of slowing down, having appeared in over a dozen films in the year 2000 alone!

Twilight Samurai is a human story, eschewing the superhuman swordsman for a gentle father, farmer, and family man. Even the one sword battle of the film is filled with humanity, a struggle between two men who learn in the course of their conflict that they have a lot in common, pitted against each other as they are by the samurai system. Their fight is stark, harrowing, right down to the sound of blood dripping on the tatami (listen for it).

Twilight Samurai opens a new chapter in the long and storied history of the samurai film, taking the genre proudly into the twenty-first century. When will it end? Let's hope it never does.

Part III
Appendix

Glossary and Cross-Index

Abayo!
"Good-bye," "So long."

Ah-so
"I see."

Adventures of Zatoichi
See pages 103–105.

Amachi, Shigeru
Sohji Tada in *Destiny's Son*
Hirate in *The Tale of Zatoichi*

Anma
Masseur.

Aratama, Michiyo
Wife in *Kwaidan (The Black Hair)*
Okiku/Kikuhime in *Samurai Assassin*
Hama in *Sword of Doom*

Asano, Tadanobu
Hyozo Tashiro in *Taboo*
Gennosuke Hattori in *Zatoichi*

Asaoka, Yukiji
Omino in *The Razor: Sword of Justice*
Miss Tomoe in *Zatoichi Challenged*

Baka
"Fool!" Variant: "Bakayaro!" ("Idiots!") Depending on tone and emphasis, baka can mean something far more insulting than merely "fool." It is a common epithet, heard frequently in samurai films.

Bakufu
Military government. See page 18.

Bakuto Gambler. See sidebar on page 87.

Bakumatsu Period of dissolution of the Tokugawa Shogunate, roughly 1854–1868. See page 18.

Band of Assassins See pages 148–151.

Banri, Masayo Miss Tadokoro in *Destiny's Son*
Tane in *The Tale of Zatoichi*
Tane in *The Tale of Zatoichi Continues*

Biwa Japanese lute. The sounding box is teardrop-shaped. See page 108.

Biwa hoshi Storyteller who sings his tales while playing the biwa. See page 108.

Bohachimono Sex slavers. See page 158

Bo-jutsu Okinawa-based martial art employing a long stick, the 6-foot Bo staff.

Bokuto Wooden samurai sword. See page 63.

Bonsai Horticultural practice involving the miniaturization of trees. See page 19.

Buri-buri Torture technique: the victim is hung upside-down, dunked in water, then spun and beaten with sticks.

Bushi Warrior.

Bushido The Way of the Warrior. See page 58.

Chambara Sword film (also chanbara).

Chamberlain Second in command to the daimyo. See sidebar on page 83.

Chikusho

"Damn it!" (literally: bestial).

Chiaki, Minoru

Tahei in *The Hidden Fortress*
Priest in *Rashomon*
Boatman in *Samurai 3: Duel on Ganryu Island*
Heihachi in *Seven Samurai*
Yoshiaki Miki in *Throne of Blood*

**Chiba, Sonny
(Shinichi)**

Samon Shimoguni in *Hunter in the Dark*
Jubei Yagyu in *Samurai Reincarnation*
Jubei Yagyu in *Shogun's Samurai*

Chushingura

See pages 93–96.

Dai

Great, giant.

Daiei Studios

See page 28.

Daikan

Regional shogunate official charged with collecting taxes, overseeing public works, and other administrative duties in the han. Often translated as "intendant" in subtitles. See sidebar on page 83.

Daikon

Cylindrical, white Japanese radish.

Daimajin

Great Devil.

Daimajin

See pages 120–122.

Daimyo

Feudal lord. See page 13.

Daisho

Practice of wearing two swords, the large (dai) katana and the small (sho) wakizashi. According to law, only samurai were allowed to wear two swords. See page 14.

Daito

Long sword, 2½ feet long.

Daruma

Japanese name for Bodhidharma, 28th Patriarch of Buddhism and founder of Zen. Also an armless, legless red doll featuring a caricature of Bodhidharma's face. See sidebar on page 105.

Date, Saburo

See sidebar on page 159.
Chuma in *Daimajin*
Bohachimono member in *Lone Wolf and Cub: Baby Cart to Hades*
Official in *Lone Wolf and Cub: Sword of Vengeance*
Gohei Zeniya in *Sleepy Eyes of Death: The Chinese Jade*
Ronin in *Yokai Monsters: 100 Monsters*

Deigan

Noh mask indicating a vengeful female spirit. See page 73.

Destiny's Son

See pages 91–93.

Do

The way (hence kendo = the Way of the Sword, Bushido = the Way of the Warrior).

Dojo

School and/or hall used for martial arts training.

Dotanuki

Battle sword, longer than the standard katana. Built for halving torsos. See page 154.

Edo

Tokyo (before 1868). See page 19.

Edo period

See **Tokugawa period.**

Eiga

Movie. See page 120.

Eijanaika

"Nevermind," "So what." See page 139.

Endo, Tatsuo

Gunjuro in *Daimajin*
Tomita in *Wicked Priest 5: Cast a Net of Drunken Anger*

Fujimaki, Jun

Kogenta in *Daimajin*
Yasutaro in *Yokai Monsters: 100 Monsters*

Fujimura, Shiho

Fujiko in *Destiny's Son*
Torizo's sister in *Sleepy Eyes of Death: Sword of Seduction*

Fujiwara, Kamatari

See sidebar on page 75.
Innkeeper in *Chushingura*
Matashichi in *The Hidden Fortress*
Manzo in *Seven Samurai*
Grandfather in *Sword of Doom*
Jinbei in *Three Outlaw Samurai*
Tazaemon in *Yojimbo*

Fukasaku, Kinji

Director.
Samurai Reincarnation
Shogun's Samurai

Gaijin

Foreigner.

Gate of Hell

See pages 54–55.

Geisha

Literally "arts person" (gei = art, sha = person). A woman trained in the traditional arts of Japan. Geisha entertained men with conversation, singing, and dancing. Although they inhabited the pleasure districts, they were not necessarily prostitutes.

Geki

Drama.

Gendai-geki

Modern drama (set after 1868). See page 12.

Giri

Obligation. See page 14.

Giri/Ninjo Conflict

Inner conflict between obligation to the daimyo and clan (giri) and personal conscience (ninjo). See page 18.

Gojuon

The 50 sounds, the phonetic foundation of the Japanese language. See page 25.

Gomi, Ryutaro

Samanosuke Odate in *Daimajin*
Official in *Lone Wolf and Cub: Sword of Vengeance*
Magistrate Uzen in *Yokai Monsters: 100 Monsters*

Gosha, Hideo

Director. See page 34.
Hunter in the Dark
The Secret of the Urn
Tenchu!
Three Outlaw Samurai

-Gumi

Group, gang. See page 44.

Haiku

Japanese poetic form consisting of three lines, the first and third of five syllables and the second of seven. The subject of haiku is traditionally some aspect of the natural world. See page 19.

Han

Feudal fiefdom, domain.

Hannya

Wickedly grinning Noh mask, usually white or pale yellow, featuring sharp horns and fangs. It expresses the rage of a woman transformed through jealousy and anger into a vengeful she-demon.

Harakiri

Suicide by disembowelment. See also **Seppuku** and sidebar on page 85.

Harakiri

See pages 84–86.

Harada, Yoshio

Yataro Tanigawa in *Hunter in the Dark*
Shusuke Tokunaga in *Lady Snowblood: Love Song of Vengeance*
Gennai Aramaki in *Roningai*
Flutist in *Shogun's Samurai*

Hashimoto, Shinobu

Screenwriter. See page 35.
Harakiri
Rashomon
Samurai Assassin

Samurai Rebellion
Sword of Doom
Tenchu!

Hayaku	Hurry.
Heaven and Earth	See pages 189–192
Hidari, Bokuzen	See sidebar on page 59. Gohei in *Red Lion* Yohei in *Seven Samurai*
Hidden Fortress, The	See pages 74–77
Hifukibaba	Fire-breathing granny ghost. See page 133.
Hinin	Non-man, lowest stratum of feudal Japanese society. See page 89.
Hira, Mikijiro	Gounosuke in *Adventures of Zatoichi* Kikyo in *Three Outlaw Samurai*
Hirata, Akihiko	Lord Suwa in *Samurai Banners* Seijuro Yoshioka in *Samurai 2: Duel at Ichijoji Temple* Samurai in *Sanjuro*
Hunter in the Dark	See pages 176–181
Iaido	Quick-draw sword technique.
Ichikawa, Raizo	See page 41. Shingo Takakura in *Destiny's Son* Nemuri Kyoshiro in *Sleepy Eyes of Death: The Chinese Jade* Nemuri Kyoshiro in *Sleepy Eyes of Death: Sword of Seduction*
Ikebana	Art of flower arranging. See page 19.

Inaba, Yoshio	Ikebe in *Destiny's Son* Keijiro Sumita in *Samurai Assassin* Gorobei in *Seven Samurai* Bizenya in *Sleepy Eyes of Death: Sword of Seduction*
Inagaki, Hiroshi	Director. *Chushingura* *Samurai 1: Musashi Miyamoto* *Samurai 2: Duel at Ichijoji Temple* *Samurai 3: Duel on Ganryu Island* *Samurai Banners*
Intendant	Shogunate official assigned to oversee a han (see **Daikan**). See sidebar on page 83.
Ito, Yunosuke	See sidebar on page 139. Retsudo Yagyu in *Lone Wolf and Cub: Sword of Vengeance* Kamio in *Red Lion* Kenmotsu Hoshino in *Samurai Assassin* Chamberlain Mutsuta in *Sanjuro*
Jidai-geki	Period drama (set before 1868). See page 12.
Jitsu	Truth, essence, substance.
Jitsuroku	True story. "Jitsuroku-eiga" was the term applied to early '70s yakuza films, such as the Battle Without Honor or Humanity (Jingi naki tatakai) series, for their cinema verité–style depictions of gang violence.
Jitte	Specialized hand-held defensive weapon used by Edo-period police consisting of 18-inch central tong and one or two curved, trident-like prongs for catching and breaking sword blades.
Kabuki	Traditional form of Japanese theater developed in the early seventeenth century. Kabuki literally translates as "song, dance, and technique." Incorporating elaborate

costumes and make-up, traditional kabuki plays are concerned with giri/ninjo conflicts, and all female parts are played by men.

Kagemusha

Double, look-alike (for political leaders). See page 54.

Kagemusha

See pages 182–185.

Kaiju

Giant monster.

Kaishaku

The ritual act of beheading someone after he has disemboweled himself (part of the larger ritual of seppuku).

Kaishakunin

Second in seppuku, one who performs the beheading following the disembowelment ritual. See page 15.

Kaji, Meiko

Yuki in *Lady Snowblood: Blizzard from the Netherworld*
Yuki in *Lady Snowblood: Love Song of Vengeance*

Kanie, Keizo

Mamushi in *The Razor: Sword of Justice*
Mamushi in *The Razor: The Snare*
Mamushi in *The Razor: Who's Got the Gold?*

Kanji

Chinese character for writing.

Karakasa

Umbrella ghost. See page 133.

Karo

Chamberlain. The Edo-karo represented the daimyo in Edo; the kuni-karo did so in the han.

Katana

Standard long sword. See also **Daito** and page 14.

Kato, Daisuke

Kichiemon Terasaka in *Chushingura*
Policeman in *Rashomon*
Toji in *Samurai 2: Duel at Ichijoji Temple*
Toji in *Samurai 3: Duel on Ganryu Island*
Shichiroji in *Seven Samurai*
Inokichi in *Yojimbo*

Kato, Go

Aka Tsuyoshi Kato.
Kanbei Magomura in *Lone Wolf and Cub: Baby Cart to Hades*
Yogoro Sasahara in *Samurai Rebellion*

Katsu, Shintaro

Aka Katsu-shin. See page 39.
Itami Hanzo in *The Razor: Sword of Justice*
Itami Hanzo in *The Razor: The Snare*
Itami Hanzo in *The Razor: Who's Got the Gold?*
Bull in *Roningai*
Izo Okada in *Tenchu!*
Zatoichi in *Adventures of Zatoichi*
Zatoichi in *New Tale of Zatoichi*
Zatoichi in *The Tale of Zatoichi*
Zatoichi in *The Tale of Zatoichi Continues*
Zatoichi in *Zatoichi Challenged*
Zatoichi in *Zatoichi: The Festival of Fire*

Kawazu, Seizaburo

Asano Official in *Chushingura*
Banno in *New Tale of Zatoichi*
Guraku Nomura in *The Secret of the Urn*
Seibei in *Yojimbo*

Kayama, Yuzo

Lord Asano in *Chushingura*
Samurai in *Sanjuro*
Hyoma Utsuki in *Sword of Doom*

Ken

Sword.

Kendo

Literally "the Way of the Sword." Traditional Japanese fencing practiced with elaborate uniform (robes, protective gloves, and face mask) and employing a shinai.

Ken-geki

Sword drama.

Kimura, Isao

Katsuhiro in *Seven Samurai*
Genzaburo Yagyu in *The Secret of the Urn*

Kirisutegomen Right of samurai to kill commoners. See page 89.

Kiru Cut, kill, slice, behead (variants: kiri, kire).

Kishida, Shin Seishiro Kikui in *Lady Snowblood: Love Song of Vengeance*
Kuruma Hidari in *Lone Wolf and Cub: Baby Cart at the River Styx*
Wicked Manager in *Red Lion*

Kitano, Takeshi Aka Beat Takeshi.
Toshizo Hijikata in *Taboo*
Zatoichi in *Zatoichi*

Koban Gold coin worth 1 ryo. See page 171.

Kobayashi, Keiju Toshizo Hijikata in *Band of Assassins*
Lord Awaji in *Chushingura*
Einosuke Kurihara in *Samurai Assassin*

Kobayashi, Masaki Director.
Harakiri
Kwaidan
Samurai Rebellion

Kogi Kaishakunin Official executioner of the shogunate. See page 152.

Koku Bale of rice equal to roughly 5 bushels, a year's supply. Standard unit of measurement for wealth of a han.

Koi Carp.

Koike, Kazuo Screenwriter.
Lady Snowblood: Blizzard from the Netherworld
Lone Wolf and Cub: Baby Cart at the River Styx
Lone Wolf and Cub: Baby Cart to Hades
Lone Wolf and Cub: Sword of Vengeance
The Razor: Sword of Justice

Kondo, Isami	Leader of the Shinsengumi following assassination of Kamo Serizawa. See page 149.
Koto	Japanese harp. See page 54.
Kubo, Naoko	Virgin Shima in *Sleepy Eyes of Death: Sword of Seduction* Lady-in-Waiting in *Samurai Reincarnation*
Kurosawa, Akira	Director. See page 31. *Kagemusha* *Rashomon* *Sanjuro* *Seven Samurai* *The Hidden Fortress* *Throne of Blood* *Yojimbo*
Kurosawa, Toshio	Ryurei Ashio in *Lady Snowblood: Blizzard from the Netherworld* Junai Mikoshiba in *The Razor: The Snare*
Kurosawa-gumi	Loose company of actors and staff used repeatedly by director Akira Kurosawa. See page 44.
Kusano, Daigo	Gun-slinging yojimbo in *Lone Wolf and Cub: Baby Cart to Hades* Knife-throwing bandit in *Lone Wolf and Cub: Sword of Vengeance* Onibi in *The Razor: Sword of Justice* Onibi in *The Razor: The Snare* Onibi in *The Razor: Who's Got the Gold?*
Kusarigama	Weapon consisting of a chain with a small weight on one end and a sickle on the other. The chain is thrown to ensnare the opponent's weapon, then the sickle is employed for hacking, slicing, and generally disabling the opponent.
Kwaidan	See pages 106–109.

Kyo, Machiko	Kesa in *Gate of Hell* Samurai wife in *Rashomon*
Kyogen	Classical comic theater. Performances usually follow Noh plays for comic relief.
Lady Snowblood: Blizzard from the Netherworld	See pages 165–167.
Lady Snowblood: Love Song of Vengeance	See pages 168–170.
Lone Wolf and Cub: Baby Cart at the River Styx	See pages 154–157.
Lone Wolf and Cub: Baby Cart to Hades	See pages 157–159.
Lone Wolf and Cub: Sword of Vengeance	See pages 151–154.
Loyal 47 Ronin	Common term for the Asano clan retainers who perpetrated the beheading of Lord Kira in revenge for the death of their master two years before. Their story is told in the *Chushingura.* See page 93.
Majin	Devil, genie, evil spirit. See page 120.
Makoto	Truth. See page 149.
Makoto no Bushi	Literally "true warrior." See page 149.
Manga	Japanese comic books. Manga are far more pervasive in Japanese culture than the standard "comic book" in Western culture, occupying more the role of "graphic novel." Manga, a term coined by legendary artist Katsu-

shika Hokusai (1760–1849), extend to all walks of Japanese life: there are manga for salarymen, housewives, kids, teenagers, professionals, government agencies, etc. The so-called "God of Manga" is artist and animator Osamu Tezuka.

Matsumoto, Koshiro
Kuranosuke Oishi in *Chushingura*
Lord Naosuke Ii in *Samurai Assassin*

Matsuo, Kayo
Oren in *Hunter in the Dark*
Sayaka in *Lone Wolf and Cub: Baby Cart at the River Styx*

Meifumado
Buddhist hell. See page 152.

Meiji Restoration
Event that ended 265 years of Tokugawa rule and reinstated the Emperor (who became Emperor Meiji) to the position of supreme power in Japan in 1868. See page 19.

Meiji Period
1868 to 1912, the period of the rule of Emperor Meiji, marked by rapid westernization and technological advance. The last vestiges of samurai tradition were effectively abolished, the country was militarized, and had its first modern war, defeating Russia in 1905. See page 19.

Metsuke
Inspector for the shogunate, performing policing and intelligence-gathering duties. See page 19.

Mifune, Toshiro
See page 36.
Isami Kondo in *Band of Assassins*
Gemba Tawaraboshi in *Chushingura*
Tajomaru in *Rashomon*
Gonzo in *Red Lion*
Tsuruchiyo Niiro in *Samurai Assassin*
Kansuke Yamamoto in *Samurai Banners*
Musashi Miyamoto in *Samurai 1: Musashi Miyamoto*
Musashi Miyamoto in *Samurai 2: Duel at Ichijoji Temple*
Musashi Miyamoto in *Samurai 3: Duel on Ganryu Island*

Isaburo Sasahara in *Samurai Rebellion*
Sanjuro Tsubaki in *Sanjuro*
Kikuchiyo in *Seven Samurai*
Lord Owari in *Shogun's Samurai*
Toranosuke Shimada in *Sword of Doom*
General Rokurota Makabe in *The Hidden Fortress*
General Taketori Washizu in *Throne of Blood*
Sanjuro Kuwabatake in *Yojimbo*

Mikuni, Rentaro

Kamo Serizawa in *Band of Assassins*
Kageyu Saito in *Harakiri*
Samurai in *Kwaidan (The Black Hair)*
Matahachi Honiden in *Samurai 1: Musashi Miyamoto*

Misumi, Kenji

Director.
Destiny's Son
Lone Wolf and Cub: Baby Cart at the River Styx
Lone Wolf and Cub: Baby Cart to Hades
Lone Wolf and Cub: Sword of Vengeance
The Razor: Sword of Justice
The Tale of Zatoichi
Zatoichi Challenged
Zatoichi: The Festival of Fire

Mito, Mitsuko

Oko in *Samurai 1: Musashi Miyamoto*
Oko in *Samurai 2: Duel at Ichijoji Temple*

Mito Tengu

Anti-shogunate rebel group based in Mito province.
Eventually became outlaws.

Miyagawa, Kazuo

Cinematographer.
Rashomon
The Razor: The Snare
Yojimbo

Miyamoto, Musashi

1584–1645. Japan's most famous swordsman, Musashi
won over 60 duels, developed the Nito-ryu (two-sword)
style, and was also an accomplished painter, sculptor,
writer, and devotee of Zen. He penned *The Book of Five*

Rings, a volume on sword fighting strategy remarkably applicable to many life situations. See page 14.

Mono

Person, thing, object.

Mori, Masayuki

Samurai in *Rashomon*
Yamibuko in *Zatoichi: The Festival of Fire*

Nakago

Base of a samurai sword covered by the hilt. Area where swordsmith's name appears. See page 14.

Nagauta

Traditional Kabuki style of singing accompanied by shamisen. See page 40.

Naginata

Spear with long, curved blade. See page 154.

Nakadai, Tatsuya

See page 37.
Hanshiro Tsugumo in *Harakiri*
Kiyoemon Gomyo in *Hunter in the Dark*
Shingen Takeda/Thief in *Kagemusha*
Minokichi in *Kwaidan (The Woman in the Snow)*
Tatewaki Asano in *Samurai Rebellion*
Hanbei Muroto in *Sanjuro*
Passing Samurai in *Seven Samurai* (uncredited)
Ryunosuke Tsukue in *Sword of Doom*
Hanpeita Takechi in *Tenchu!*
Unosuke in *Yojimbo*
Ronin in *Zatoichi: The Festival of Fire*

Nakamura, Kanemon

Kannai in *Kwaidan (In a Cup of Tea)*
Nobukata Itagaki in *Samurai Banners*

Nakamura, Katsuo

Hoichi in *Kwaidan (Hoichi, the Earless)*
Nobusato Itagaki in *Samurai Banners*

Nakamura, Kinnosuke

Aka Kinnosuke Yorozuya.
Shingen Takeda in *Samurai Banners*
Tange Sazen in *The Secret of the Urn*
Tajima Yagyu in *Shogun's Samurai*

Narita, Mikio	Gosun in *Hunter in the Dark* Izumori Matsudaira in *Samurai Reincarnation* Bansaku Tonami in *The Razor: Who's Got the Gold?* Imperial courtier in *Shogun's Samurai*
New Tale of Zatoichi	See pages 97–99
Ninja	See **Shinobi**.
Ninjo	Human feelings, compassion, conscience. See page 18.
Nishimura, Ko	See sidebar on page 171. Dokai in *Lady Snowblood: Blizzard from the Netherworld* Magobei Onishi in *The Razor: Sword of Justice* Magobei Onishi in *The Razor: The Snare* Magobei Onishi in *The Razor: Who's Got the Gold?* Shichibei in *Sword of Doom* Kuma in *Yojimbo* Migi in *Zatoichi—The Festival of Fire*
Nito-ryu	Two-sword fighting technique developed by Musashi Miyamoto. See page 67.
Nodachi	Extra-large war sword. See page 57.
Noh	Haunting classical Japanese drama incorporating dance, music, and poetry into a highly stylized form of performance art. The singing is drone-like, often to minimalistic percussion interspersed with occasional yelps and cries. The performers wear masks and move slowly, as in a dream.
Nopperabo	No-face goblin. See page 133.
Oda, Nobunaga	Powerful warlord of the Sengoku period and first to initiate the political unification of Japan (followed by Hideyoshi Toyotomi and Ieyasu Tokugawa). See page 17.

Ohaguro	Teeth-blackening, a fashion among married ladies in medieval Japan. See sidebar on page 54.
Ohara, Reiko	Okuni in *Shogun's Samurai* Okiyo in *Zatoichi—The Festival of Fire*
Okada, Mariko	Akemi in *Samurai 1: Musashi Miyamoto* Akemi in *Samurai 2: Duel at Ichijoji Temple* Akemi in *Samurai 3: Duel on Ganryu Island*
Okamoto, Kihachi.	Director. *Red Lion* *Samurai Assassin* *Sword of Doom*
Okubi	Big-head ghost. See page 133.
Oni	Ogre. See page 133.
Onoe, Kuroemon	Takuan in *Samurai 1: Musashi Miyamoto* Takuan in *Samurai 2: Duel at Ichijoji Temple*
Otafuku	Comical Kyogen mask of fat, jowly woman.
Oyaji	Middle-aged man; literally "Dad" or "Boss."
Pinku-eiga	Pink film, softcore porn.
Rashomon	See pages 51–53.
Razor: Sword of Justice, The	See pages 160–162.
Razor: The Snare, The	See pages 162–164.
Razor: Who's Got the Gold?, The	See pages 170–173.
Red Lion	See pages 137–140.

Rokurokubi	Long-necked lady ghost; literally "potter's wheel neck." See page 133.
Ronin	Masterless samurai. See page 16.
Roningai	See pages 192–194.
Ryo	Gold coin worth 1 koku. Equivalent to 4,000 mon = 4 kan = 50 momme.
Sake	Rice wine. Ranging from 15–20% alcohol, it is clear, strong, and normally served hot in the winter.
Sakamoto, Ryoma	Political architect of the Meiji Restoration. Sakamoto worked behind the scenes during the Bakumatsu period, traveling all over Japan to unify factions behind the overthrow of the Tokugawa Shogunate. He was assassinated in 1868. See page 141.
Samurai	Clan retainer, warrior, ruling class during the Tokugawa period. See sidebar on page 87.
Samurai 1: Musashi Miyamoto	See pages 62–66.
Samurai 2: Duel at Ichijoji Temple	See pages 66–68.
Samurai 3: Duel on Ganryu Island	See pages 69–71.
Samurai Assassin	See pages 115–117.
Samurai Banners	See pages 134–137.
Samurai Rebellion	See pages 126–129.
Samurai Reincarnation	See pages 185–189.

Samurai Trilogy

Term for the three films (*Samurai 1: Musashi Miyamoto, Samurai 2: Duel at Ichijoji Temple,* and *Samurai 3: Duel on Ganryu Island*) made by Hiroshi Inagaki from 1954 to 1956.

Sanada, Hiroyuki

Kirimaru Iga in *Samurai Reincarnation*
Hayate in *Shogun's Samurai*
Seibei Iguchi in *Twilight Samurai*

Sanjuro

See pages 81–83.

Sashimi

Thinly sliced raw fish.

Sato, Masaru

Composer.
Band of Assassins
Hunter in the Dark
Red Lion
Samurai Assassin
Samurai Banners
Sanjuro
Sword of Doom
Tenchu!
The Hidden Fortress
Throne of Blood
Yojimbo

Sawamura, Sonosuke

Boss Kanbei in *The Tale of Zatoichi Continues*
Lord Nariyasu Maeda in *Sleepy Eyes of Death: The Chinese Jade*

Secret of the Urn, The

See pages 117–120.

Sekigahara, Battle of

Decisive battle won by Ieyasu Tokugawa in 1600, marking the end of the Sengoku period and leading to the establishment of the Tokugawa Shogunate. See page 17.

Sengoku period

1478–1603. Period of turmoil and civil wars. Also known as the Warring States period. See page 61.

Sensei	Teacher, learned person. The term is also used for doctors and other highly educated professionals.
Seppuku	Ritual disemboweling ceremony. Preferred method of suicide by the samurai class. See page 15 and sidebar on page 85.
Serizawa, Kamo	First leader of the Shinsengumi. Assassinated by his second in command, Isami Kondo.
Seven Samurai	See pages 56–62.
Shakai-mono	Social awareness films. See page 32.
Shakuhachi	Bamboo flute.
Shamisen	Japanese banjo-style stringed instrument. The sounding box is square. See page 97.
Shikami	Noh mask indicating a demon spirit. See page 73.
Shimura, Takashi	Hyobu Chisaka in *Chushingura* Head priest in *Kwaidan (Hoichi, the Earless)* Woodcutter in *Rashomon* Narihisa Ichijo in *Samurai Assassin* Court Official in *Samurai 3: Duel on Ganryu Island* Kambei in *Seven Samurai* Boss Wajima in *Wicked Priest 5: Cast a Net of Drunken Anger* Tokuemon in *Yojimbo*
Shinai	Fencing foil for kendo consisting of four bamboo staves held together with leather and string.
Shinchogumi	Special police force stationed in Edo. Similar to the Shinsengumi.
Shinobi	Spy. Shinobi were highly trained professionals skilled in martial arts, acrobatics, specialized weaponry (those

deadly shuriken, for example), and the fine art of invisibility. They specialized in explosives, diversionary tactics, assassinations, and all manner of "special ops." Surveillance experts, they spent their time running, jumping, climbing trees, scaling walls, and slipping in and out of heavily guarded compounds. Shinobi were active during the Sengoku and Tokugawa periods.

Shinsengumi

Paramilitary group of pro-shogunate ronin formed in Kyoto in 1863, at the height of the Bakumatsu period as the Tokugawa Shogunate was disintegrating. Essentially an ad hoc police force, they were in fact a brutal gang of killers led initially by Kamo Serizawa, a corrupt former member of the Mito Tengu. Serizawa was murdered by Isami Kondo, who took over, but their numbers dwindled as the Tokugawa period drew to a close.

Shinto

Indigenous pantheistic religion of Japan. See page 19.

Shochiku Studios

See page 29.

Showa period

1926–1989. The reign of Emperor Showa, otherwise known as Hirohito.

Shogun

Military dictator, generalissimo, supreme member of the samurai class.

Shogun's Samurai

See pages 173–176.

Shogunate

The administrative core of the government under the shogun.

Shorinji Kempo

Martial art utilizing strikes, kicks, and throws with hands and feet.

Shuriken

Deadly spiked throwing disks used by ninja.

Sleepy Eyes of Death: The Chinese Jade

See pages 99–102.

Sleepy Eyes of Death: Sword of Seduction	See pages 112–114.
So ka	"Is that so?" Exclamation of realization, i.e., "Ah ha" or "You don't say."
Superintendent	Executive representative of the shogunate stationed in a han (see Daikan). See sidebar on page 83.
Sword of Doom	See pages 122–125.
Taboo	See pages 195–197.
Tachikawa, Hiroshi	Lord Tsuzuki in *Throne of Blood* Yoichiro in *Yojimbo*
Takada, Miwa	Miss Saki in *Adventures of Zatoichi* Kozasa in *Daimajin* Okiku in *Yokai Monsters: 100 Monsters* Mitsu in *Zatoichi Challenged*
Takahashi, Etsushi	Gen'an Sugino in *The Razor: Who's Got the Gold?* Hanzo in *Red Lion* Izu Matsudaira in *Shogun's Samurai*
Takeda, Shingen	Powerful warlord during the Sengoku period nicknamed "The Mountain." His armies wore red armor. [Pg. #]
Tale of Zatoichi, The	See pages 87–89.
Tale of Zatoichi Continues, The	See pages 89–91.
Tamba, Tetsuro	See page 42. Hikokuro Omodaka in *Harakiri* Okitsugu Tanuma in *Hunter in the Dark* Ghost Samurai in *Kwaidan (Hoichi, the Earless)* Muramasa in *Samurai Reincarnation* Genshinsai Ogasawara in *Shogun's Samurai*

Tsushima Yagyu in *The Secret of the Urn*
Shiba in *Three Outlaw Samurai*
Tozaemon Iguchi in *Twilight Samurai*

Tanaka, Kunie

Magohachiro in *Roningai*
Samurai in *Sanjuro*

Tanto

A short blade (under 12 inches) used for seppuku. Easily concealed, it was also popular for general dagger duties. See page 15.

Tatami

Woven straw mat roughly 3 feet by 6 feet used in Japanese households as floor covering. To keep tatami clean, shoes are removed when entering household. Tatami are also used as a unit of measurement for living space.

Tekiya

Peddler, subset of the yakuza. See sidebar on page 87.

Tenchu

Heaven's punishment.

Tenchu!

See pages 140–142.

Tengu

Mountain goblins skilled in martial arts. Some are bird-like; others have red faces with huge noses and dress as Yamabushi. Legend has it that Munenori Yagyu's sword sensei was a Tengu.

Tengu of Mito

See **Mito Tengu.**

Tenno

Emperor. See page 32.

Three Outlaw Samurai

See pages 109–112.

Throne of Blood

See pages 71–74.

Toei Studios

See page 29.

Toho Studios

See page 27.

Tokugawa

Clan that dominated Japan from 1603 to 1868 through control of the shogunate.

Tokugawa Period

1603–1868. The period of the Tokugawa Shogunate, marked by sustained peace achieved by national isolationism. To maintain power, the Tokugawa clan and government sought to weaken and eliminate rival clans, creating ever-increasing numbers of ronin. Mounting corruption, political intrigue, and cultural stagnation ultimately left Japan vulnerable to more technologically advanced Western powers. See page 17.

Tokugawa, Ieyasu

First Tokugawa shogun. Brilliant strategist and nation-builder, he codified the structure of Japanese society for centuries to come, stratifying it into rigid classes and dictating how the classes were to behave and interact down to the most minute detail. Architect of the Tokugawa Shogunate. See page 17.

Tomikawa, Akihiro

Daigoro in *Lone Wolf and Cub: Sword of Vengeance*
Daigoro in *Lone Wolf and Cub: Baby Cart at the River Styx*
Daigoro in *Lone Wolf and Cub: Baby Cart to Hades*

Tono, Eijiro

See sidebar on page 80.
Seigoro Kisoya in *Samurai Assassin*
Baiken in *Samurai 2: Duel at Ichijoji Temple*
Thief in *Seven Samurai*
Gonji in *Yojimbo*

Tosa Clan

Anti-shogunate clan active during the Bakumatsu period, staging raids and assassinations. See page 141

Tsuchiya, Yoshio

Matanosho Shiota in *Chushingura*
Samurai in *Sanjuro*
Rikichi in *Seven Samurai*
Washizu Samurai in *Throne of Blood*

Tsuchikorobi

Huge, furry Cyclops ghost. See page 132.

Tsuruta, Koji

Kojiro Sasaki in *Samurai 2: Duel at Ichijoji Temple*
Kojiro Sasaki in *Samurai 3: Duel on Ganryu Island*

Twilight Samurai

210–203.

Ueda, Kichijiro

Boss Jinbei in *Adventures of Zatoichi*
Commoner in *Rashomon*
Agon in *Samurai 3: Duel on Ganryu Island*

Wakayama, Tomisaburo

Aka Kenzaburo Jo. See page 41.
Ogami Itto in *Lone Wolf and Cub: Baby Cart at the River Styx*
Ogami Itto in *Lone Wolf and Cub: Baby Cart to Hades*
Ogami Itto in *Lone Wolf and Cub: Sword of Vengeance*
Tajima Yagyu in *Samurai Reincarnation*
Chen Sun in *Sleepy Eyes of Death: The Chinese Jade*
Chen Sun in *Sleepy Eyes of Death: Sword of Seduction*
Yoshiro in *The Tale of Zatoichi Continues*Shinkai in *Wicked Priest 5: Cast a Net of Drunken Anger*

Wakizashi

Short sword (12 to 24 inches) worn with the katana in the daisho configuration. See page 14.

Warring States period

See **Sengoku period.**

Watari-kashi

Samurai for hire. Usually employed by daimyo for protection on journeys to and from Edo. See page 157.

Wicked Priest 5: Cast a Net of Drunken Anger

See pages 145–148

Yachigusa, Kaoru

Otsu in *Samurai 1: Musashi Miyamoto*
Otsu in *Samurai 2: Duel at Ichijoji Temple*
Otsu in *Samurai 3: Duel on Ganryu Island*

Yagyu Clan

Ancient and venerable clan serving the Tokugawa shoguns as their private fencing instructors. Munenori Yagyu became the first, serving Ieyasu Tokugawa, the first Tokugawa shogun. Renowned for their sword prowess, the Yagyu were also powerful, exercising influence at court through their unique relationship with the shogun. See sidebar on page 175.

Yakuza

Umbrella term for the demimonde of Japanese organized crime (like "mob" or "mafia"). See sidebar on page 87.

Yamabushi

Mountain monks.

Yamagata, Isao

Wataru Watanabe in *Gate of Hell*
Genba Sawatari in *Lone Wolf and Cub: Baby Cart to Hades*
Samurai in *Seven Samurai*

Yanagi, Eijiro

Matsudaira in *Destiny's Son*
Sukegoro in *The Tale of Zatoichi*
Sukegoro in *The Tale of Zatoichi Continues*

Yojimbo

Bodyguard.

Yojimbo

See pages 78–81.

Yokai

Ghost, demon, monster, goblin.

Yokai Monsters: 100 Monsters

See pages 131–134.

Yorozuya, Kinnosuke

See **Nakamura, Kinnosuke.**

Yosh

"Alright," "Very well." Spoken with gusto by samurai and yakuza, usually right before going into action.

Zato

Blind man or masseur.

Zatoichi

See pages 197–201.

Zatoichi Challenged	See pages 129–131.
Zatoichi: The Festival of Fire	See pages 143–145.

Bibliography

Print

Anderson, Joseph L., and Donald Richie	*The Japanese Film: Art and Industry.* Princeton, NJ: Princeton University Press, 1982.
Galbraith, Stuart IV	*The Emperor and the Wolf.* New York: Faber and Faber, 2001.
Kael, Pauline	*5001 Nights at the Movies.* New York: Henry Holt and Company, 1991.
Kurosawa, Akira	*Something Like an Autobiography.* New York: Random House, 1982.
Macias, Patrick	*Tokyoscope: The Japanese Cult Film Companion.* San Francisco: Cadence Books, 2001.
Nakane, Chie, and Shinzaburo Oishi, eds.	*Tokugawa Japan: The Social and Economic Antecedents of Modern Japan.* Tokyo: University of Tokyo Press, 1990.
Nolletti, Arthur, Jr., and David Desser, eds.	*Reframing Japanese Cinema.* Bloomington and Indianapolis: Indiana University Press, 1992.
Richie, Donald	*A Hundred Years of Japanese Film.* Tokyo: Kodansha International, 2001.

——— *The Films of Akira Kurosawa.* Berkeley and Los Angeles: University of California Press, 1996.

Schilling, Mark *The Encyclopedia of Japanese Pop Culture.* Trumbull, CT: Weatherhill, 1997.

——— *The Yakuza Movie Book: A Guide to Japanese Gangster Films.* Berkeley, CA: Stone Bridge Press, 2003.

Silver, Alain *The Samurai Film.* Woodstock, NY: The Overlook Press, 1983.

Internet

Kung Fu Cinema http://www.kungfucinema.com/

Kung Fu Cult Cinema http://www.kfccinema.com/

Raizo's World http://www.raizofan.net/eng/

Samurai Liner Notes
from AnimEigo http://www.animeigo.com/SamLiner/

The Internet Movie
Database http://us.imdb.com/

The Ninja Dojo http://www.ninjadojo.com/

Samurai Archives http://www.samurai-archives.com/

Other Titles of Interest from Stone Bridge Press

Available at bookstores and online, or contact the publisher.
Stone Bridge Press, P. O. Box 8208, Berkeley, CA 94707
sbp@stonebridge.com • www.stonebridge.com

The Midnight Eye Guide to New Japanese Film
TOM MES AND JASPER SHARP
376 pp, paper, 1-880656-89-2, $22.95

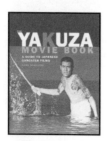

The Yakuza Movie Book: A Guide to Japanese Gangster Films
MARK SCHILLING
336 pp, 1-880656-76-0, $19.95

Hayao Miyazaki: Master of Japanese Animation
HELEN MCCARTHY
240 pp, 1-880656-41-8, $18.95

Tokyo Story: The Ozu/Noda Screenplay
YASUJIRO OZU AND KOGO NODA; TRANS DONALD RICHIE AND ERIC KLESTADT
128 pp, 1-880656-80-9, $12.95